T0319704

TECHNOLOGICAL LEARNING

... for my parents, Abdul Kareem, Lerlyn Marcelle and Anthony Applewhite

Technological Learning

A Strategic Imperative for Firms in the
Developing World

Gillian M. Marcelle

Edward Elgar
Cheltenham, UK • Northampton, MA, USA

Published by
Edward Elgar Publishing Limited
Glensanda House
Montpellier Parade
Cheltenham
Glos GL50 1UA
UK

Edward Elgar Publishing, Inc.
136 West Street
Suite 202
Northampton
Massachusetts 01060
USA

A catalogue record for this book
is available from the British Library

ISBN 1 84376 692 2

Printed and bound in Great Britain by MPG Books Ltd, Bodmin, Cornwall

Contents

List of Figures   vi
List of Tables   vii
Abbreviations and Acronyms   ix
Preface   xi

1. Introduction   1

2. The TCB System Approach   25

3. A Quantitative Exploration of Technological Learning   63

4. Management, Culture and Leadership for Learning   83

5. Managing Supplier Relationships   107

6. Role of the Innovation System   135

7. Strategic Balance   159

Appendices   175

References   199

Index   207

Figures

1.1	Interaction of firm-level and country-level factors	11
2.1	Three main constituent elements of technological capabilities	27
2.2	Elements and indicators of firm-level technological capability	29
2.3	Ten types of learning for developing country firms	45
2.4	Five critical components of a technological capability building system	52
3.1	Distribution of sample firms across three categories of TCB system development	65
3.2	An unbalanced TCB system	79
4.1	Key processes in learning systems	99

Tables

1.1 Summary of primary data gathering   7
1.2 Main characteristics of sample firms   8
1.3 Distribution of sample by market segment code   9
1.4 Sample firms distributed by ownership structure   9
1.5 Economic profiles Uganda, Ghana, Tanzania and South Africa   13
1.6 Key features of technological change in telecommunications   16
2.1 Key texts on organizational learning and technological   26
     capability building
2.2 Key routines for innovation management in developing country
     firms   41
2.3 Core abilities for managing innovation   42
2.4 Adapting the Hobday (1990) typology of learning mechanisms   48
3.1 Composition and characteristics of the seven groups of TCB
     mechanisms   64
3.2 Patterns of usage for firms across three categories of TCB   67
     system development
3.3 ANOVA table for frequency of TCB mechanisms   68
3.4 Sum of intensity scores for three levels of TCB system development   70
3.5 TCB gaps with the highest reported incidence   72
3.6 Correlation between TCB system development and reported gaps   73
3.7 Correlation matrix – TCB mechanisms used, years in operation   74
     and firm size
3.8 Correlation matrix – TCB mechanisms used, market segment,   74
     ownership type and country of operation
3.9a Intensity scores for three categories of TCB system development   77
     and ideal
3.9b Difference and ranks for three categories and ideal   77
4.1 Usage of internally orientated TCB mechanisms   85
4.2 Data on expenditure on TCB activities by sample firms   91
5.1 Selection criteria ranked in order of importance   108
5.2 Suppliers of equipment and services   109
5.3 Routines used for acquisition of technology capability   111
     from suppliers

5.4   Suppliers assessment of operating company capability   122
6.1   Desired public sector support for TCB in firm   137
6.2   Interaction between sample firms and national public policy 139
      and regulatory bodies

Abbreviations and Acronyms

AAT	Altech Telecommunications Ltd
ADH	Asynchronous Digital Hierarchy
ADSL	Asynchronous Digital Subscriber Line
AFRALTI	African Advanced Level Telecommunication Institute
ANOVA	Analysis of Variance
ATM	Asynchronous Transfer Mode
ATU	African Telecommunication Union
AXE	Ericsson family of telecommunication networking equipment
CCITT	Comité Consultatif International Télégraphique et Téléphonique (an ITU committee)
CLI	Caller Line Identification
CNET	Centre National d'Etudes des Télécommunications: National Center for Telecommunications Studies (France)
CSIR/STEPRI	Council for Scientific and Industrial Research/Science and Technology Policy Research Institute
CSF	Critical Success Factor
CTO	Commonwealth Telecommunication Organization
DECT	Digital European Cordless Telecommunications
DTM	Digital Terrain Model
ESRF	Economic and Social Research Foundation
ETSI	European Telecommunication Standards Institute
FCC	Federal Communications Commission (US)
FDI	Foreign Direct Investment
GIS	Geographic Information System
GMPCS	Global Mobile Personal Communication Service
GPRS	Global Packet Radio Service
GSM	Global System for Mobile Service
HIPC	Highly Indebted Poor Countries Initiative
HRD	Human Resource Development
IDD	International Direct Dialling
ICT	Information and Communication Technology
ISDN	Integrated Services Digital Network
IT/IS	Information Technology/Information Systems
ITU	International Telecommunication Union
JIT	Just in Time

JV	Joint Venture
MIS	Management Information Systems
NCA	National Communications Authority
NGO	Non Governmental Organization
NIS	National Innovation System
NTT	Nippon Telegraph and Telephone Corporation
OECD	Organisation for Economic Cooperation and Development
Oftel	Office of Telecommunication (UK)
PABX	Private Automatic Branch Exchange
PARUC	Pennsylvania Regulatory Utilities Commission
PATU	Pan-African Telecommunication Union
PTO	Public Telecommunication Operator
R&D	Research and Development
SATRA	South African Telecommunications Regulatory Authority
SC	Strategic Competence
SDH	Synchronous Digital Hierarchy
SETA	Sector Education and Training Authority
SMME	Small, Medium and Micro Enterprise
SNO	Second National Operator
TCC	Tanzania Communications Commission
TCP/IP	Transmission Control Protocol/Internet Protocol
TDMA	Time Division Multiple Access
TNC	Trans-National Corporation
TNS	Telecommunication Network-based Services
TSh	Tanzania Shilling
TT	Technology Transfer
UCC	Uganda Communications Commission
UTL	Uganda Telecommunication Ltd
UMTS	Universal Mobile Telephone Service
UNDP	United Nations Development Programme
USTTI	United States Telecommunication Training Institute
Westel	ACG Systems (Ghana) Ltd
WAN/LAN	Wide Area Network/Local Area Network
WLL	Wireless Local Loop
Z-Comms	Zakheni Communications Strategies

Preface

This book investigates how developing country firms undertake technological learning and capability building efforts. The main focus of the analysis is explaining variation in ability to effectively manage technological capability building (TCB) and learning at the individual firm level. The conceptual framework developed for this study – the TCB system approach – draws on a number of intellectual traditions, including organizational development, strategic management, innovation studies, development studies and evolutionary theory of the firm.

The main conclusion of this study is that for developing country firms, adopting a balanced systematic and coherent approach to technological learning yields significant benefits. The study will show that when developing country firms implement systems that simultaneously, proportionately and systematically direct effort at the following five key elements that is financing, management and co-ordination, culture and leadership, managing relationships with suppliers and with the innovation system, they increase the effectiveness of TCB and learning. This approach extends development studies perspectives on capability accumulation by paying greater attention to specific and general organizational learning routines and practices within firms.

An indicator is developed and applied that measures the extent to which firms are involved in an investment process that is likely to lead to greater effectiveness in capability accumulation. The results of the study demonstrate that there appears to be a structural dimension of TCB insofar as firms that are effective in capability development were found to have invested simultaneously and proportionately in all of the key elements suggested by the TCB system framework. The learning systems of firms that are effective in TCB were found to have a morphology that differed significantly from the 'systems in use' by novices and laggards.

A key insight of the analysis is that endogenous factors rather than the specific characteristics of the policy environment appear to be most important in distinguishing between the levels of performance of firms. Specifically, the breadth of learning routines, the effective integration of learning routines, and the existence of specific routines within firms appear to contribute to improved effectiveness of the firms' capability development efforts. The results of the study are likely to be particularly relevant for firms operating in service sectors, for firms that are not aiming to generate radical innovations at the changing technological frontier, and for firms facing challenges arising from the speed, complexity and extensive effects of technological change. These factors make the findings and conclusions relevant to many industries in developing countries and, especially, to the telecommunication operating company sector.

These conclusions are drawn from an in-depth study, which develops an original conceptual framework to carry out a detailed cross-sectional analysis of technological learning and capability building in a sample of 26 telecommunication operating companies in Uganda, Ghana, Tanzania and South Africa. The unit of analysis in this study is the telecommunication operating company, that is the firm that owns or controls telecommunication networks and uses these to provide services to final customers. The empirical setting, therefore, is a fast-moving dynamic industry that is both a site of technological change and, in parallel, a site of industrial restructuring. Examining the processes that developing country firms use to build technological capabilities under these conditions has shed new light on some of the uncharted areas of science and technology policy studies.

This research would not have been possible without financial contributions from the Graduate Teaching Centre, SPRU and the Information Networks and Knowledge (INK) Research Group, University of Sussex (UK). I am also particularly grateful for the in-country support provided by my many hosts: in Uganda, Hon. Winnie Byanyima and Paul Nalikka; in Ghana, Hon. Cmdr (Rtd) PMG Griffiths; in Tanzania, Prof. Samuel Wangwe and his team at the Economic Social Research Foundation, and in South Africa, Dr Derrick Cogburn, then Director CISDA, and Ms Alison Gillwald, Director of the LINK Centre, University of Witswatersrand. In South Africa, Matsuma Marunyana provided valuable assistance for the quantitative exploration and Heather van Niekerk produced the illustrations and diagrams. I am tremendously indebted to the managers, engineers, policy makers, regulators and consultants who work in the telecommunication industry that provided access to materials and were willing to spend time having interesting discussions about capability development activities.

This book was written in Johannesburg in 2004, but my interest in the subject goes back 20 years, when Trevor Farrell taught me an undergraduate course in Science and Technology Policy at the University of the West Indies, St Augustine, Trinidad. I continue to draw inspiration from Caribbean scholars, particularly Prof. Norman Girvan, Drs T.M.A Farrell, Ralph Henry, Elizabeth Parsan, Auliana Poon, Rosina Wiltshire and Lloyd Best, who have always insisted that academic writing should be relevant to real-world development challenges.

At a personal level, several people have contributed to the completion of the research on which the book is based. The skilful guidance of my doctoral supervisor, Prof. Robin Mansell helped me to translate the intuition and observations that I gathered over several years working in industry into a more rigorous framework. She continues to be a source of motivation, invaluable insight and advice. Members of the intellectual community at the University of Sussex particularly Martin Bell, Prof. Keith Pavitt, Dr Aldo Geuna and Prof. Michael Hobday were interested in the project and often engaged me in challenging discussions. The library staff at SPRU provided invaluable assistance. Cynthia Little, who edited this volume, held my hand at many difficult stages along the way and helped to improve the final product. My friends and family have been with me in this project. I am grateful for the generosity and interest of Ainsley, Antonio, Barbara, Benu, Cathy-Mae, Cherrie-Anne, Gem, Karen, Kenneth, Kafi, Patrice, Louanne and Tuere. I also wish to specially thank Vittoria de la Grenade for her boundless enthusiasm and Chantal Collet for her unconditional support.

.... a luta continua

1 Introduction

This book makes a contribution to knowledge by investigating how developing country firms undertake technological learning and capability building efforts. The main focus of the analysis in the study is explaining variation in ability to effectively manage technological capability building and learning at individual firm level. Drawing on a number of intellectual traditions, including organizational development, strategic management, innovation studies, development studies and evolutionary theory of the firm, the analysis sheds light on the processes by which firms accumulate and systematically deploy a broad range of technological capabilities and acquire technological capabilities from external sources including suppliers and the innovation system.

The main conclusion of this study is that for developing country firms a systematic approach to technological learning yields significant benefits. The study will show that, when developing country firms implement systems that simultaneously, proportionately and systematically direct effort at the following five key elements, that is financing, management and co-ordination, culture and leadership, managing relationships with suppliers and with the innovation system, they increase the effectiveness of technological capability building (TCB) and learning. As will be shown, even in very poor developing countries in Africa there are firms that have been able to deploy systems that conform to this ideal and these firms have been effective in technological capability and learning. The firms that demonstrated effectiveness in learning and capability development, developed and implemented TCB systems including: mechanisms for allocating financial resources to learning and capability development; and an appropriate organizational culture and specific management practices to encourage and support technological learning, as well as to manage the relationships between firms and their equipment and service suppliers and the innovation system.

It will be shown that the ability of firms to implement effective systems for learning and capability building is characterized by path dependency insofar as the initial stock of accumulated technological capability has an influence on effectiveness. However, it will also be shown that developing country firms can compensate for weaknesses in their context and environment by a variety of management practices and boundary relationships, including forging relationships with the global innovation system.

These conclusions are drawn from an in-depth study, which develops an original conceptual framework to carry out a detailed cross-sectional analysis of technological learning. and capability building in a sample of 26 telecommunication operating companies in Uganda, Ghana, Tanzania and South Africa. The unit of analysis in this study is the telecommunication operating company, that is the firm that owns or controls telecommunication networks and uses these to provide services to final customers. The empirical setting, therefore, is a fast-moving dynamic industry that is both a site of technological change and, in parallel, a site of industrial restructuring. Examining the processes that developing country firms use to build technological capabilities under these conditions has the potential to shed new light on some of the uncharted areas of science and technology policy studies, specifically with respect to the capability accumulation processes of service sector firms and the impact of rapid technological change on the prospects for technological capability development. The conceptual framework developed in this research and the empirical strategies employed also have the potential to be extended to other industries, and may be more generally applicable in the field of technological learning.

The central research question investigated in this study is: how do firms in developing countries implement learning processes for building technological capabilities? This study differs from other work in the field of capability development because it integrates the approaches from diverse traditions and extends them by applying their insights to developing country firms. Specifically, it is argued that a systemic approach to developing technological capability is an essential requirement. The conceptual framework extends the development studies approach to understanding intra-firm processes of capability development by centrally integrating insights from organizational development and strategic management theory. The second differentiating feature is that this study of capability accumulation extends the development studies tradition by focusing on how rapid technological change affects capability development processes in service sector firms and by examining processes that enable firms to manage assets that are not under their direct control. Although the processes for acquiring technological capabilities from external sources have received attention, the processes through which firms learn how to manage these boundary relationships to more effectively acquire technological capabilities is an under-researched area.

The rest of the chapter is organized as follows. Section 2 highlights key features of the conceptual framework; this is followed by Section 3 which summarizes the methodology. Section 4 provides an overview of the empirical context, including economic and industry features. Section 5 locates the contribution of this study within the academic literature and summarizes the implications for research, policy and firm strategy. The introduction concludes by presenting an overview of the organization of the book.

THE TCB SYSTEM APPROACH

Technological capability (TC) in this book is understood as a collection of firm-specific assets, both material and non-material, that are built up over time through non-linear processes of investment characterized by uncertainty. Building technological capabilities at firm level requires purposive co-ordinated activities over time. For this to be effective, firms must develop TCB systems consisting of internal processes and boundary relationships.

TC is defined as a firm-specific collection of equipment, skills, knowledge, aptitudes and attitudes that confer the ability to operate, understand, change and create production processes and products. The aspects of technological capability associated with human beings are referred to as the embodied elements of a technological capability, that is skills, attitudes, tacit knowledge and aptitude. These aspects of TC are coupled with non-embodied elements, such as codified knowledge, equipment and software. Firms require the tight integration of embodied and non-embodied capabilities if they are to derive benefit. If either of these broad types of capabilities is missing, or if their implementation is not well co-ordinated, it is suggested that the overall effect of having a capability may be diminished. To be operational and effective, technological capabilities should not exist in isolation, but should be integrated across an entire organization. This is defined as the organizational integration element of a TC and is similar to the concept of organizational coherence (Leonard-Barton 1995; Pettigrew and Whipp 1991) and the Tushman and Nadler (1996) concept of organizational congruence. At the detailed level, organizational integration is understood to include activities related to setting conditions for realizing the benefits from embodied and non-embodied capabilities, and management systems for decision-making, implementation and resource allocation and the establishment of a facilitating organizational culture.

The framework applied in this book builds on the resource-based approach to understanding capability development (Teece 1987; Teece and Pisano 1994; Teece et al. 2000), which suggests that a capability is only meaningful in terms of the services it delivers to the firm. This framework extends that treatment by delineating some of the human attributes that are required to

confer meaning. Unlike some other approaches, here institutional
relationships are excluded from the definition of a capability (see Bell and
Pavitt 1997). Instead, it is suggested that the management of institutional
relationships is part of the capability building process.

The process of technological capability building (TCB) is defined as a
process of assembling or accumulating technological capabilities and is
regarded as an investment activity undertaken by firms. In developing the
conceptual framework, the study draws upon four distinct, but related,
scholarly traditions of research into organizational learning in firms. The
TCB system approach draws on insights into the behavioural, structural,
environmental and functional enablers of learning, and specific development
studies approaches to analyzing capability development, particularly studies
such as Bell (1984); Bell and Pavitt (1997); Dutrenit (2000); Ernst et al.
(1998); Hobday (1990); Hoffman and Girvan (1990); Kim (1999); Leonard-
Barton (1995); Pettigrew and Whipp (1991); and Tidd et al. (1997).

By treating capability development as a learning process this study permits
an exploration of the aspects of TCB that are not linear, sequential or orderly.
The TCB system approach argues that firm-level variation in the
effectiveness and intensity of TCB effort cannot be fully explained by
country-level factors and is likely to be influenced by developments that
occur endogenously within the firm. The TCB system approach is designed
explicitly to investigate those aspects of firm performance that cannot be
explained by exogenous factors. It argues that firms may go further in
capability development than is suggested by the environment in which they
are located. The TCB system permits investigation and explanations of why
some firms are able to compensate for external conditions that are not
conducive to technological learning.

TCB activities are expected to have the potential to produce economic
benefits in the medium to long term for firms and the national contexts in
which they are located. Technological capability building activities are not
regarded as consumption activities; rather they are regarded as having the
potential to yield productivity gains, increases in output, improvements in
quality, reductions in operational costs, greater operational efficiency and
increased scope and range of outputs. Expectations of such outcomes provide
incentives for firms to undertake the required investment. Achieving
potential benefits from investments in TCB activities, however, is not
expected to be automatic. It involves a learning process in which existing
capabilities are transformed over time through a process of trial and error
into improved or enhanced capabilities. Nevertheless, as trial and error
implies, investments in TCB may not always produce enhanced outcomes.
There may be failures that result in improved understanding and lead
eventually to improved capabilities. The impetus for undertaking TCB

activities may also derive from internal factors, such as recognition of technological trends and existing capability gaps, or from external factors, such as changing market structure, the behaviour of competitors, actions of regulators and policy makers and information from suppliers and other knowledge creating institutions.

Firms are likely to improve the effectiveness of their learning and capability building by deploying a set of five integrated processes and mechanisms to: (1) allocate financial resources to TCB effort; (2) implement and support the TCB effort through appropriate management practices, systems and decision-making rules; (3) enable an organizational culture in which the TCB effort is exercised with committed and skilled leadership; (4) access external TC resources from suppliers; and (5) access TC resources from the innovation system (local and global).

The application of all five elements is considered to be necessary for increasing the stock of technological capabilities. There are internal processes – financing, management practices and culture and leadership – which are under the control of the firm and external (or boundary processes) – managing relationships with suppliers and with the innovation system, which are only partially under the firm's control.

Much of the policy literature on developing countries' capability accumulation experiences advocates a proactive role for public sector institutions in influencing TCB activities within firms (Lall 1987, 1992; Stewart 1984). The framework in this work positions developing country firms as active respondents to signals from public sector institutions rather than as passive agents. This contrasts with more conventional views that often see public sector bodies as 'omniscient' and better placed than the decision makers in firms to select suppliers, choose technological platforms and adjust technological capability building efforts. There is support for the need to critique this view from studies in many regions of the developing world, and particularly in Africa, where the 'state-in the lead' model of stimulating TCB performance in firms has met with dismal outcomes (Abiodun 1997; Cooper 1994; Enos 1995; Forje 1991; Pickett 1991; Stewart et al. 1992; UNCTAD 1996; Wangwe 1995).

EXAMINING LEARNING IN AFRICAN TELECOMMUNICATION FIRMS: RESEARCH STRATEGY, METHOD AND ANALYSIS

This section discusses the strategy, methodology and approach to analysing research findings. As stated earlier this study focuses on how firms in developing countries implement learning processes for building technological capabilities. Following on from this, the study also considers:

1   What specific learning processes are implemented to accumulate technological capabilities?
2   What are the implications of the management of internal processes for the accumulation of capabilities?
3   What are the implications of relationships with supplier firms for the accumulation of capabilities?
4   What are the implications of relationships with policy and regulatory bodies, as representative bodies of the innovation system, for the accumulation of technological capability?

The study involves a detailed cross-sectional analysis of technological learning and capability building in this sample of 26 telecommunication operating companies in Uganda, Ghana, Tanzania and South Africa. The firms selected for detailed analysis all owned or leased telecommunication networks and use these to deliver services to end customers.[1] These firms had features in common with the telecommunication network-based services (TNS) concept defined by Mansell (1987) as firms that offer 'services that combine information production, manipulation, storage and or distribution with the use of telecommunication facilities and software functions' (p. 33). This study drew tighter boundaries around the definition in order to operationalize the concept. These firms offer a diverse array of services, their service range and the technologies used to supply changes in services over time.

The principal technique of data collection used was the case study method, because as an 'intensive' research method it is particularly well suited to the task of generating and analysing qualitative information (Sayer 1992). The opinions, judgements and views of the representatives of operating companies, policy and regulatory bodies, equipment supply companies and independent experts served as the primary sources of information. In addition, the views of key actors in the industry, such as officials from central government, science and technology institutions, regulatory authorities, international investors and international organizations, were also solicited to corroborate the views of the representatives of the operating companies and to provided insights into contextual variables. To elicit this information, semi-structured interviews were conducted personally with all respondents, with each interview taking, on average, one and half hours. In implementing these research techniques the guidelines and approaches suggested by Argyris (1993b); Argyris and Schon (1996a); and Oppenheim (1992) were employed.

The main empirical research was conducted over two years (1998–1999) with the researcher spending an average of four weeks in Uganda, Ghana and Tanzania and seven weeks in South Africa on primary data collection.

Additional interviews were conducted with suppliers in South Africa in September 2000. During the course of this study, 96 individuals from 58 organizations were interviewed. Table 1.1 provides a summary of the types and number organizations and individuals interviewed.

The primary data collection phase yielded rich results. Being active in a number of professional networks and having had considerable experience providing advisory services in the African telecommunications industry, I was able to access senior management in the operating companies and also government officials. My success in persuading respondents to participate in the research was also positively influenced by the reputation of my host organizations in each of the four countries. These included a government ministry responsible for telecommunications, two research centres and an NGO headed by a well-known member of parliament. My hosts were also generous enough to provide administrative and logistical support.

Table 1.1 Summary of primary data gathering

	Uganda	Ghana	Tanzania	SA	Inter-national	Total
Organizations	12	13	15	13	5	58
Individuals	18	21	23	29	5	96
Telecom operating companies (fixed, mobile, data, satellite, signal distribution)	3	6	8	9		26
Public sector organizations (regulatory, public policy, academic institutions, other research and knowledge production)	7	6	4	3		20
Individual experts, commentators, consultants, officials of multilateral institutions	2	1	3	1		7
Telecommunication equipment suppliers					5	5
Total	12	13	15	13	5	58

Source: Compiled by author.

The 26 telecommunication operating companies that comprised the sample provided great variety in terms of length of establishment, size, business models, ownership structures and the range of market structures in which they operated. Table 1.2 provides summary data on the 26 sample firms, including the date the firm began operation, number of years of operation, firm size based on number of employees, and market segment and ownership codes. The table also indicates the year in which data were gathered.

Table 1.2 Main characteristics of sample firms (based on company data)

Date of interview	Company	Start date	Years	Staff count	Market segment	Type of ownership
1998 Uganda						
	Uganda Telecom Ltd	1983	15	1,900	2	9
	CelTel	1995	3	90	3	4
	MTN Uganda Ltd	1998	0.25	10	2	7
Ghana	Ghana Telecom Co. Ltd	1995	3	3,548	2	2
	ACG Telesystems (Ghana) Ltd (Westel)	1997	1	74	2	3
	Mobitel (Ghana)	1992	6	150	3	4
	Celltel Ltd	1995	3	55	3	3
	ScanCom Ltd	1996	2	70	3	5
	Network Computer Systems Ltd (NCS)	1994	4	60	4	8
1999						
Tanzania	Tanzania Telecom Co. Ltd (TTCL)	1992	7	3,705	1	9
	Mobitel (Tanzania) Ltd	1994	5	150	3	4
	TRI Telecom Tanzania Ltd (TRITEL)	1996	4	230	3	2
	Datel Tanzania Ltd	1996	3	17	4	4
	Wilken Afsat (Tanzania) Ltd	1997	2	12	4	7
	Africa On-Line (Tanzania)	1997	2	16	4	7
	Planetel Communications Ltd	1998	0.6	12	6	7
	Computer Corp. of Tanzania Ltd (CCTL)	1996	3	68	4	3
South Africa	TELKOM SA Ltd	1991	8	59,012	1	1
	MTN SA Ltd	1995	4	2,000	3	8
	Vodacom	1995	4	2,500	3	4
	ESKOM-Telecoms division	1993	6	300	6	9
	Transtel	1992	7	2,000	6	9
	Orbicom	1993	6	77	5	8
	Sentech	1994	5	460	5	9
	UU-Net (SA) Pty Ltd	1994	5	130	4	3
	ICO Global Communications	1999	0.6	7	6	6

Source: Compiled by author based on company data and interview accounts.

Table 1.3 defines the market segment codes shown in Table 1.2. The data show that the sample firms operated within six types of business models from vertically integrated firms operating in national monopoly markets to firms operating private networks not subject to market competition.

Table 1.3 Distribution of sample by market segment code

Market segment code	Definition	No of firms
1	Monopoly on fixed voice, competition on mobile, data and value added services	2
2	Fully competitive on fixed voice, mobile, data and value added services	4
3	Competitive mobile operator	8
4	Competitive datacommunication, value added services and ISPs	6
5	Duopoly signal distribution and multimedia value added services	2
6	Precompetitive or prelaunch	4

Source: Compiled by author based on secondary data.

Table 1.4 shows the distribution of ownership structures for the sample firms as well as the definitions of shareholding codes. As can be seen from the table, there were nine types of ownership structure ranging from public sector companies owned by national African governments to branches of international corporations.

Table 1.4 Sample firms distributed by ownership structure

Shareholding codes	Ownership structure	No. of firms
1	Malaysian and US shareholding	1
2	Malaysian shareholding	2
3	US shareholding or joint venture	4
4	European shareholding	5
5	Lebanese shareholding	1
6	Branch of global company	1
7	100% private sector cross-border African shareholding	4
8	100% private sector single African country	3
9	100% state owned African state	5

Source: Compiled by author based on secondary data and interviews.

A complete list of all interviews conducted and the semi-structured questionnaires used for the interviews with operating companies, policy and regulatory officials and supplier companies are provided in the appendix to Chapter 1. In addition to primary data collection, a number of secondary sources were consulted, which were particularly important for providing basic information on the operations of the companies, the market structures in which they operated, the nature of the extended institutional system, policy objectives and regulatory philosophy and practice.

This empirical dataset on the TCB practices of the sample firms was used in a series of quantitative and qualitative analyzes to answer the research questions and operationalize the conceptual framework.

The quantitative analysis involved several steps: constructing indicators of TCB system development, using these indicators to develop categories of TCB system development, and testing to check the extent to which there was conformity to a hypothetical ideal across different categories of TCB system development. Detailed correlation analysis was conducted, which permitted exploration of the relationship between the level of TCB system development and independent variables, such as length of time in operation, firm size as measured by staff count, market segment, ownership type and country of operation, as well as the relationship between TCB system development and the likelihood of having a directed and problem-focused approach to TCB effort. TCB indicators were constructed and ANOVA computations and Kruskal–Wallis and Wilcoxon Sign tests conducted on their application and use in testing the hypotheses from the conceptual framework. The implications of the results of these tests are described in Chapter 3.

Qualitative data analysis techniques were used to identify and explore patterns of variation across the sample of firms. Firstly, the observable patterns of TCB were organized and mapped. Secondly, features common to all firms as well as the specific patterns within categories of TCB system development were identified. In order to probe more deeply in order to explain what might account for variation across categories of TCB system development, the patterns across categories were compared and contrasted.

This research strategy, which combined qualitative and quantitative analysis to test *a priori* relationships and hypotheses, proved fruitful. It provided analyzes and conclusions that can be used as the basis for making analytical generalizations about technological capability building and learning in developing country firms. These analyses and conclusions, while not representative in the strict sense, are sufficiently robust to provide a foundation for drawing conclusions about the effectiveness of TCB and learning and the role of a systematic approach to their accumulation.

The main focus of the analysis in this work is explaining the variation in ability to manage technological capability building and learning at the individual firm level. The approach adopted is that, although the capability building and learning processes of developing country firms are context dependent, a fuller explanation of effectiveness in technological learning can only be achieved by a dual focus on country-level factors that may facilitate or impede technological learning, and on endogenous, intra-firm factors. Figure 1.1 depicts a model that illustrates the hypothesized interaction between country-level and firm-level factors. The TCB system approach suggests that the most desirable position for any firm would be in the top right-hand side (Q4), where firm level and country level factors combine to produce a positive effect on the effectiveness of TCB. Conversely, the least attractive position would be in the lower left-hand side (Q2), where neither country-level nor firm-level factors are strongly supportive of technological capability building and learning.

Figure 1.1 Interaction of firm-level and country-level factors

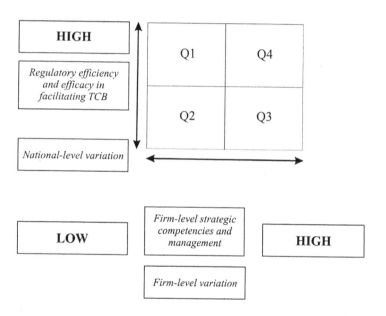

Source: Compiled by author.

It is also possible for the combined effect of firm-level competencies and country-level factors to be insufficiently strong to produce a large positive influence on the effectiveness of learning, an event that would correspond to the lower right-hand side (Q3). The position represented by the upper left-hand side (Q1) is one where country-level factors outweigh the impact of firm-level competencies.

EMPIRICAL CONTEXT: ECONOMIC ENVIRONMENT AND
INDUSTRY SPECIFIC FACTORS

This section provides a summary of the economic context in which the
sample firms included in this study are located. The first subsection considers
the economic performance of the African region. The analysis of regional
trends and the main features of the economic structure and performance of
the four countries – Uganda, Ghana, Tanzania and South Africa – are based
on secondary data. This material on economic context is followed by a
review of the main trends in policy and regulation in the telecommunication
sector in the region. This discussion draws upon documentation from
multilateral agencies, particularly the International Telecommunication
Union (ITU/BDT 1996, 1998b, 1998c, 2000) and national government
agencies. The material in the policy analysis section is based on primary and
secondary data. The final subsection provides an analysis of the main
features of technical change in the global telecommunication industry drawn
from a review of academic research.

Economic Structure and Performance

The macroeconomic conditions in the four sub-Saharan African countries[2]
selected as case studies during the period 1998–2000 were characterized by:

- increasing optimism about the African region's economic recovery.
  Some 37 countries registered positive per capita GDP growth in 1997,
  21 of which grew at a rate of 5 per cent or more. In 1998, the average
  African country's GDP grew 4.6 per cent, slightly lower than in 1996
  (4.8 per cent);
- significant expansion of exports at rates that were exceeding growth in
  output;
- reduction in fiscal deficits and inflation, which were also considered
  to have boosted growth rates;
- World Bank-inspired and managed macroeconomic reforms, which
  had encouraged a reshaping of the role of the state and sought to
  create business environments that would encourage private investment
  and private sector development. The Bank also focused on 'helping
  African people take advantage of global communications systems for
  accessing information' (World Bank 1998a: 1) and identified
  telecommunication sector reform as a prerequisite to achieve this
  objective;
- changes in the management of debt, including proposals for the
  development of special initiatives, such as the Highly Indebted Poor

Countries (HIPC) Debt Initiative, which would permit governments to shift resources to aid development and alleviate poverty rather than to achieve debt repayment.

In addition to these changes in the economic and policy environment, the African region has faced many serious challenges to progress towards its social and economic development goals including:

- the impact of the pandemic HIV/AIDS on economic activity and the social fabric;
- continuing dependence on development assistance;
- the rapid rise of domestic debt in some countries; and
- the dampening effect of the East Asian crisis in the late 1990s and declining foreign investment flows to the region.

Table 1.5 Economic profiles Uganda, Ghana, Tanzania and South Africa

1998–1999	Uganda	Ghana	Tanzania	South Africa
Population – millions	21	18.4*	32.4	41.4
GDP per capita US$	317	372	244	3,107
GDP growth	7.8	4.2	3.8	0.7
% contribution of transport and communications sector to GDP	n.a.	5	4	n.a. **
% contribution of agricultural sector to GDP	45	36	49	4

Source: Compiled by author based on Economist Intelligence Unit Country report 1999.[3]
*Notes: *Population estimated based on actual for 1997.*
*** South African service sector contribution to GDP at factor costs is more in line with OECD levels, (60–70% of total) and during the 1990s the communications sector was a fast growing segment.*

Table 1.5 summarizes key demographic and economic characteristics of the four countries for the period 1998–999. As can be seen from the table, South Africa is the largest economy measured in terms of gross domestic output, followed by Tanzania, Uganda and Ghana, respectively. The relative ranking of these four economies is the same for both population size and gross domestic output. Uganda was the fastest growing over the period 1998–99; real GDP grew at a rate of more than 7 per cent. Ghana and Tanzania averaged real growth rates of approximately 4 per cent, while South Africa struggled to achieve a 1 per cent growth rate in real GDP in that period. Analysis of these data suggest that for 1998/99 in Uganda, Ghana and

Tanzania the agricultural sector made the largest contribution to national output, accounting for more than 40 per cent of GDP. In South Africa in 1999, the contribution of the service sector was more than seven times that of the agricultural and mining sectors combined. In all four countries, the share of the transport and communication sector as a percentage of GDP increased.

Summary of Telecommunication Policy and Regulatory Environment

At the time of the field research, Uganda, Ghana, Tanzania and South Africa were among the leaders in Sub-Saharan Africa in terms of progress in undertaking a fundamental restructuring of their telecommunication sectors to achieve the following similar broad objectives:

- expansion of national telecommunication networks and range of services available;
- attracting foreign investment to facilitate the injection of capital, technology and management skills necessary to achieve this expansion;
- harmonization of approaches to sector development with international 'best practice', in particular, with respect to reducing direct state ownership and control of operating companies and achieving a separation of the regulatory function of the state from ownership and policy making.

As a result of their success, these four countries had a number of market players, a variety of market structures, a considerable range of services on offer, relatively good institutional development and significant foreign investment. Notwithstanding these broad commonalties, in each of these countries there were variations in terms of the priorities assigned to these objectives and also in the strategies used by national governments.

All four countries were also similar in so far as national policy makers demonstrated little awareness or understanding of the importance of the processes through which telecommunication companies build technological capabilities. Rather than being given explicit attention, technological capability building appears to have been treated as an 'automatic' by product of the process of the restructuring of the operating companies in the sector in the bid to attract foreign investment. Rather than technology capability building, the priorities for national policy and regulatory agencies were found to be defined as: market access rules and licensing; interconnection rules; and technology and facilities access, including spectrum pricing. Furthermore, the international advice that was available to national governments is shown to have given much more emphasis to the need to change the market structure and ownership of the telecommunication operating companies than to regulatory or policy oversight of the companies' technological capability building processes.

This empirical context represents a challenging environment for technological learning and capability building. In selecting this particular context, the study sheds light on how developing country firms in a services sector build technological capabilities in a fast-moving dynamic industry that is both a site of technological change and, in parallel, a site of industrial restructuring. Further details on the telecommunications industry structure in these four countries can be found in Appendix A1.3. The appendix to Chapter 6 provides factual details on the legal and policy institutional arrangements for facilitating TCB and Chapter 6 provides a detailed assessment of the effectiveness of these arrangements.

Technical Change in the Telecommunication Industry: A Brief History

The main features of technological change in the global telecommunication industry are summarized in Table 1.6. These features or *stylized facts* regarding telecommunication technologies and associated learning regimes[4] are subject to localized variation and refer primarily to trends in wealthy countries. As shown by these data, the telecommunication industry has experienced variation in the rate at which technical change has taken place. It has also experienced shifts in the focus of innovation, which has emphasized digitization, shift to modularity of network architectures, the incorporation of decentralized intelligence, global standards and the development of the Internet.

Fransman (2000), using a dynamic analysis, stresses that in responding to changes in the industry firms often go through processes that are difficult to manage and argues that the most significant technology shifts are often not smooth or uncontroversial. For example, the transition to new generations of switching equipment was accompanied by debates about whether the new generations were needed and whether improvements could be made to existing technologies. In his assessment, the adoption of packet switching was a particularly hard fought battle. The replacement of electromechanical devices by digital equipment and the widespread deployment of the TCP/IP in networks are other examples of disruptive technical change in the telecommunication industry.

Table 1.6. Key features of technological change in telecommunications

Era	Major technological change	Features and improvements in technology	Characteristics of learning regime
Up to 1950s	Electromechanical to electronic switches.	Electromechanical devices were reliable and robust and well suited to voice transmission.	Required precision engineering and knowledge of multiple engineering disciplines. Equipment suppliers vertically integrated firms producing equipment and services.
1970s	Fully digital switching and transmission.	Increased speed, reduced maintenance, feature rich equipment, large range of data formats. Use of packet switching replaced circuit switching for data transmission.	Partnership between public research laboratories and equipment suppliers; small number of specialist equipment suppliers; very high cost R&D investment; long lead time, often as much as ten years, for evolution from invention to commercial deployment and emphasis on trials and prototype development. Digital systems developed with principles of modularity and divisibility and emphasis on design engineering. Generalized knowledge base with emphasis on IT and software development.
1980s	Incremental innovation in switching and transmission equipment. Dramatic shifts in network architecture with adoption of open architecture.	Focus on increasing system capacity and customer satisfaction. Improvements in the end-to-end connection and management of networks, automation of testing and maintenance, development of flexible charging systems, some customer control of configuration, calling party verification, information security and authentication.	Competition based on equipment functionality and system integration capability of equipment vendors and network operators. More focus on integration of technological knowledge. Increasing number of specialist equipment suppliers facilitated by liberalization of service provision markets. Co-operation between operators and service providers with a division of labour, suppliers focus on R&D, service providers on customer service, and product differentiation.

		Features located in processor communication and software protocols within and peripheral to the network.	
1990s	Incremental innovation in switching and transmission equipment.	Shift in focus to increasing advanced functionality of switches and provision of enhanced services. Development of asynchronous transfer mode (ATM) switching and synchronous digital hierarchy (SDH) transmission systems. Focus on mobility and radio signalling access networks.	Equipment suppliers extend to local manufacturing in developing countries and learn how to transfer technology. Greater opportunity for acquiring manufacturing know-how from international suppliers. Equipment suppliers and service providers simultaneously collaborate and compete with competition based on product innovation and first to market advantages. Pace of technological change accelerates and the demand for R&D spending increases, while some equipment unit prices decline.
Late 1990s & early 21st century	Radical innovation in network architecture.	Focus on internetworking based on TCP/IP and providing access to the Internet.	Network operators rely on specialist equipment suppliers through subcontracting and other relationships, while specialist equipment suppliers remain R&D intensive and become focused on satisfying customer requirements and more experimentation. There is rapid concurrent innovation and remote innovation.

Source: Author based on Brock (1981); Crandall and Flamm (1989); Davies (1996); Fransman (2000); Hobday (1990); Mansell (1987); and Mytelka (1999).

The transition to TCP/IP took place within the period considered in the empirical research for this book. Under conditions of disruptive change, the capability to select technologies becomes essential, particularly for developing country firms, which have limited financial resources to undertake these significant investments and are likely to be influenced by suppliers who are not disinterested, but rather are supporters of particular technological configurations. Although the sample firms and their contexts are geographically and psychologically distant from the characteristics of technological change and learning described here, the prospects for these firms to develop technological capability are likely to be decidedly influenced by these trends.[5]

Technical change has also had implications at the component and subsystem level of telecommunication networks. A telecommunication network can be considered as an expandable system of independent units or system elements. The equipment – switching, transmission and access networks – that makes up these system elements has become increasingly computer controlled and software subsystems control the intelligent and efficient connection and transmission of messages. As the 'embeddedness' of intelligence in equipment has increased, the microelectronic systems and subsystems have become more important (Fransman 2000; Hobday 1990; Mansell 1987)[6] and telecommunication networks have become more similar to computer networks. Proprietary knowledge is held at the machine code and electronic circuitry levels and this has implications for differentiating service offerings from competing suppliers. But access to this type of knowledge is not the core competence required by service providers. For the telecommunication operator, access to this proprietary knowledge may not be as important as access to advanced systems integration capability to ensure that components provided by different suppliers function and integrate well with other components. When telecommunication companies were vertically integrated there may have been a coupling of knowledge about equipment and about how to make that equipment work (Davies and Brady 2000; Fransman 2000; McKelvey et al. 1998).

However, in the structure of the 1990s telecommunication market, the sellers of equipment regarded knowledge about how best to make their equipment work in a given customer's location as a core selling factor and distinguished this from proprietary knowledge. They used their ability to facilitate operators in making best use of their equipment as a competitive factor in their market share battles (Davies and Brady 2000; McKelvey et al. 1998). This illustrates that technological change has impacted on the constraints facing developing country firms. Technical change in the telecommunication industry has contributed to making sources of technological inputs for the utilization of equipment, the integration of new varieties of technological solutions and knowledge about performance more widely available than in the past. This is important for telecommunication operators in developing countries, as the external suppliers of equipment and related services are the main sources of these inputs – they are usually not substitutable by domestic sources or the internal resources of the firms.

All telecommunication operators are faced with the challenge of keeping up with these changing technical characteristics. However, it is the large and influential users in the host countries of equipment supply companies (Europe, Japan, South Korea and USA) that often play a role in specifying the direction of technical change. The changes in demand by users, user–producer and supplier–user dynamics in the telecommunication industry play an important role in the innovation process (Davies 1997; Davies and Brady 2000; Ernst and Lundvall 1997; Fransman 2000; Lundvall, 1988; Mansell 1993, 1995; McNamara 1991; OECD 1992); developing country firms are also affected by these trends.

Mansell (1995) in her analysis of innovation in telecommunication argues that the digitization of networks and the changing market structure of the supply industry were the focus in the analysis of the innovation processes until the 1980s. However, the supplier–user interface is 'a site of negotiation of technical and organizational design alternatives' (Mansell 1995: 235). In the 1990s the producers of telecommunication equipment identified the system and large system management capabilities as areas of core competence and sources of competitive advantage.[7] Equipment suppliers have been taking increasing responsibility for activities previously undertaken in-house by operating companies, including systems integration, project management and network planning. 'Economies of repetition' gained over time by improving project effectiveness may help to increase incentives for long-term mutually beneficial relationships between suppliers and their operating company users. They may also provide an incentive for organizational capability development by suppliers (Narduzzo et al. 2000).

Telecommunication network operators have been identified as 'sophisticated users' Fransman (2000: 12). They play a role in the innovation process through learning-by-using and through experience gained in making improvements in running networks. Operators have been innovative in changing their services and relationships with customers. Network operators have made many changes to enhance their competitiveness that did not require R&D investment (p. 19). Operators that are not involved in R&D learn by outsourcing to specialist suppliers and by buying in the 'fruits of this learning in the form of tangible assets such as telecommunication equipment or intangible knowledge such as occurs when technical advice is given' (p. 21).

Network operators face a differentiation constraint, since they are dependent on equipment suppliers, and all operators have access to the same tangible technologies. In this case, operators compete on the basis of being able to provide superior quality of service 'provisioning time, quicker restoration of disrupted service, superior customer case – do you really mean case or base, better understanding of customer needs, greater ability to provide solutions on the basis of common technology, to customer problems' (p. 24).

In the late 1990s there was considerable experimentation as 'many kinds of equipment and software can be tested on-line at a far earlier stage in the development process' (p. 40). A process of co-evolution of consumer tastes and preferences, involving substantial 'interpretative ambiguity' was underway.[8] Equipment supply firms' employees become sources of capability. These employees moved around and often provided resources to operating companies (p. 20). In the 1990s equipment suppliers, as producers supplying to operating companies, appeared to become more attentive to customer demand. Operating companies, in turn, appeared to have increased their focus on the requirements of their end–customers. The capability development process for telecommunication operating companies in developing countries is likely to be influenced by the demand as well as the supply conditions.

Specialized equipment suppliers play a leading role in the innovation effort, primarily through R&D investment in this industry.[9] Fransman notes that the supply industry has changed and this author characterizes the last decade as being defined by increasing competition across segments of supply chains, particularly between firms specialized in computer networking equipment and the telecommunication equipment suppliers.

This characteristic may have the potential to assist in the capability development effort of developing country operating firms by increasing the possible sources of technological inputs. The sources of capability inputs now include suppliers of 'codified' knowledge such as information brokers, specialist suppliers of equipment and IT firms. Hobday (1990) emphasizes that the technological knowledge required to manufacture digital telecommunication systems includes generalized high-level software design and development skills and in principle these are available from a wide range of suppliers. The importance of these skills for the design and management of telecommunication networks is also stressed (Davies 1996; Mansell 1987). This may increase the number of means for acquiring capability inputs, for example through the international migration of skilled labour, including the repatriation of nationals. These factors may reduce the constraints on developing country firms and provide greater opportunities for gaining access to technological knowledge.

IMPLICATIONS FOR KNOWLEDGE, POLICY AND PRACTICE

The study in this book meets its aims of improving understanding of the nature of learning and technological capability building (TCB) processes in firms, where the external environment presents challenges of dramatic and fundamental industry restructuring and institutional development; and of providing an analysis that can be used as a guide for firm strategy and the design of policy and institution building in developing countries that face these challenges.

This study sheds new light on how developing country firms learn to build technological capabilities. It is important that the empirical setting for the research is a service sector in which the sample firms run and manage telecommunication networks, but are not engaged in the manufacture of telecommunication equipment, which is an under-researched area.

The results arising from applying the TCB system approach are applicable not only to the telecommunication industry, but also to other sectors where developing country firms are forced to interact with technology that is at the frontier when their local innovation system is not able to operate at the frontier. It is also of interest to understand how developing country firms undertake learning and technological capability building when the purpose and motivation is not to generate radical innovation, but to use frontier technologies for economic and social development. The firms in this study face demand conditions that are influenced by the structure and performance of the poor developing economies in which they simultaneously operate and negotiate supply conditions that are influenced by the global industry. The supply conditions that influence their design of telecommunication networks and the equipment used in these networks are directly impacted by global trends, although these firms operate in small, peripheral countries that are not at the frontier of technology. Some of the other sectors where these insights are likely to be relevant include banking, electricity and road transport, all of which are sectors where developing country firms interact with large technical systems (Hughes 1987), and their effectiveness has a significant impact on development prospects.

Another product of this study is that it sheds light on how developing country firms face specific challenges arising from the speed, complexity and extensive effects of technological change. The information and communication technology (ICT) sector is increasingly being recognized as a sector in which technological mastery and responsiveness are important and challenging. Moreover, it is now accepted that the ability to harness ICT has implications for overall performance in meeting development goals (Bhagavan 1997; Mansell and Wehn 1998; UN 1997, 2000). In this context the results of this study are pertinent, since they move beyond diagnosis to providing an analysis that can guide firm level and national strategies for improving technological capability development in this critical domain.

The analysis provides new insights into the processes through which developing country firms build technological capabilities using internal firm processes and management of relationships with suppliers and policy and regulatory institutions. The TCB system approach departs from previous treatments of capability accumulation in developing country firms. In particular, capability development is considered to be a dynamic, path dependent and uncertain process, and, in analyzing the sources of effectiveness, emphasis is placed on both endogenous factors and national policy intervention. The results provide insights that demonstrate that a simultaneous focus on both **internal** processes and **boundary** relationships is necessary if firms are to be effective in learning and capability accumulation. This is a useful extension of the development studies' perspectives on capability development, which also provides room for firm agency. By demonstrating that some firms are able to be effective in learning and capability development in this high-technology sector through adopting a systematic and proactive approach to internal competency development and management of boundary relationships, the framework presented here provides a basis for strategic action.

ORGANIZATION OF THE STUDY

This book is structured into seven chapters. The introductory chapter, which sets out the purpose, methodology and context of the study is followed by Chapter 2, which presents the conceptual framework. In Chapter 3 a detailed exploration of the quantitative analysis is presented. Chapter 4 presents a discussion of the management, culture and leadership elements of the TCB system. Chapter 5 discusses the part played by management of supplier relationships and Chapter 6 analyzes the role of the innovation system. Chapter 7 offers some concluding reflections and implications of the study for improved knowledge and practice. The central observation is that a systematic, balanced and coherent approach to the simultaneous development of internal processes and the management of boundary relationships was found to have yielded improvements in the effectiveness of capability development and learning.

NOTES

1   Fransman (2000: Exhibit 7, p. 37) provides a six-layer model of the infocommunication
     industry: layer 1 equipment and software; layer 2 network layer; layer 3 connectivity

layer; layer 4 navigation and middleware layer; layer 5 applications layer including content packaging; and layer 6 customers. The sample firms operate in layers 1 and 2 only and do not include the facility-less service providers that operate from layer 4 upwards.

2   Main sources are World Bank (1998a, 1998b, 2000).

3   See Economist Intelligence Unit (1999a,b,c,d).

4   Learning regime is understood as defined by Fransman (2000: 7) as the 'learning regime that determines the kinds of learning paths and patterns in which the firms and other organizations involved in the industry will engage'. The learning regime is considered to be related to the technological regime defined as 'the conditions under which technological knowledge is created – which determine the rate of technical change and the kinds of technologies that are created – and the opportunities and constraints that exist in the use of that knowledge'.

5   Hobday (1990) and Mytelka (1999) provided a detailed examination of the capability development experienced by developing country firms in Brazil and South Korea seeking to manufacture telecommunication equipment. While manufacturing is not the concern of this book, these studies provide useful insights for understanding the capability development of telecommunication network operating companies and for developing an argument about how technological change at the frontier influenced the capability development efforts of non-frontier firms (see Chapter 2 in this volume).

6   Hobday (1990: 43) succinctly describes this trend towards increasing embeddedness of technological knowledge when he says that '..intelligence for interconnection, storing and transmitting many thousands of messages simultaneously, and at the same time controlling hardware operations, recording subscriber traffic, and routing is encoded in software routines in telecommunication equipment. [These software routines] absorb the greatest share of R&D budgets of [equipment suppliers]'.

7   See Davies and Brady (2000). The empirical illustration is the effort made by Ericsson to develop network implementation capabilities in which 'time to profit' advantages were critical. To achieve this, the equipment supplier improved its project execution capability by setting up project management specialization, standardizing project management disciplines and recruiting to match identification of this core competence. Where there were gaps such as site acquisition and construction, Ericsson developed that competence. Although the empirical study was based on the UK, the trend identified may be relevant for relationships between developing country operating companies and their equipment suppliers.

8   Defined as 'when currently available information left significant ambiguity regarding what should be inferred' (Fransman 2000: 50).

9   Fransman (2000: 10) identifies the central research laboratories of monopoly telecommunication operators as the engine of innovation in the early period, naming as representatives of this trend: AT&T's Bell laboratories, BT's Martlesham Laboratories, France Telecom's CNET Laboratories and NTT's Electrical Engineering Laboratories. Mytelka (1999) and Davies and Brady (2000) add to this list Ericsson's joint venture with the Swedish telecommunication operator that led to development of the AXE digital switch. As an indication of the dynamics of the industry, Fransman (2000:19) notes that by the mid 1990s, the R&D engine had decisively moved to specialist technology suppliers.

2 The TCB System Approach

The conceptual framework developed in this chapter is used to investigate the proposition that for firms in developing countries to be effective in building technological capabilities they must systematically deploy technological capability building (TCB) systems that incorporate specific internal processes and management of two sets of boundary relationships. The TCB system approach suggests that the key internal processes are: mechanisms for allocating financial resources to the TCB effort; development of an appropriate organizational culture and management practices to encourage and support technological learning. It also suggests that developing country firms must have the ability to manage relationships with equipment and service suppliers and with the innovation system.

The strategy employed in constructing the conceptual framework was to examine the received theory on the themes of organizational learning, innovation management, technological capability development and technology transfer, as developed by their leading proponents, and then to extract the insights that could meaningfully be applied to developing country firms. This process of review and extraction identified broad principles of successful technological capability building and, second, identified gaps and blind spots in the existing theory that could be filled through an original and detailed examination of the technological capability building processes of firms in developing countries.

The extraction and amplification process was undertaken using the following distillation questions as a guide. How might an insight, argument or concept be relevant to the analysis of technological capability building processes undertaken by firms in developing countries? What would need to be added to or deleted from the existing literature to make it more specific and applicable to developing country settings? Are the 'general' observations in the existing literature likely to be applicable only when firms reach a certain threshold level in building capabilities? Will the observations with respect to capability building continue to apply to firms in developing countries?

By employing the review-extraction-amplification methodology it was possible to produce a critical synthesis of a vast and rich academic terrain and to produce new information and insights on how firms have managed technological capability building and learning. The key texts that were examined are presented in Table 2.1. The organizational development and strategic management approaches to understanding learning in organizations, which is almost exclusively concerned with how organizations in wealthy countries, operating at the technological frontier, implement systems of learning, produced valuable insights although their context was considerably different from the empirical context of this study. Studies in the field of innovation management located within the broad 'schools' of management science, strategic management and innovation studies contributed to the conceptual framework by providing insights into how firms, operating in an age when generic technologies and paradigm changing technologies are pervasive, should go about technological learning and successful product/process innovation. Empirical and conceptual research in the development studies tradition, including the technology transfer literature, were particularly useful for examining the role of suppliers and the policy-making apparatus, which attempts to stimulate and support firms' technological capability development. The conceptual framework integrates these insights from different traditions, as well as adapting and amplifying them for developing country settings.

Table 2.1 Key texts on organizational learning and technological capability building

Organizational development	Strategic management
Argyris 1993a, 1993c, 1996;	Teece 1987; Teece & Pisano 1994;
Argyris & Schon 1996b	Teece et al. 2000
Starkey 1996;	Prahalad & Hamel 1990, 1994
Vaill 1996	Baden-Fuller & Stopford 1994
Schein 1992	
Senge 1992, 1999	
Watkins & Marsick 1993	
Integrative approaches	**Evolutionary theory of the firm**
Leonard-Barton 1988, 1992a, 1992b, 1995	Nelson & Winter 1982;
Moingeon & Edmondson 1996	Winter 1987
Pettigrew & Whipp 1991; Garvin 1993;	Dosi et al. 2000b
Weick 1987	
Innovation management and national innovation systems	**Development studies**
	Bell 1984
Tidd et al. 1997	Bell & Pavitt 1993, 1997
Lundvall 1988, 1995, 1992; Lundvall &	Dutrenit 2000
Johnson 1994; Nelson 1993	Ernst et al. 1998; Kim 1999; Kim &
Edquist 1997; Freeman 1995; Mowery	Nelson 2000
1994; Patel & Pavitt 1994	

Source: Compiled by author.

TECHNOLOGICAL CAPABILITY BUILDING AS LEARNING

Technological capability (TC) is defined as a firm-specific collection of equipment, skills, knowledge, aptitudes and attitudes, which confers the ability to operate, understand, change and create production processes and products. The assets that constitute a firm's TC are likely to include elements with intensive scientific and technological content, such as disciplinary-specific technical knowledge, codified product and process specifications and tacit knowledge about production processes, as well as organizational elements that enhance the ability of a firm to benefit from the presence of these technical components. The non-technical organizational elements of a firm's TC are vital components that support the acquisition of technological knowledge and learning, both at individual and firm levels. In the TCB system approach, a firm's TC is considered to be made up of three main constituents, namely embodied, non-embodied and organizational integration (see Figure 2.1).

Figure 2.1 Three main constituent elements of technological capabilities

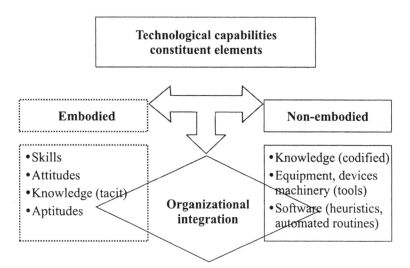

Source: Author.

Embodied elements refer to those aspects of technological capability that are associated with human beings, such as skills, attitudes, tacit knowledge and aptitudes. Non-embodied elements include codified knowledge, equipment and software. In the TCB system approach, it is explicitly stated that for firms to realize benefit, disembodied elements of a TC must be effectively coupled with the embodied elements through the third element, organizational integration. Firms that are effective in their technological capability building do not accumulate technological capabilities in isolation, but deploy mechanisms to ensure that the effort is integrated across the entire organization. If any of these three elements of a TC is missing, the overall effect of the capability is likely to be diminished. By placing emphasis on the role of human attributes, as well as on the material and organizational aspects of technological capabilities, the conceptual framework builds on the integrative approach to strategic management and extends the resource-based theory of the firm by delineating the human attributes that are required to confer meaningful capability and provide services to a firm.

To enable the operationalization of the TCB system approach, the conceptual framework identifies the observable sub-elements of TCs and develops indicators that can be used to identify whether or not a particular TC element is present in the firm. These indicators are depicted in Figure 2.2. The use of 'existence indicators', which go deeper than the simple definition of capabilities and measure the constituent elements (Garvin 1993), has the advantage of proposing a measure that is feasible to observe in practice and is not restricted to input measures, such as expenditure on R&D.

Following from this definition of technological capabilities, the process of technological capability building (TCB) is defined as an investment process in which firms learn to accumulate technological capabilities under conditions of uncertainty. TCB effort is not linear, sequential and orderly, nor is it guaranteed to succeed without sustained, purposive co-ordination. To be effective at TCB, firms must acquire basic organizational capabilities, specific functional capabilities and the ability to manage complex change. Firms that are successful in technological learning are likely to overcome the challenge of reconciling tensions between activities that may stimulate innovation, but reduce short-term productivity gains, and must have the ability to simultaneously update old ways knowing and old ways of doing while acquiring new technological knowledge. Thus, in order to be successful at TCB, firms must also be able to manage complex change effectively (Pettigrew and Whipp 1991).

The TCB system approach draws on evolutionary theories of the firm, incorporating many basic assumptions, and departs from neo-classical theorizing about economic growth at the macro and micro levels. First, firms are viewed as information processing units that do not operate under conditions of perfect information and are considered to make boundedly rational decisions (Barnett and Burgelman 1996; Foss 1999; Levinthal 2000; Nelson and Winter 1982). Second, the approach acknowledges informational failures and imperfect decision processes as possible causes of under-performance and ineffectiveness. Third, the approach considers boundary conditions between firms to be important (Thomson 1993). Finally, the TCB approach maintains the focus on explaining variation in firm performance (Nelson 1991) and uses a methodology that lends itself to appreciative theorizing and related methods of investigation, such as development of economic histories, detailed chronological accounts, case studies and other qualitative techniques for data collection and analysis (Nelson and Winter 1982). This contrasts with the formal modelling approach, which characterizes much of the evolutionary economics field.[1]

Figure 2.2 Elements and indicators of firm-level technological capability

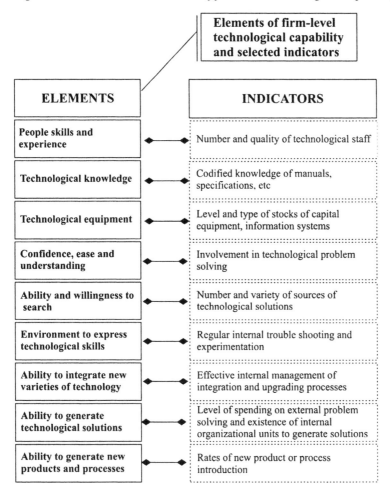

Source: Author.

In applying an evolutionary theory of the firm, the conceptual framework draws on Dosi et al.'s (2000a) innovation as learning approach by taking into account that:

- particular ways of learning or learning routines[2] can be developed within firms and when these routines are difficult to replicate they can confer competitive advantage;
- learning is a trial and error process, which involves uncertainty and risk;
- learning activity requires sustained investment
- learning requires management attention and must be a process, not a haphazard process;[3]
- learning activity often involves local searches and, therefore, the environment contiguous to the firm affects the ability to learn;
- management of boundary relationships involves exchange of tacit information and the mastery of such exchange across organizational boundaries is considered to be an integral element of TCB (Winter 1987).

Firms undertake TCB efforts primarily because they expect them to produce economic benefits (for the individual firms and for the national contexts in which they are located), such as productivity gains, increases in output, improvements in quality, reductions in operational costs, improvements in operational efficiency and/or increased scope and range of outputs. These benefits are expected to accrue in the medium to long term and to yield returns on the investment. The motivation for this investment of effort is facilitated by internal factors, such as recognition of technological trends and an assessment of existing capability gaps, and from external factors, such as changing market structures, the behaviour of competitors, actions of regulators and policy makers and information drawn from suppliers and other knowledge creating institutions.

However, it can be shown that firms are unlikely automatically to achieve benefits or to respond smoothly to external stimuli or internal evaluations and assessments. In the light of this, TCB is best characterized as a learning process in which existing levels of capability inputs are transformed over time through a process of trial and error into an improved or enhanced capability level. In such learning processes failures often occur, but, with appropriate responses, these failures can provide lessons that lead to improved understanding and, eventually, to improved capability.

Endogenous factors, such as management competence, organizational culture and leadership, are important influences in the abilities of firms to manage these learning processes and reap potential benefits. There is also considerable evidence that these abilities are not evenly distributed. This framework investigates this variation in firms and offers an explanation of why, within a single country, there are firms that respond with alacrity to changes in external factors by carrying out a range of technological capability building activities and, at the same time, there are other firms that respond much more slowly and deploy a much less developed range of technological capabilities.

The framework focuses on the processes rather than on the outcomes of learning. In this regard it has more in common with the approaches of Argyris and Schon (1996b), Senge (1992) and Starkey (1996) than studies of organizational learning conducted by economists, who tend to focus on the outcomes of the process and the comparative efficiency of its technological inputs (Cohen and Levinthal 1989; Dodgson 1993; Tidd et al. 1997). To this extent this study throws new light on innovation management by going beyond the narrow concerns of directly or indirectly measurable outcomes.[4]

In this approach we look at the human dimension of TCB and see TCB as a learning process with many features in common with Dodgson's (1993) definition of organizational learning: 'the ways firms build, supplement, and organize knowledge and routines around their activities and within their cultures, and adapt and develop organizational efficiency by improving the use of the broad skills of their workforces' (p. 377).

The following characteristics of technological capability building as a learning process are emphasized:

- firms can learn by making mistakes;
- there is a distinction between individual learning and learning by the organization as a whole;
- group and organizational processes can assist with individual learning and amplify its usefulness;
- learning in organizations requires attention to contextual and internal stimuli in order to support active learning;
- learning does not take place in isolated parts of the firm, but is distributed across a number of activities. Its overall effectiveness, therefore, requires coordination.

These features of the approach are in line with organizational development theorists (Argyris 1996; Argyris and Schon 1996b; Schein 1992; Senge et al. 1999; Starkey 1996; Vaill 1996), the strategic management approaches (Baden-Fuller and Stopford 1994; Leonard-Barton 1995; Pettigrew and Whipp 1991; Senge 1992) and scholars who identify firm-specific structural enablers for organizational learning (Barney 1991; Nelson 1991; Nelson and Winter 1982; Rumelt 1984; Teece et al. 2000).

The TCB system framework considers capability development from the perspective of a firm attempting to achieve its strategic objectives. It also explicitly treats TCB as a learning process that arises in response to multiple motivations, including the need for developing countries to adjust and adapt to uncertainty (Freeman and Perez 1988; Perez 1983, 1985). The TCB system approach considers that firms in developing countries will be more likely to have defensive rather than offensive motivations for pursuing their TCB or organizational learning goals.

To explain further, the typical firm in a developing country is considered to be more likely to be concerned with undertaking organizational learning to adapt to changes in a techno-economic paradigm. The decision makers in developing country firms are likely to be aware that failure to adapt is likely to have deleterious consequences for market share, competitive position, ability to source and use equipment and, in extreme circumstances, firm survival. This is a very different context from that envisaged by theorists who apply Schumpeterian analysis to explain how firms pursue organizational learning to support 'creative destruction processes' and to realize profit and create wealth. The majority of developing country firms are located within the wave of creative destruction, but their starting points, perceived futures and motivations for adapting to technological change are very different from those of firms at the frontier. These non-frontier firms need particular capabilities to cope with technological change and how these differ from the TCB of frontier firms matters for the types of learning processes that are necessary.

For instance, there will be significant differences in the TCB effort required to respond to a defensive motivation, such as the need to respond to external shifts in sources of technological knowledge, and an offensive objective linked to competitive demands associated with the need to create new products or processes or to improve operational efficiency and quality levels (Nonaka 1994; Perez 1985). While firms are not expected to achieve a perfect match between their overall strategic objectives and technological capability building management activities, those that achieve greater coherence between overall strategic objectives and capability development will be better able to master the accumulation of capabilities. Ability to manage this process of integration is therefore considered to be a source of differentiation in the effectiveness of TCB. This argument builds on the work of strategic management scholars on strategic change management, and Freeman and Perez's analysis of macro-level technological change and its impacts at a firm level (Freeman and Perez 1988; Pettigrew and Whipp 1991; Weick 1987).[5]

In learning processes, initial conditions matter. Conditions of fiscal austerity, low national purchasing power, limited capital markets, low levels of technological know-how and underdeveloped innovation systems generally typify conditions in developing countries. As will be shown, although these contextual factors do exert an influence on learning processes (Bell and Pavitt 1993; Ernst et al. 1998; Kim 1999) some firms are able overcome these difficult initial conditions to acquire technological knowledge and capability.

In summary, the process of technological capability building is considered to be a complex learning process implemented by firms through trial and error during which they invest in increasing stocks of people, skills, knowledge and tangible assets. Firms improve effectiveness and the returns on their investment by implementing managerial routines and developing values that facilitate learning. Developing country firms are considered to face particular challenges in undertaking these processes because of their difficult initial conditions. The main amplification to previous organizational development and technological learning research is to consider capability development to be a learning process that is not automatic, which improves over time and which involves more than the selection of core competencies. This makes the approach more suitable for novice innovators.

Having defined the key concepts and assumptions, we now turn to recommendations for improving effectiveness in learning and capability development.

IMPROVING EFFECTIVENESS IN LEARNING AND CAPABILITY BUILDING

The TCB system approach argues that to be effective in technological learning and capability building, developing country firms must organize their learning and capability accumulation efforts as a systematic, organized process, involving five critical components, namely financing, management and co-ordination, culture and leadership, managing relationships with suppliers, and managing relationships with the innovation system. It is further argued that proportional and simultaneous investment in all these elements is likely to increase the stock of technological capabilities and to improve effectiveness of technological capability building. The TCB system approach argues that firm level variation in the effectiveness and intensity of TCB effort cannot be fully explained by country-level factors and is likely to be influenced by developments that occur endogenously within the firm. The approach specifically takes into account the challenges faced by developing country firms because their learning and technological capability processes must take account of difficult initial conditions.

This argument draws on insights from various traditions that all suggest that firms with behavioural, structural and environmental enablers are likely to be more successful in learning and capability building.[6] Strategic management research provides evidence of the benefits that may arise as a result of a purposive focus on capability development. Within the dynamic capabilities and resource-based theory of the firm perspective, it is argued that technological knowledge and other technological assets constitute the linchpin of competitive advantage, since these core capabilities are not easily reproducible. Scholars in this tradition also focus on tacit elements of information and knowledge, regarding them as an important component of firm-specific assets from which competitive advantage may be derived (Barney 1991; Rumelt 1984; Teece and Pisano 1994; Teece et al. 2000). The normative conclusions associated with this tradition suggest that firms should invest in technological knowledge and assets and should master routines for identifying, developing and defending the core capabilities that derive from combinations of technological knowledge and assets. These propositions are used as the point of departure; however, the problem of insufficient skills, knowledge and/or assets is given greater prominence here, and the assumption that there is a relatively smooth supply of skills, knowledge and technological assets is relaxed in the TCB system approach.

The more integrative approaches (Edmondson and Moingeon 1996; Leonard-Barton 1995; Pettigrew and Whipp 1991) are particularly helpful because they consider the processes through which firms can build, maintain and renew these enablers. These studies also focus on internal factors that might impede learning within the firm and, also, on how the firm's environment might impact on the ability to implement learning strategies. The TCB system approach specifically focuses on how firms can create conditions that enable human learning. Building on the insights of writers such as Argyris and Schon (1978, 1996b), Schein (1992), Senge et al. (1999), Senge (1992) and Watkins and Marsick (1993), the approach emphasizes the methods that firms use to facilitate individual and team learning through 'active inquiry' techniques and 'mental models' and the techniques used by firms to influence and change organizational culture, to encourage and maintain levels of learning and to promote transformative learning.

The conceptual framework draws on the approach of Leonard-Barton (1995) who defines a firm's core capabilities as a system comprising: (1) technical competencies in the form of people's skills; (2) knowledge embedded in physical systems; (3) managerial systems that support the growth and development of skills and knowledge; and (4) values that direct the development of beneficial knowledge and skills. Her framework identifies key activities that firms can engage in to develop these systems and lays great stress on the role of knowledge building and learning. Following on from this, she identifies four key activities for managing and renewing core capabilities: (1) creative integrated problem solving across different functional and cognitive barriers; (2) implementation of innovative methodologies, operational tools and process tools; (3) experimentation; and (4) importing know-how from outside technological and market sources. Leonard-Barton's vision of the management of knowledge building is a broad one that focuses on firm-wide activities and embedded values and behaviours rather than on the narrower issues of research and development (R&D) as being the main functional driver of improvements in knowledge building. Leonard-Barton (1995: 260) suggests that firms that are successful at renewing their 'wellsprings of knowledge' have organizational consistency,[7] which she defines as 'a pattern of thought and behaviour that is observable at all levels and that gives the organization its character' (p. 260). Organizational consistency is considered to be a key determinant in the ability of firms to create and continuously renew their core technological capabilities. The key elements, activities, embedded values and behaviours identified as critical success factors (CSFs) are:

1 **Enthusiasm for knowledge** – as reflected in respect for and encouragement of the accumulation of knowledge, valuing the ability to learn and encouragement of curiosity and information seeking attitudes.
2 **Drive to stay ahead in knowledge** – expressed in the capability to enter technological markets or use technologies by keeping up with the knowledge about the latest technologies, experimenting with technologies, promoting active transfer of knowledge and stimulating creativity. Maintaining permeable organizational boundaries and facilitating rapid and ready access to activities outside the boundaries of the firm, particularly with customers. Promoting empathetic design and listening to improve ability to anticipate customer needs and technological change.
3 **Tight coupling of complementary skill sets** – expressed through creating teams of people from a variety of disciplinary and cognitive backgrounds. Building 'deep reservoirs of knowledge and skill' and creating roles for 'boundary spanners' – defined as 'people who understand the world of the source and the receiver and translate as well disseminate knowledge' (Leonard-Barton 1995: 158),[8] having multiple conduits for information flow and maximizing transfer and absorption of tacit knowledge.
4 **Iteration of activities**. Promoting return-loop and continuous learning mechanisms through investment of fresh resources, renewed attention and new insights combined with space for reflection, and explicitly allowing prototyping, field trials and other 'try it and learn' methods.
5 **Promotion of higher–order learning** – facilitated by actively

encouraging reflection and enquiry into the objectives of learning, introduction of 'meta-routines' that evaluate all firm activities in terms of their effect on learning and introducing long-term orientation into decision making.

6   **Exercising engaged leadership**. Promoting decentralized responsibility for active leadership at all levels to ensure that individuals at all levels have the requisite skills. Taking action to inspire people to invest in knowledge creation and renewal.

A major strength of this framework is that the characteristics of organizational consistency apply equally to firms that are either novices or experienced innovators. There are few restrictive assumptions about the state of initial conditions within firms. Therefore, the framework applies to firms that already have the capabilities needed to support innovative performance and also to those that must compensate for unfavourable initial conditions. This strength derives from Leonard-Barton's consideration of factors that, although outside those functions in the firm directly involved in innovation-related activities, contribute to overall success in innovative performance. Compared with the propositions in the management of innovation tradition the critical success factors identified by Leonard-Barton are generic and not specific to firms at the frontier of technology. By including generic organizational capabilities in her framework, these propositions are applicable to those firms that have not yet built up the infrastructures commonly associated with innovation activity.

The TCB system approach also uses the insights of Pettigrew and Whipp (1991) about how the ability to manage complex change is itself a key success factor in capability building. Pettigrew and Whipp in discussing the management of cultural change introduce a concept of organizational coherence, which is defined as the ability to manage a series of interrelated and emergent changes. Their analysis suggests that a firm's ability to accommodate and manage the compound processes of competition and strategic change is the decisive strategic asset.[9] These authors suggest that firms that develop the ability to handle the demands of simultaneity and continuity can reap advantages, since these abilities are not easily appropriated by competitors. Their model identifies five key features, which, they argue, must be possessed by firms if they are to achieve competitive advantage. These assets are: environmental assessment, leading change, linking strategic and operational change, human resources and, finally, coherence in the management of change.

Pettigrew and Whipp's (1991) treatment of organizational coherence is very detailed. They suggest that organizational coherence derives from implementing change processes that are consistent and not contradictory;

consonant, in that they are appropriate adaptations to the environment; advantageous and not purely traditional or expected; and, finally, feasible, in that they are not overly demanding or near impossible. The framework suggests that these four primary conditions for organizational coherence are possible only through attention to secondary features, such as appropriate leadership and senior management, behaviours that unite intent and implementation, an apposite knowledge base generated through interorganizational linkages and the ability to create and apply mechanisms continuously and consistently over time and not as episodes or initiatives.

This analysis of organizational coherence also identifies detailed activities that firms can undertake to provide the analytical, educational and political competences that are required to master these primary and secondary conditioning features. The activities suggested for developing analytical competence, for example, include: providing planning tools and information systems; encouraging questioning of assumptions; providing access to quantitative and qualitative information; ensuring credibility of top–down and bottom–up communication processes; and providing for thematically arranged groups and working parties. To develop educational competence activities should include: communicating goals clearly and widely; explaining goals of strategic change processes; encouraging localized learning; encouraging senior management to become more sophisticated in their learning goals; and becoming more open to personal learning and rotation of staff. To improve political competence Pettigrew and Whipp (1991) suggest the following routines: identifying and managing internal conflict; using working parties as a safety valve and as an integrative mechanism; using resource allocation rules that emphasize fairness and promote transparency; improving appraisal systems to include strategic change goals; introducing leadership training to minimize friction at senior management level; and, finally, making adequate preparation for major changes and introducing these in non-threatening ways, such as use of 'islands of progress', trials and experiments, and 'learning cells'.

Pettigrew and Whipp (1991: 243) explicitly consider how firms go about mastering strategic change. In so doing, their study contributes considerably to understanding how organizations can undertake learning, which is considered to be 'mastering the ability to hold an organization together while simultaneously reshaping it'. This focus on the strategic change aspect of learning is a key insight, which is incorporated in the conceptual framework developed in this book. Pettigrew and Whipp consider strategic change to be a creative and unpredictable process because strategic positions are impermanent and the forces of competition are often fragile. They argue further that:

it is this unpredictable quality **which leads the more successful firms to develop learning processes at all levels in the organisation**. Such learning is seldom through orderly progressions but through untidy iterations and learning spirals. Such a process may be better served by not necessarily punishing apparent failures of contradictions but by using them more productively. (Pettigrew and Whipp 1991: 277 emphasis added)

The ability of a company to learn ... in other words to reconstruct its knowledge base (made up of skills, structures and values) should be **a key task**. ... [T]he firm should be able to break down outmoded attitudes and practices, **while at the same time**, building up new more appropriate competences. (Pettigrew and Whipp 1991: 290 emphasis added)

By linking the incentive for undertaking organizational learning, that is to achieve competitive advantage, with the mechanisms through which organizational learning can be implemented and improved, the analysis developed by these authors is very valuable. In addition, this approach specifies how an intangible asset – organizational coherence – is important for learning and provides a detailed analysis of the mechanisms for creating this asset. These insights are used in the development of the conceptual framework; however, the Pettigrew–Whipp framework is amplified to include other motivations for developing and mastering strategic change processes, that is, those that are defensive rather than offensive.

The insights of Tushman and Nadler (1996), who suggest that for organizations to perform learning effectively they must design and develop organizational systems and structures that are congruent with the objective of facilitating learning, are also used in the TCB system approach. These authors define organizational congruence as a good fit between tasks, individuals, organizational arrangements and informal organization and a good match between these features and the basic requirements of organizational strategy. They argue that congruence improves overall organizational effectiveness by developing patterns of behaviour that are reinforced over time and become associated with shared norms and values. They further suggest that the contribution of congruence to organizational effectiveness changes over time, since the stability conferred by congruence can produce inertia by locking an organization into behaviour that matches strategies, and an environment that has ceased to be appropriate. When congruence produces dysfunctional stability, they suggest that this can result in organizations becoming complacent, inert and responding with conformity to the status quo.

Tushman and Nadler (1996: 142) show that in highly regulated industries, such as telecommunication, the dominant firms, such as AT&T and GTE, often achieved congruence in the past that was better suited to obsolete technologies rather than to the implementation of new technologies.

Conversely, when innovative organizations have congruent systems and structures, they suggest that they are able to acquire information about customers, competitors and technology, and are also able to rapidly process, assimilate, validate, evaluate and disseminate this information and the associated knowledge. The organizational congruence required by innovating firms is that which enables these firms to function as effective learning systems.

The insights into environmental enablers of learning are also used in the TCB system approach. In particular, the conceptual framework retains the distinction between enablers that are under the full or partial control of the firm and those that exist in the external environment in which the firm is located or does business. The endogenous factors that assist with technological capability building include environmental scanning, improving environmental responsiveness and improving organizational absorptiveness. To provide these environmental enablers, firms must include in their stock of firm-specific assets those that extend beyond the boundaries of the firm. These boundary resources are defined by Nanda (1996: 105) as 'relationship-specific intangible assets which link the firm with external constituencies'. Boundary assets include consumer loyalty, worker human capital, and public trust; these asset stocks are not considered to be owned by the firm, although the flows that emanate from them enter as inputs into the production process and can add value to the firm. These assets, therefore, can be likened to bridges that span organizational boundaries and have the potential to secure benefits outside the firm's boundaries.

Studies of the innovation process within firms offer considerable evidence that a firm's sources of learning are not restricted to its own internal resources. Early work (Hobday 1995) identified the role of access to resources outside the firm's boundaries as a mechanism for learning and considered learning from joint ventures, installation of capital goods, training, hiring key individuals, reverse engineering, imitating inward investors, assembly and mass manufacturing, exporting, investment abroad and learning through a variety of collaborations. More recent work considers the important role played by knowledge bases that derive from organizational network relationships (Brusoni and Prencipe 2001; Pavitt 2002; Prencipe 2000).

Organizational development studies on boundary relationships tend to focus on how environmental changes can facilitate organizational learning. This work suggests that firms do not have automatic and similar responses to environmental factors. One firm may respond to external stimuli with changed behaviour and attitudes, others may respond differently and yet others may not respond at all. Firms with individuals or units playing the role of a 'boundary spanner' are more likely to be able to be responsive to the signals from customers, suppliers, markets and other agents, which facilitates organizational learning (Leonard-Barton 1995).

The TCB system approach also draws on insights from the innovation management tradition. It specifically adapts Tidd et al.'s (1997) framework making it more relevant to developing country firms. The first step in adapting their framework is to identify a selection from the total number of routines that may be considered to be particularly relevant to developing country firms. This selection of routines is presented in Table 2.2.[10]

The second step is to analyze Tidd et al.'s framework of core abilities for successful innovation management and construct a new set that is more applicable to firms in developing countries. The revisions take into account that consideration of the core abilities required by developing country firms must recognize that the majority of these firms are likely to be novice innovators, as opposed to the more experienced innovators considered in the original framework.

Table 2.3 presents an adapted version of the Tidd et al. core abilities framework. The adaptations include adding the ability to learn how to innovate and distinguishing between what are core and non-core abilities for novice innovators. Learning how to manage innovation and acquiring technology from external sources are considered to be core abilities for novice innovators, while routines for generating new technology are not emphasized. These adaptations are important in the context of the present investigation because the work of Tidd et al. is concerned with the learning processes of experienced innovators. It is less focused on firms that are learning how to innovate.

These writers appreciate that the requirements for successful innovation management vary across firms because of different starting levels in terms of accumulated technical competence, size and financial resources. For example, they refer to novice learners having 'no substitute for the long and experience-based process of learning' and they insist that successful innovation management routines are 'not easy to acquire' (p. 34). However, they do not elaborate on the distinctiveness of innovation management in these different contexts. Tidd et al.'s framework embraces firms that survive with no in-house capability to generate technology, but have a 'well developed network of external sources that can supply technology' and the ability to put that externally acquired technology to effective use becomes a 'source of competitive advantage' (p. 250). This feature is incorporated in the TCB system approach. However, since their detailed specification of routines does not appear to apply equally to firms with well-developed capabilities to generate technology and to firms that lack these capabilities; in the latter case, it is to be expected that these firms will need to learn to find, select and integrate technology from outside the firm. They are also likely to have to develop routines for selecting, negotiating and appropriating the benefits of technology supplied by commercial providers.

Table 2.2 Key routines for innovation management in developing country firms

Scanning
– Recognizing market and technology related signals including market forecasting, technology forecasting; developing extensive links with sources of technology, demonstration projects, benchmarking; and communicating with external and internal customers.

Resourcing innovation through technology transfer
– Improving selection processes and ability to choose between suppliers.
– Negotiating full technology transfer to include intangible elements of technologies and reduce dependency on suppliers. Working effectively with external sources to combine internally generated knowledge and external sources.

Process innovation
– Careful project planning and monitoring and ability to manage projects across departmental boundaries over extended periods of time.
– Managing continuous improvement processes through frameworks and tools.
– Managing *structural* and *infrastructural* improvements in processes, where structural aspects refer to the basic building blocks of a process – for example, the telecommunication equipment in a network improvement – and the infrastructural elements refer to the less tangible, but no less important, elements such as the operational systems for managing quality, ensuring information flow and maintaining equipment and the quality, age, experience and flexibility of the workforce, systems of work organization and co-ordination of different functions and organizational culture.
– Auditing strengths and weaknesses and exploring options for developing competencies as required.
– Implementing process innovation as a mutual adaptation between technology and organization, managing resistance to change and incorporating organizational development requirements.

Change management and learning
– Establishing clear strategy at top level and communicating throughout the organization.
– Involving managers and staff early in decision making and design of implementation process.
– Creating an open climate and setting clear targets.
– Investing in training in specific skills and in capabilities for understanding change processes and managing change.
– Reviewing innovation and learning activities through open and informed review.

Source: Adapted by author from Tidd et al. (1997: 241–71).

Table 2.3 Core abilities for managing innovation: learning vs experienced innovators

Basic ability	Contributing routines	Applicability to learning innovators
Recognizing	Searching environment for technical and economic clues to trigger change.	Strong
Aligning	Ensuring good fit between overall business strategy and proposed change – not innovating because of fashion or as knee jerk response to competitors.	Strong
Acquiring	Recognizing limitations of inhouse technology base; being able to connect to external sources of knowledge, information, equipment, etc. Transferring knowledge from outside sources and connecting it to the relevant points in the organization.	Core
Generating	Ability to create some aspects of technology in house, e.g. through R&D, engineering groups.	Weak
Choosing	Exploring and selecting most suitable response to environmental triggers that fit strategy and internal resource base/external technology network.	Strong
Executing	Managing developmental projects for new products/processes from initial idea to final launch. Monitoring and controlling projects.	Strong
Implementing	Managing introduction of technical and other change in the organization to ensure acceptance/effective use of innovation.	Strong
Learning	Having ability to evaluate and reflect on innovation process; identify lessons for improvement to management routines.	Strong
Developing the organization	Embedding effective routines in structure, processes, underlying behaviours, etc.	Strong
Building portfolio of basic abilities	Developing learning routines to enable enterprises to recognize–align–acquire–choose–execute–implement–improve and undertake organizational development.	Core

Source: Author's adaptation and amplification of Tidd et al. (1997: 36).

Tidd et al. identify a number of differences in the successful innovation management approaches of small and large firms. They note, for example, that in small firms much less importance is placed on routines for the integration of specialized technical functions with other functions and resource allocation to R&D. They argue that the key tasks involved in innovation strategy in small firms are not accomplished using the same approaches of organizational design and formal procedures that are employed by large firms, but rather through the efforts of skilled senior managers. For small firms:

> it is the level of training, experience, responsibilities and external linkages of senior managers that play a central role, and in particular their level of technical and organizational skills that determine whether or not [small firms] will be able to commercially exploit a firm-specific technological advantage. (Tidd et al. 1997: 156)

The innovation management approaches that are feasible for the majority of firms in developing countries are more likely to mirror the approaches of small firms in wealthy countries. By adapting Tidd et al.'s framework to take into account small size, low levels of accumulated technical competence, limited experience in innovation and absence of a capability to generate technologies in-house, the current research is more applicable to developing countries.

An important foundation element in the TCB system approach is Bell and Pavitt's (1993) framework which defines[11] technological capability development as: 'the resources needed to generate and manage technical change, including skills, knowledge, and experience, and institutional structures and linkages' (p. 261). The conceptual framework in this study maintains the sharp distinction between the processes necessary to generate technical change, to manage change, to consciously and deliberately learn how to acquire the capabilities necessary for changing and improving production processes (technological capability) and the learning that occurs through cumulative experience in production (production capacity). Production capacity is regarded as the resources used to achieve static efficiency, that is to produce industrial goods at given levels of efficiency and given input combinations, while technological capabilities are considered to confer dynamic efficiency and to be necessary to manage and to adapt to technical change. Several important features are used in the development of the conceptual framework employed here:

- detailed definition of technological accumulation specifies actions taken to build the minimum initial stock of capabilities required for any meaningful capability building to take place;

- emphasis on considering that building or accumulation of capabilities requires purposive investment is retained;
- defining capability building as uncertain, non-linear, path dependent and not guaranteed to succeed;
- considering technological capability development as including a wide range of activities through which firms accumulate various kinds of engineering capabilities.

These authors suggest that TCB allows firms to generate:

continuous incremental change in technologies initially acquired from industrialised countries, for synthesising diverse elements of increasingly complex imported technology into new plants and products, for independently replicating technologies already developed elsewhere, and for developing more original innovations. (Bell and Pavitt 1997: 114)

This view explicitly recognizes that for developing country firms, technological capability development involves more than allocating internal funds to R&D to be carried out in specialist units. These authors note that in developing country firms, technical capability building involves migration of skilled people, for example. They identify the hiring of science and technology graduates – whether foreign nationals on expatriate contracts, nationals returning from overseas or locally trained specialists – as being among the important elements of a technical capability building strategy. The mobility of these individuals within and across firms is an important feature of the capability development process. Bell and Pavitt (1997) argue that these flows of people-embodied technology were often especially important in providing key nuclei of competence that laid the basis for effective accumulation in new areas of technology. The skills and capabilities embodied in highly qualified, trained individuals provided a major impetus for technological accumulation and, in particular, for the assimilation of imported technology and the establishment and maintenance of international networks with science and technology professionals.

The emphasis on learning in Bell and Pavitt's (1993, 1997) framework draws on Bell (1984), who elaborates a simple typology of learning activities consisting of seven main types: learning-by-doing operating, changing, searching, hiring, training activities and system performance feedback. This typology incorporates considerable diversity by naming different types of capability building activities. It also makes an important distinction between passive and active modes of learning. The former are defined as accumulated knowledge and skill, derived 'automatically' from production activity. The latter are considered to result from firms undertaking additional effort outside production, yielding the benefits of capability accretion. This distinction is central to the Bell and Pavitt (1993, 1997) framework and it is used in the TCB system approach. Technical capability building is not treated as an automatic process resulting from well-chosen policy interventions or from accumulated production experience. Bell uses the typology to identify and to discuss modes through which firms learn. He maintains that certain modes are better suited to different types of learning. This matching and selection of appropriate modes suggests that technical capability building may be a strategic undertaking. If the ability of firms to undertake strategic change is itself a capability, then it follows that the ability of firms to identify, select and manage modes of TCB will not be uniform. Bell (1984) also considers active learning to be an aggressive and purposeful investment. This is consistent with the expectation that there will be variation in firms' abilities to formulate and implement technical capability building strategies. Finally, the author points to the difficulties that arise from the embeddedness of the technical capability building learning process. He suggests that firms do not control some of the conditions that affect their ability to undertake some of these purposeful investments in learning. This observation is helpful because it suggests that firms may need to compensate for country level factors in their technological capability building activities.

Figure 2.3 Ten types of learning for developing country firms

Bell (1984)

Learning by doing
Learning by operating

....

Learning from changing
Learning by searching
Learning by hiring
Learning by training
Learning by system performance feedback

....

Updating Bell's types of learning

Learning by sharing
Learning by field experimentation (not R&D)
Learning by large-scale project management

Source: Author's adaptation of Bell (1984).

The insights in Bell (1984) on the importance of the ability to fit technical capability building mechanisms to capability development objectives are extended by the acknowledgement of Pettigrew and Whipp (1991) that strategic change competence in firms is likely to vary. This gives explanatory power to an analysis of why technological capability building performance varies across firms. The theoretical framework I have developed here also amplifies Bell's learning framework by adding three forms of active learning to the original seven types. The adapted learning framework is depicted in Figure 2.3. The new forms of active learning are: learning by sharing, for instance, through participating in technology communities (Nelson and Winter 1982); learning by experimentation, including field trials and other pilot or incremental introductions of capability development; and learning by large-scale project management.[12]

LEARNING AND CAPABILITY DEVELOPMENT IN THE TELECOMMUNICATION SECTOR

The TCB system approach also builds on the insights from two studies that examined the experiences of developing country firms, which established telecommunication equipment manufacturing operations in South Korea and Brazil (Hobday 1990; Mytelka 1999). Some of the features, such as the emphasis on considering learning and capability development as a time-consuming costly process in which endogenous factors matter, are retained, while the conceptual framework developed here suggests that there is more need for a focus on explaining variation in the responses of firms to signals from policy institutions.

The 1980s was a period when developing country firms were able to accelerate their entry into technologically intensive manufacturing of telecommunication equipment. The fact that international suppliers were keen to license production technology as a strategy to stimulate growth in new markets was an important facilitating factor. The relatively slow pace of change from electromechanical to microelectronic equipment also contributed by creating an opening for 'technological leap-frogging' and 'catch-up' strategies (Hobday 1990; Mytelka 1999). The important features of these strategies included:

- greater concentration of technological skills in operating companies and public R&D labs;
- reduced reliance on specialist telecommunication and mechanical engineering skills, with increasing importance of generalized IT and software programming skills, and design engineering skills;
- the possibility for developing countries to produce digital exchanges that were scaleable, because of modularity and the divisibility of microelectronics technology; and
- gradual learning with time for investment in experimentation.

Mytelka (1999) suggests that the shift to microelectronics technology does not provide as benign or favourable an environment for developing country firms seeking to survive or succeed with 'keeping-up strategies'. She argues that the pace of technological change accelerated in the 1990s and the focus shifted to service differentiation. Developing country firms would be invariably prepared to translate their catch-up strategies into keeping-up strategies. While Hobday (1990) recognizes the discontinuity of technical change, his research suggested that Brazilian firms would be able to cope with technical change in the 1990s.

By contrasting Brazilian technological capability effort with that of South Korea, Mytelka (1999) arrives at a different conclusion as to how well developing country firms may cope with technological discontinuities. She emphasizes the importance of 'learning how to learn' as a capability for effectiveness in keeping up strategies, and states that 'by turning themselves into learning institutions, firms which learn to learn during the catch-up phase' (p. 18) are in a position to sustain their competitiveness over the longer term.[13] Both authors place a great deal of emphasis on the role played by public research laboratories, universities and technical colleges as important sources of technological knowledge used by telecommunication manufacturing companies (Hobday 1990; Mytelka 1999). Hobday (1990) presents information about how Telebras, the Brazilian holding company for telecommunication manufacturing and service delivery, undertook a range of learning and TCB methods including: collaborative technology agreements with domestic firms, foreign firms, research institutions, government bodies and universities;[14] securing technical assistance, training and capital goods from external suppliers; and using internal sources such as national universities to provide feasibility studies, graduate training and project development. Similarly, Mytelka (1999) provides evidence about the dynamic role played by national and local institutions in firm-level capability development efforts by telecommunication equipment manufacturers in South Korea and Brazil.

The evidence from Brazil and South Korea suggests that the innovation system in those countries played a positive role that was similar to that of policy and regulatory factors in the OECD area. Non-market incentives stimulated innovation during the early stages of diffusion, enhanced co-operative competition among small numbers of specialized suppliers and created political pressures and incentives to improve telecommunication services (Brock 1981; Crandall and Flamm 1989; Fransman 2000; Mansell 1987, 1993; McNamara 1991; OECD 1992).

Table 2.4 presents Hobday's (1990) typology of five learning mechanisms.

Table 2.4 Adapting the Hobday (1990) typology of learning mechanisms

Five learning types and associated key success features for developing country manufacturers	Definition	Adaptation for telecommunication operating companies
Learning by searching (a) knowledge centres (b) physical proximity to advanced knowledge centres (c) risk assessment and management (d) investment programmes of suitable duration (e) continuous reassessment and reformulation of goals and strategies (f) selecting an appropriate entry point	Preinvestment investigation that provides an overall appreciation of the range of production technologies available, and a critical assessment of whether and how any elements of the technology can be developed domestically.	Scan and search mechanisms that focus on identifying equipment suppliers that can provide technology components that suit the operator's network development strategy and fill technological gaps, as well as generalized search to keep up with technological trends.
Learning by setting up electronic capital goods (a) physical handling of complex equipment to gain/enhance confidence (b) careful staging of processes (c) training to support continuous assessment of goals and strategy	Installation and commissioning of capital equipment for production, including developing testing, design, support and infrastructural facilities.	Commissioning, testing, operation of complex equipment remain important. Operators focus on efficient operation of a system that interacts with end customers. Producing according to design specification not important, thus timing of measurement in production cycles and indicators of success vary.

Learning by training and hiring Systems that are designed to communicate and share technological knowledge.	Organized learning courses including those provided by universities, international organizations, equipment suppliers, research institutes. Hiring of skilled professionals including consultants on short-term and longer-term assignments.	Embodied knowledge imported informal and informal exchanges is vital and is provided by a variety of sources.
Learning by designing and adaptation of product designs Depth of knowledge of broad technological principles and product-specific familiarity and mastery of production processes.	Redesigning products to suit local conditions; mastering production technology well enough to transfer know-how to other producers.	Ability to design and adapt 'product' specifications such as network parameters is a core capability. Requires mastery of design and control of standardized telecommunication network components so that service differentiation benefits are realized and networks are responsive to customer requirements.
Learning by installing information feedback systems Development and use of appropriate computerized tools and communication systems.	Developed computerized mechanisms for synchronizing engineering effort and managing/monitoring performance of design engineers. Includes developing codified methods for guiding production processes, e.g. blueprints, design specifications, formalized working methods.	Mechanisms to improve effectiveness of learning remain important, however, focus on design aspect unlikely to be sufficient since network operators require more dispersed learning effort.

Source: Author's adaptation of Hobday (1990: 134–9).

While all of these mechanisms are considered to be relevant to telecommunication network operating companies, they require adaptations to make them more relevant to service providers as the types of technological knowledge required; the applications of this knowledge and the sources of knowledge vary between goods manufacturers and service providers.

Hobday (1990) suggests that the telecommunication industry offers a promising site for examining how developing country firms respond to conditions of fundamental and rapid technological change, such as the introduction of microelectronics technology and the Internet, and characterizes the process of capability development as Schumpeterian learning.[15]

Hobday (1990) concluded that Brazil was successful in its attempt to respond to technological change associated with a fundamental shift in telecommunication technologies from electromechanical to microelectronics systems. Dynamic learning was central to the strategy of using local institutions to expand the telecommunication infrastructure, secure industrial development and acquire design, bargaining and investment capabilities. The specific characteristics of digital technology, that is modularity and divisibility, seemed to allow gradual technological accumulation, selective development and progressive upgrading of skills. In the Brazilian case, the process of capability development was characterized as being costly, difficult, gradual and involving active government participation in policy decisions and in investment. Brazil 'slowly and painfully learned its way gradually and selectively progressing up the scale of technological complexity' (Hobday 1990: 197) and was expected to continue with the same momentum.

Mytelka (1999) characterizes capability development as an interaction between firms and a system of 'policy dynamics' and emphasizes that deliberate effort is required by developing country firms in order to understand and respond to technological change.[16] She also offers a distinction between the capabilities of firms that pursue 'catch-up' as opposed to 'keep-up' or 'get-ahead' strategies. The capabilities identified as being important for manufacturers interested in pursuing get-ahead strategies appear to be similar to those that would be required by telecommunication network operating companies, that is:

* introduction of variety;
* improvement in quality;
* reduction in costs;
* incremental change.

These capabilities are mainly concerned with process management, the core competencies needed by service providers. Mytelka (1999) suggests that firm habits and learning practices influence the types of capabilities that are required by firms and also influence firm-specific processes of capability development. She concludes that in the 1990s, firms in Brazil were unable to cope with the acceleration of technological change and were ill-prepared to respond to market liberalization.

In summary, previous research suggests that capability accumulation in the telecommunication industry is a time-consuming costly process in which endogenous factors matter. These studies also suggest that policy institutions and their interaction with firms can have a positive influence on firm level capability development effort, under particular circumstances. These studies imply that a dynamic analysis, which includes consideration of technological change, is required. All of these suggestions provide guidance for the research described in this book; however, as we will see, the TCB system approach, presented in the next section, extends these frameworks so that the requirements of telecommunication operating companies are taken into account.

AN IDEAL SYSTEM FOR TECHNOLOGICAL CAPABILITY BUILDING

The TCB system approach presents a hypothesized 'ideal' system for developing country firms. It is suggested that for firms' TCB efforts to be effective, they require a system consisting of five critical components: (1) allocating financial resources to TCB effort, (2) management practices, systems and decision-making rules that implement and support the TCB effort, (3) practices to establish and maintain an organizational culture in which the TCB effort is exercized with committed and skilled leadership, (4) accessing external TC resources from suppliers, and (5) accessing external TC resources from the innovation system (local and global).

Figure 2.4 is a graphical representation of the ideal system for TCB, showing the five constituent elements. The symmetrical form indicates the proportional and balanced investment of all of the elements in the system. In the TCB system approach, both the internal processes that are considered to be under the direct control of the firm and the external or boundary processes that are only partially under the firm's control are considered to be equally important. The base of the pyramid represents the existing stock of accumulated technological capability and is included to take account of the path-dependent characteristic of capability development. This is also an important feature of the approach, since it makes the TCB system especially well suited to examining technology capability building activities that take place under severe resource constraints and in settings that vary considerably from those in the industrialized countries. The TCB system is explicitly designed to take account of capability development in a wider range of industry contexts than previous work on capability development in poor countries. Most firm-level empirical studies have focused on manufacturing activities or heavy industrial process technologies (for example, steel, petrochemicals). The conceptual framework developed here is applicable to both manufacturing and service sector firms.

Figure 2.4 Five critical components of a technological capability building system

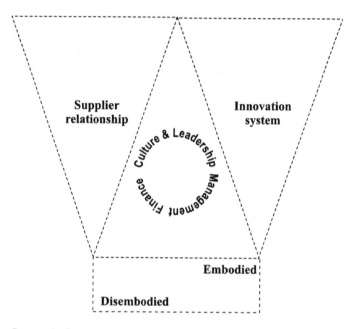

Source: Author.

Internal Processes in the TCB System

There are three internal processes of the TCB system that are considered to be essential.

Financing mechanisms to identify and allocate resources to TCB
Since TCB is essentially an investment activity, developing country firms require decision-making systems that support the analysis of technological investment projects and make allocations of financial resources, despite uncertainty and complexity (Leonard-Barton 1995; Tidd et al. 1997). In the

TCB system approach, it is assumed that there will be variety in the sophistication of these financing processes. It might be expected that small and inexperienced firms in developing countries would not have sophisticated information technology-based decision-making systems, but are likely to rely on the judgement of entrepreneurs or corporate leaders. These formal and/or informal allocation rules, as well as the practices to undertake TCB expenditure, are a vital part of the capability accumulation process.

Management practices to implement and manage TCB
The processes for setting rules and establishing decision-making systems for undertaking TCB include co-ordination mechanisms and systems for aligning TCB with overall firm objectives. These practices provide organizational coherence and operationalize firms' intentions to invest in technological capability building. The following management practices are likely to be important and relevant for developing country firms' technological capability building efforts.

1   Recruitment and retention systems to identify, attract and keep people with technical skills, including recruitment of both overseas nationals with skills and expatriates.

2   Human resource development systems to train staff, carry out performance evaluation, design and implement reward and incentive systems and implement promotion and staff development systems, which increase individual motivation and performance.

3   Design and implementation of organizational structures to support learning, including cross-functional teams, staff rotation, assignment of responsibility for technological learning to line managers and specific units.

4   Efforts to increase organizational integration using planning as an active learning mechanism; implementation of project feedback mechanisms; active environmental scanning; vision setting and future assessment. The system should include management practices that permit feedback and evaluation mechanisms, so that learning from failure can take place.

5   Design and implementation of technological capability evaluation and assessment systems.

6   Implementation of formal and informal active technology scanning and search mechanisms.

7   Implementation of knowledge management systems to capture, organize and disseminate technological knowledge across the firm.

Culture and leadership to support TCB

These activities provide legitimacy, encouragement and motivation for sustained technological capability building effort. In the TCB system approach, the culture and leadership activities are not assumed to be the preserves of the senior management team. All actions taken that contribute to creating an environment and culture in which staff at all levels of the firm perceive that they are able to undertake the complex, risky, problem-solving activities associated with technological capability building are considered to be part of this facilitating process. These elements of the TCB system have many characteristics in common with firms in industrialized countries. For example, in both contexts there is a need for inspired leadership that is focused on vision setting, motivation and communication. The TCB system considers that leaders play an important role in establishing the legitimacy of the technological capability building effort and ensuring sustainability of effort. Effective leaders recognize the inherent challenges of capability development, are concerned about the human aspects of the process and ensure that the technological capability building system is coherent with organizational goals and position.[17] Firms with an organizational culture that allows risk taking and experimentation, promotes open communication, supports ongoing challenges to existing ways of thinking and doing business, promotes 'learning how to learn' and encourages personal achievement are more likely to support capability development. The TCB system approach suggests that the possibility for developing and nurturing leadership talents and building this learning culture exists everywhere, but developing country firms face specific difficulties.

This specification of the internal processes of the technological capability building system draws on insights from the organizational development, strategic management and innovation management fields. However, the work in these areas is extended to provide a theory that may be more relevant to developing country firms. A major distinction between the TCB system proposed here and organizational development frameworks for analysing organizational learning is that the former specifies multiple motivations for technological capability building investment. The internal processes in the TCB system therefore include both processes for learning how to accumulate TCs and those concerned with the implementation of what is accumulated. Activities that firms undertake to improve their competitive positions, as well as those that are necessary to compensate for deficiencies in the external environment, are part of the TCB system. The latter have received relatively little attention in the innovation literature.

The next section discusses boundary processes in the TCB system.

Boundary Processes in the TCB System

Two boundary processes are important components of the technological capability building system framework. The first is the set of mechanisms for accessing technological knowledge and artefacts through relationships with suppliers. The second is the relationship between the firm and the innovation system. The prominent role given to the analysis of boundary relationships is based on the resource-based theory of the firm where core capabilities are defined to include boundary assets (Prahalad and Hamel 1990; Teece 1987; Teece et al. 2000), on insights drawn from the national innovation system (NIS) approach (Freeman 1995; Lundvall 1988, 1992; Nelson 1993; Patel and Pavitt 1994) and development perspectives on capability development (Bell 1984; Bell and Pavitt 1997; Cooper 1991; Hoffman and Girvan 1990; Kim and Nelson 2000; Kumar 1996).

Interaction with suppliers
The TCB system approach recognizes that, for the majority of developing country firms, importation of technological inputs is a major source of capability development. Drawing on empirical research, including the influential studies noted above, the TCB system approach identifies internationally operating firms or local branches of such firms as the main source of technological inputs. However, the approach suggests that it is necessary to go further to examine in detail the variety of mechanisms used by firms to acquire technological capabilities from these external sources and to investigate the various processes involved in the acquisition of technological capability inputs. Some of these processes include selecting suppliers, procuring equipment and services from external suppliers under suitable terms and conditions and integrating this supply process with other aspects of technological capability building. The TCB system approach emphasizes the need to balance the development of indigenous capacity with the importation of know-how (Bell and Pavitt 1997; Ernst et al. 1998) and suggests that although developing country firms must rely on imported technological inputs because their local innovation systems are inadequate, sources of advanced technological knowledge, equipment, software and technical services, managing the interface with suppliers becomes an important aspect of technological capability. In addition, the approach suggests that effectiveness in boundary management will draw on the internal processes described earlier. In the technology transfer literature these capabilities are referred to as 'absorptive' capacities or the ability to manage technology transfer. The TCB system approach extends the concept of absorptive capacity by specifying the types of supplementary capabilities that include the ability and willingness to search for and the ability to integrate

new varieties of technology. These abilities are likely to include intensive efforts and management practices, as well as supportive corporate culture and leadership styles that facilitate joint management of importation and local capability development activities (Cohen and Levinthal 1990). Although there is acknowledgement of the long-term benefits of implementing such approaches, evidence suggests that it is still rare in developing country firms.[18]

In the TCB system approach, the effectiveness of developing country firms in implementing these capability acquisition mechanisms is considered explicitly to be under the partial control of these firms. The other important factors are the willingness and ability of external suppliers to play a role in capability development and the nature of the technological inputs that the developing country firm is seeking to acquire. Therefore, the technology acquisition process in the TCB system is considered to be a boundary relationship in which developing country firms exercize 'constrained agency'. The firms are not purely passive actors at the mercy of TNCs, but neither are they fully in control of the extent to which they can maximize capability development objectives using externally acquired inputs. This characterization is similar to that provided by Bell and Pavitt (1997) and Hoffman and Girvan (1990). The amplification in the TCB system is that it provides a detailed analysis of the conditions that influence the acquisition of different types of capabilities and emphasizes industry–specific factors as one of the explanatory factors.

In the TCB system framework, the limitations and opportunities for making effective use of supplier relationships for technological capability building are expected to be derived from the nature of the specific technological inputs being sought, and the willingness and ability of supplier firms to provide these inputs. In the early technology transfer literature, represented here by Lall (1987) and Stewart (1990), developing country firms are often assumed to have less access to technological inputs as a result of the concentration of innovation activity in the industrialized countries. The secular trend of the increasing concentration of innovation activity is not questioned here, but an alternative reading of its consequences for developing country firms is offered. By specifying at a greater level of detail what is meant by technological capability and delineating some of its constituent elements (see Figure 2.2), the TCB system approach suggests that, while the inputs for generating innovation do tend to be affected, many of the capabilities that are required by developing country firms may be unaffected by concentration in innovative activities. As industry concentration increases, supplier firms are less likely to facilitate the acquisition of the inputs necessary to generate new knowledge, products or processes. Radical innovation and incremental innovative activity are being concentrated in large, transnational corporations, which invest heavily in professional R&D facilities and other supporting infrastructures and seek to appropriate returns through the enforcement of intellectual property rights. However, if a firm in a developing country is not seeking to acquire the ability to generate new products or processes, this increased concentration is unlikely to have a major impact. Many of the early studies of technology transfer focused on the manufacturing sector, where firms in developing countries were seeking to produce the same output (at lower cost) as their suppliers. As a result, the threat of the extension of proprietary rights to production technologies may have been overstated. In service sectors, the purchaser of imported inputs often does not compete directly with suppliers and the threat of non-disclosure of technological functionality etc. is therefore reduced.

As discussed earlier, Bell and Pavitt (1997) noted that the trend towards increasing concentration in innovation activities has been accompanied by a trend towards increased specialization in many technological markets. This latter trend has led to an increase in the sources of technological inputs, particularly those that are not aimed at generating new products and processes. For instance, there are many more suppliers of codified knowledge and there have been increases in the number of specialized suppliers of equipment. Other factors that may facilitate access to external inputs include increased international migration of skilled labour and information and communication technologies that assist in the technological search process. The TCB system also considers that technological change has implications for the relationship between the suppliers of technological inputs and their customers.[19]

By presenting a more detailed analysis of the types of technological capabilities that are likely to be desirable for developing country firms, and by considering the constituent elements of technological capabilities, the TCB system approach provides a more nuanced analysis of the technological acquisition process. In the approach developed here, capability building using external inputs includes elements that can be provided by external suppliers, for example, tacit and codified knowledge, software, etc., and others that must be built by the firms themselves. The management of supplier relationships requires active investment and cannot be provided by suppliers. Effectiveness in managing supplier relationships includes the ability to search for alternative sources, to negotiate supply on appropriate terms and conditions and to integrate external inputs from a variety of sources. Another key feature of the TCB system approach is the emphasis on understanding how the changing nature of the relationship between supplier and user and the technological characteristics of the inputs affect the process of technological acquisition.

Relationship to the innovation system

The second boundary relationship included in the technological capability building system framework is the process through which firms interact with the innovation system. The institutions within the domestic innovation system that are considered to be important sources of technological inputs in this study are knowledge creating institutions, such as universities, technical vocational training colleges, training institutes, national research centres, etc., and policy making and regulatory bodies (Edquist 1997; Freeman 1995; Lundvall 1988; Nelson 1993; Patel and Pavitt 1994). Development scholars such as Bell and Pavitt (1997), Ernst et al. (1998), Hobday (1995) and Katz (1987) also offer useful insights in this area.

Innovation systems can provide firms with access to a number of different types of technological inputs including codified and tacit knowledge, which contribute to an improved understanding of technological trends and patterns ('know-why'). Public institutions are also likely to provide reliable and independent technological information on sources of technology ('know-who'). Innovation system institutions have the potential to be a source of embodied skills and codified knowledge on how to use artefacts in production processes ('know-how'), but often this is limited by relatively poor access to up-to-date equipment in the local setting. Policy and regulatory bodies can provide information on what technological capability building activities are permissible or feasible under legislative and regulatory rules, and advise on changes to those rules. Domestic innovation system institutions may also support cost effectiveness in technological search activities.[20]

Early policy research on developing country capability development experiences tended to advocate a proactive role for public sector institutions in directing technological capability building activities and tended to imply that public sector bodies were better equipped to direct technological capability building activities than firms. The evidence for the positive effects of policy intervention come from a relatively narrow range of studies in southeast Asia (Amsden 1989; Enos and Park 1988; Hobday 1995; Kim 1997; Lall 1987, 1992, 1997; Stewart 1984).

Many empirical investigations that utilized this traditional approach failed to problematize the ability of public sector organizations to influence technological capability building activities in firms. These approaches therefore provide little insight into how public organizations needed to improve their effectiveness and, in particular, into what capabilities these organizations would need to possess to be successful in influencing firm-level technological capability building activities. Critiques have suggested that traditional studies over-emphasized the positive role of developing R&D capabilities in public research centres. These writers suggest that influencing technological capability building activities in firms requires much more varied competencies (Bell and Pavitt 1997; Cooper 1980, 1991; Ernst et al. 1998; Salter 1999).

The TCB system approach regards firms as active respondents to signals from public sector institutions rather than as passive agents. Public sector bodies are not regarded as being omniscient or better placed than decision makers in firms to select suppliers, choose technological platforms, or adjust technological capability building efforts. This approach is relevant to many regions of the developing world, and particularly to Africa where the performance of innovation systems in support of technological capability building by firms is reported to have been dismal (Abiodun 1997; Cooper 1994; Enos 1995; Forje 1991; Pickett 1991; Wangwe 1995a,b). The TCB system approach focuses on why some firms respond favourably to positive signals and inducements from the domestic innovation system, while others do not. It therefore offers an explanation of why some firms may be able to compensate for ineffectiveness in the domestic innovation system and succeed in technological capability building to a greater extent than other firms in the same context.[21]

The TCB system framework assumes that technological capability building activities will have multiple objectives and, therefore, does not take a firm's ability to achieve incremental or radical innovation as a benchmark in evaluating capability development.

In summary, the TCB system framework consists of an approach to understanding capability development in which management practices, financial allocation rules and routines and cultural change to support learning, as well as the management of boundary relationships with suppliers and the innovation system are considered to be the key elements of an effective TCB programme. This framework provides the basis for investigation of the main research question in this study – how do developing country firms build technological capabilities? The conceptual framework TCB system approach is designed so that it can be operationalized through measurable indicators of technological capability building and the empirical application through a detailed study of 26 firms in the telecommunication sector in Uganda, Ghana, Tanzania and South Africa will be explored in subsequent chapters.

This chapter has presented a conceptual framework that can be used to understand the technological capability building processes in developing country firms. In the TCB system approach, technological capability building is defined as an investment process that is characterized by path dependency, non-linearity and uncertainty. The management of strategic change is considered to be an important competence within this framework. The technological capability building process is understood as a learning process in which meaningful change takes place through people. The conceptual framework was developed by integrating and amplifying insights drawn from organizational development, innovation management and development perspectives. The resulting conceptual framework is the TCB system approach, which suggests that firms can develop effective learning processes for capability development by implementing systems consisting of five core elements. The elements required are internal processes for investing in capability development, management practices to implement and coordinate the effort, leadership and culture to support learning and two processes to manage boundary relationships with suppliers and the innovation system.

NOTES

1	See Miyazaki (1995), Kim (1997) and Nelson and Winter (1982) as often cited studies of capability development that use evolutionary economic methodologies, and a more recent study using the cellular industry as the empirical context (Narduzzo et al. 2000). The study does not use the formal modelling methods that are the norm in evolutionary economics. For examples of this approach see Carlsson and Stankiewicz (1991), Jovanovic (1995) and Silverberg and Verspagen (1994).
2	Used in the context of the evolutionary theory of the firm, after Nelson and Winter (1982), this term is used to mean 'ways of doing' things rather than implying that the approaches are unfixed and unchanging.
3	Studies in the evolutionary tradition, such as Chiesa et al. (1996), extend the strategic management literature by probing the meanings of strategic competence (SC) and seeking to identify and measure types of SCs.
4	For instance, improved efficiency is measured by Arrow (1962) and Rosenberg (1982). Improvement in operational margins, market share and other indicators is examined by writers in the strategic management tradition (Prahalad and Hamel 1990; Teece 1987).
5	This assumption that firms can match TCB to overall strategy does not override the foundation assumption of uncertainty, but suggests that firms behave with bounded rationality (Foss 1999).
6	See Baden-Fuller and Stopford (1994); Pettigrew and Whipp (1991) for examples in the UK, and Leonard-Barton (1992a, b) and Prahalad and Hamel (1990) for US case studies.
7	Leonard-Barton (1995) suggests that the mathematical properties of fractals provide a useful metaphor for understanding how consistency works in organizations and how it differs from homogeneity and conformity. A fractal occurs with geometric regularity, scale invariance and self-similarity. Where organizations display these properties in learning, this provides a function of organizational integration for knowledge building activities, although they are dispersed throughout the firm.
8	Leonard-Barton (1995) distinguishes between T-shaped skills, defined as application integration skills and deep functional knowledge, and A-shaped skills, defined as two areas of deep functional knowledge. She further suggests that since boundary spanners often have both T and A-shaped skills, they facilitate knowledge flows and so are particularly important for producing positive interactions and system-wide positive externalities from stocks of disciplinary knowledge.
9	Unlike other strategic management researchers (see Barney 1991; Rumelt 1984; Teece and Pisano 1994), these authors do not focus on managerial knowledge as a purely codifiable tangible asset, but include the intangible and embodied aspects of management of change.
10	Many of the routines selected here as being relevant for firms in developing countries are similar to those that Tidd et al. (1997) identify as being important for small firms, such as

technology scanning, resourcing innovation through technology transfer, process innovation and change management and learning. The criteria for selection are a reflection of the assumption that in many developing countries both small and large firms are resource constrained.

11 Unsurprisingly, research on technological capability building in developing countries does not adopt a single definition of technological capabilities. Stewart (1984) defines indigenous technological capability as the capacity to create, adapt and modify technology thus including in the process, local adaptation and development of technology already known elsewhere as well as the creation of some completely new technology. Enos (1991) distinguishes three fundamental components of technological capability – the individual constituents, their organization and their purpose – and views all three components as important for the effects of technological capability to be realized. By defining technological capabilities as a composite of managerial resources, knowledge, skills, experience and institutional structures, Bell and Pavitt (1993, 1997) adopt a systemic view of technological capability; each of the elements is required to build capabilities and there are links between these elements.

12 The importance of such mechanisms and the culture change management benefits associated with them have been highlighted for firms in wealthy countries by many of the authors discussed in Section 2.2 including Garvin (1993; Leonard-Barton (1992b, 1995; Nonaka and Takeuchi (1995) Pettigrew and Whipp (1991).

13 Mytelka acknowledges that this term is based on work by J. Stiglitz (unreferenced in Mytelka's text), and suggests that 'learning how to learn' is a generic capability relevant to many different processes and products.

14 For further detail see Hobday (1990) Table 5.7 pp. 132–3).

15 Defined by Hobday (1990: 194) as referring to learning that occurs between firms as well as at the sectoral, government and macroeconomic level.

16 Mytelka (1999: 19) makes an important point – 'not all firms, however, pursue innovation strategies, whether of the catch-up, keep-up or get-ahead variety. Much depends upon the set of habits and practices [the firms] have developed to deal with challenges of change and competition'.

17 Coherence does not imply certainty or complete rationality. It is used in the same sense as the Pettigrew and Whipp (1991) notion of organizational coherence. This ability is not common and often serves as the critical distinguishing factor among firms that successfully manage change and those that fail to do so.

18 See Girvan and Marcelle (1990).

19 In the telecommunication industry, the focus of the empirical study in this book, technological change has led to increases in the embeddedness of knowledge within equipment. While a thorough discussion of this trend is outside the scope of this study, the implications for the capability development process in developing country telecommunication network providers are considered in Chapters 1, 2 and 5 in this volume.

20 The conceptual framework also considers that different types of knowledge can be acquired from suppliers (Johnson et al. 2002; Lundvall 1988, 1995).

21 For OECD countries there is a growing body of empirical analysis on the failure to innovate at the firm level, which considers these questions (Freeman and Soete 1997).

3 A Quantitative Exploration of Technological Learning

This chapter presents the results of the quantitative exploration of patterns of technological learning and capability building for the sample of developing country firms. This quantitative exploration of variation in the patterns of learning and TCB, involved constructing indicators of TCB system development and testing to see the extent to which there was conformity to a hypothetical ideal across different categories of TCB system development. The statistical exploration also permitted testing associations between the level of TCB system development and a number of independent variables and investigates the association between the level of TCB system development and the ability to organize a focused learning effort.

WIDE RANGE OF ROUTINES FOR TECHNOLOGICAL LEARNING AND CAPABILITY BUILDING

As shown in Table 3.1, firms in the sample used seven groups of 61 discrete TCB mechanisms. Of the total of 61 mechanisms used by sample firms, 39 (Groups I, II, III, V and VII) were internally focused, and 22 were externally focused (Groups IV and VI). The internally focused mechanisms included recruitment, organizational development, technological evaluation and search and funding of learning. The externally focused mechanisms enabled learning through interaction with industry and the innovation system. The full list and definition of all 61 mechanisms is provided in the Appendix to Chapter 3.

Table 3.1 Composition and characteristics of the seven groups of TCB mechanisms

Group number & function	TCB mechanisms	Type of orientation/ TCB system element	Functional characteristics of TCB mechanisms
I Increasing people skills base	M1–15	Internal / management practices	Focus on attracting people with skills, providing in-house training and retaining people with technical and commercial skills.
II Organizational development	M16–31	Internal/ management practices culture & leadership	Establishing and implementing organizational systems for targeted skills development, supporting learning and integrating TCB activities with systems for productivity growth and quality improvement. Undertaking activities to create an organizational culture that facilitates learning.
III Technological Search	M32–34	Internal/ management practices	Using search and evaluation systems to support technology choice, selection of suppliers and to maintain a high level of awareness of technological trends and developments.
IV Acquiring complementary knowledge from industry	M35–53	External/ supplier relationship	Acquiring technical information, knowledge and skills from a variety of sources, including equipment suppliers, international organizations and other private sector training organizations and transferring this information and skill to staff members.
V Acquiring expatriate people skills	M54–57	Internal/ management practices	Bringing knowledgeable and highly skilled people into the firm for limited duration, and transferring their information, knowledge and skills to permanent staff members.
VI Interaction with innovation systems	M58–60	External/relationship with innovation system	Accessing information and knowledge from institutions in the local and global innovation system, including universities and vocational training colleges.
VII Funding TCB	M61	Internal/financing TCB	Allocating budgets to TCB activity.

Source: Author.

The frequency counts of TCB mechanisms used by each firm were used in a statistical technique to order the sample with the usage categories taken as analytical categories of the level of TCB system development. The results of this operation showed that the sample was distributed into three categories with the following characteristics:

High (well-developed TCB system): # TCB mechanisms used greater than or equal to 16; n = 10.

Medium (moderately developed TCB system): # TCB mechanisms used between 9 and 15; n = 9.

Low (poorly developed TCB system): # TCB mechanisms used equal to 8 or fewer; n = 7.

The allocation of firms across the three analytical categories is graphically shown in Figure 3.1. The ten firms with well-developed TCB systems included representative firms from each of the four countries, and a variety of business segments, with South African firms being in the majority.

Figure 3.1 Distribution of sample firms across three categories of TCB system development

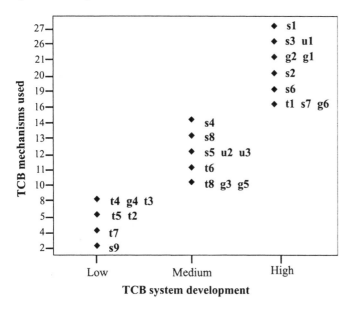

Source: Interview data analyzed by author: N=26 firms.

Among the seven firms that had made very little progress in establishing functioning TCB systems, Tanzanian firms were over represented. The remaining nine firms that had made some progress in establishing TCB systems were fairly evenly distributed across the four countries, but there was more clustering of data communications companies than fixed line or mobile communications providers.

These patterns of distribution were subjected to detailed and rigorous statistical exploration to test whether firms with more developed TCB systems did display patterns of learning and capability development that differed from firms with less well-developed TCB systems, and also to test whether any of the sample firms displayed properties similar to the hypothetical ideal system. The first step in this analysis involved computing an intensity of usage score and then using this to examine patterns across the seven functional groups of TCB mechanisms defined in Table 3.1. The composite intensity of usage score was computed for the three categories of TCB system development for each of the seven groups as follows: *number of firms using any mechanism/total number of firms in category* multiplied by *number of mechanisms used/total number of mechanisms available*. The score attempts to capture and indicate the extent to which firms used all the mechanisms in a particular group and the extent to which this was representative of the behaviour of the firms in that category of system development. If few firms in a given category used particular mechanisms, the intensity score would be reduced. Similarly, if firms in a given category used only a few mechanisms from the total number within a group, the intensity score would be reduced. The score attempts to represent intensity in both senses – usage by a large number of firms and use of many types of mechanisms within a group. The minimum score is zero, representing the event that no firms use any of the mechanisms in that group. The maximum score is one, where all firms use every type of mechanism in a group. Table 3.2 presents data on the intensity of usage for firms in the three levels of TCB system development. As shown in the table, the expected score for the ideal system would be one for each group of TCB mechanisms.

Preliminary analysis of the data in Table 3.2 indicates that firms in the high category of TCB system development appeared to have a greater intensity of usage of all groups of TCB mechanisms, and this conforms to a priori expectations. Firms with well-developed TCB systems used Group II mechanisms, that is organizational systems to support learning and capability development with the greatest intensity. This was followed by mechanisms in Group IV, that is processes for reaching outside the firm boundaries for external sources of knowledge and information. Firms in the medium category scored high for Group IV mechanisms, but did not make intensive use of organizational development to support learning. Firms with limited TCB system development scored only reasonably for Group VII mechanisms, which are associated with maintaining capital investment levels. The preliminary analysis of usage patterns appears to indicate that development of the TCB system was associated with the type of mechanisms that the firm selects and the breadth range of TCB mechanisms in use, two features that could improve effectiveness. The second stage of exploration involved carrying out statistical tests to investigate whether or not patterns of usage across the various groups of TCB mechanism were statistically different across the three levels of TCB system development.

Table 3.2 Patterns of usage for firms across three categories of TCB system development

Group no. & function	TCB mechanism	Orientation	Usage intensity scores ideal/high/medium/low			
I Increasing people skills base	M1–15	Internal	1.00	0.80	0.75	0.40
II Organizational development	M16–31	Internal	1.00	1.00	0.29	0.21
III Technological search	M32–34	Internal	1.00	0.80	0.37	0.00
IV Acquiring complementary knowledge from industry	M35–53	External	1.00	0.95	0.79	0.19
V Acquiring expatriate people skills	M54–57	Internal	1.00	0.70	0.56	0.43
VI Interaction with innovation systems	M58–60	External	1.00	0.70	0.67	0.05
VII Funding TCB	M61	Internal	1.00	0.80	0.78	0.57

Source: Interview data analyzed by author; N = 26.

Having computed these intensity scores and observed how they were distributed across firms with varying levels of TCB system development, a number of statistical tests were conducted to investigate these patterns. Statistical analyses were used to investigate whether the analytical categories of TCB system development are valid and then to explore variations in the patterns of usage across these categories. Procedures were also used to investigate associations between the gaps in capability identified by firms and their level of TCB system development. Finally, a thorough examination was made of whether there is variation between the observed patterns and the hypothesized 'ideal', and the associations between the level of TCB system development and independent variables. These tests are discussed below.

VARIATION IN DEVELOPMENT OF TCB SYSTEMS REFLECTED IN TCB SYSTEM INDICATOR

The first test was an analysis of variance (ANOVA) used to investigate whether there was variation in overall usage of TCB mechanisms across the three analytical categories of TCB system development. This test, which is a reliable test of variation among groups, established the validity of the categories of TCB system development. Variation across the three categories was found to be statistically significant at the 5 per cent significance level. Prior to undertaking this test, it was confirmed that the frequency of TCB usage was normally distributed using a superimposed normal curve on a histogram. By using an ANOVA the hypotheses are tested as follows:

H_o: High = Medium = Low; H_1: High $\neq$ Medium $\neq$ Low.

Table 3.3 ANOVA table for frequency of TCB mechanisms

Treatment	Observations	Total	Average
1 High	27 26 26 21 21 20 19 16 16 16	208	20.8
2 Medium	14 13 12 12 12 11 10 10 10 8 8 8	128	10.67
3 Low	5 5 4 2	16	4
	5972	352	35.47
Source of variation	Sum of squares	Degrees of freedom	f
Treatments	990.2	2	43.43
Errors	216.3	23	
Total	1206.5	25	

Source: Interview data analyzed by author.

Since the test statistic is greater than the critical value of

$$F_{(2,23)(0.05)} = 3.42 < 43.43$$

the null hypothesis can be rejected and it can be concluded that at the 5 per cent significance level the three categories of TCB development are statistically different and that the samples are independent.

PATTERNS OF LEARNING VARY WITH TCB SYSTEM
DEVELOPMENT

To further investigate variation in the patterns of usage across the three
categories of TCB system development, a Kruskal Wallis test was applied to
the intensity of use scores calculated for the three categories of TCB system
development. This test is used to compare two or more populations and can
be used on data that are ranked, but that do not require any assumption about
the normality of the distributions to be made. In addition, the Kruskal–Wallis
test requires that the samples are independent. The latter was confirmed using
an ANOVA.

The sum of the intensity scores for each of the three categories of TCB
system development are presented in Table 3.4; these are used to compute

$$H = \left[\frac{12}{n(n+1)} \sum \frac{T_j^2}{n_j} \right] - 3(n+1)$$

Therefore $H = 22$. Kruskal–Wallis is a Chi-Square test $\chi^2_{(0.05)(2)}$. So
$\chi^2_{(0.05)(2)} = 3.841$.

Since the null hypothesis that the three levels of intensity are the same at the
5 per cent significance level can be rejected, it can be concluded that the
intensity scores are different.

Interpretation of these results suggests that firms in the three categories of
TCB system development did display different intensities of mechanism
usage across the seven groups. The analysis suggests that firms that have
different levels of TCB system development vary in the manner in which
they deploy their TCB investment effort. This is an important result because,
as will be shown, it confirms the differences suggested by the qualitative
assessment of the TCB efforts across the sample. The discussion in
subsequent chapters also shows that firms with an absolute higher number of
TCB mechanisms in use were also the firms that achieved the most effective
TCB efforts. The findings from the Kruskal Wallis test suggests that the
development of TCB systems is associated with increases in the range of
TCB mechanisms used and the intensity of use of different types of
mechanisms. This supports the hypothesis that diversity is an important
element in the quality and effectiveness of a TCB system.

Table 3.4 Sum of intensity scores for three levels of TCB system development

Category/ group of TCB mechanism	High	Medium	Low
I	0.8	0.75	0.4
II	1	0.29	0.21
III	0.8	0.37	0
IV	0.95	0.79	0.19
V	0.7	0.56	0.43
VI	0.7	0.67	0.05
VII	0.8	0.78	0.57
Sum	5.75	4.21	1.85

Source: Interview data analyzed by author.

SERIOUS GAPS IN FIRMS' TECHNOLOGICAL CAPABILITY

The sample firms reported 55 specific gaps in existing levels of technological capability and/or in their efforts to build technological capability. It was also reported that there were gaps in technical knowledge, deficiencies in the stock of skilled human capital, ineffective or underdeveloped organizational systems and problems that were outside the direct control of the firms.

These reported gaps were grouped as follows:

1 (G1–G9) Employees have inadequate levels of technical knowledge, expertise and competence and there are insufficient numbers of skilled employees.

2 (G10–G22) Workforce lacks areas of skill and aptitudes necessary for efficient and competitive performance (not necessarily directly related to technical knowledge).

3 (G23–G39) Ineffective organizational systems and culture for commercial and customer-service orientation.

4 (G40–G46) Lack of effective internal training programmes and systems

5 (G47–G50) Supply bottlenecks that limit numbers of skilled people entering workforce and reduce effectiveness of graduate recruits and new entrants and the usefulness of local knowledge creating institutions, and

6 (G51–G55) Gaps arising out of South Africa's legacy of racial discrimination.

The group of gaps with the highest reported incidence was taken to be an indicator of where the sample firms faced the most problems in their TCB effort. It will be shown that this was not always where TCB efforts were focused. Further details of the gaps with the highest reported incidence are reported in Table 3.5.

Table 3.5 TCB gaps with the highest reported incidence

Definition and code	No of firms
G5 Missing specific areas of telecommunication technical competence:	12
Advanced access network management (WLL & ADSL) knowledge and skills; advanced mobile communications technologies WAP, GPRS UMTS; automated service order processing; basic mobile communications technologies; broadband communications design and engineering; data communications security (firewalls, etc); digital switching; digital multimedia; data broadcasting; internet service provision; internetworking technologies and systems; logistics management (J.I.T provisioning of spares and repairs management), network planning using computerized tools; network strategy and evolution and major and minor network modification planning; Optical fibre systems; satellite communications; SDH & ADH transmission systems; spectrum management and traffic engineering.	
G7 General lack of familiarity with state of the art equipment and lack of operational experience with advanced equipment.	9
G6 Insufficient IT/IS expertise for billing, MIS and customer service management.	7
G15 Poor problem-solving ability and skills.	7
G23 Attitudes and values not suited to competitive environment or rapid learning. Orientation towards bureaucratic, slow, rigid work practices or internal (non-market based) provision of service.	7
G24 Inadequate systems for customer service management and poor attitudes to customer service.	6
G8 Lack of up-to-date knowledge and familiarity with specific equipment and lack of know-how on the operational and maintenance routines for this equipment.	6

Source: Interview data analyzed by author; N = 16.

Interpretation of these data suggests that developing country firms, such as those in this sample, often experience gaps in terms of specific areas of technological knowledge. In a fast-moving field, such as telecommunications, the respondents from African firms were concerned about lacking technical knowledge about network management techniques as well as advanced access technologies and new product offerings. It should also be noted that, although production processes for telecommunications operators have become increasingly computerized, with information technology being involved in almost every process, the supply of IT skills has not grown at the same rate. As a result, representatives of the sample firms reported that there has been a growing interdependence between the need for technological capability in telecommunication disciplines and information technology disciplines and expressed concern about the existing gaps in IT skills. Seven firms reported having inadequate levels of expertise for design, modification and implementation of information systems for billing, management information, customer service management and operation of computerized network functions.

The firms were also concerned about weaknesses in core general technological knowledge, limited technological awareness, poor operational aptitudes, underdeveloped organizational systems and cultural mismatches between their management systems. There was also concern that firms lacked the capability to perform effectively in a fast-paced, technology intensive industry, in which an excellent customer service culture was an important determinant of competitive advantage. Other problem areas that were identified include lack of long-term strategic orientation and the challenges associated with making the transition from a bureaucratic environment to an organizational climate more suited to competitive markets. The sample firms also reported that they faced attitude and aptitude gaps in terms of lack of problem solving skills, limited capacity for fast decision making, lack of confidence and low aptitudes for technical experimentation on the part of their technical and operational staff. In a bid to overcome this there was a great propensity to employ expatriates, overseas experts and other persons considered to have greater aptitude for problem solving in technical environments. In terms of factors outside their direct control, the sample firms identified the lack of fit between local knowledge creating institutions and the requirements of telecommunication operating companies as a major problem.

The overall set of reported gaps contains a high proportion (32.7 per cent) of gaps reported by a single firm: this relatively high percentage may indicate that companies' perceptions of gaps in their capabilities or capability building efforts are not generalizable, but are rather company specific. As noted earlier, there were also country-specific gaps in TCB activity, defined as those arising from South Africa's legacy of racial discrimination. This set of country-specific gaps was related to companies' attempts to include black and other excluded groups in TCB activities.

Preliminary inspection of the data indicates that companies with high numbers of reported gaps identified gaps from several different categories, while firms with fewer reported gaps identified a limited range of gaps. This pattern suggests that ability to identify gaps may be associated with effort spent on TCB activities. Analysis of the data on problem-focused TCB effort also suggests that representatives of companies with more developed TCB systems generally reported a higher number of gaps in absolute terms and a greater variety of types of gaps. For example, among the firms that reported being challenged by the move to more competitive environments, only those with well developed TCB systems deployed a variety of mechanisms to solve these transition problems, such as change management and leadership development programmes and this is reflected in the firms being able to create an organizational climate that facilitates learning. Firms with well-developed TCB systems also reported more company-specific gaps.

The relationship between the problem-focused nature of TCB effort, as reflected in the number of reported TCB gaps, and the extent of TCB system development, was investigated using correlation analysis. The TCB system approach would suggest a priori that there would be a positive relationship between TCB system development and the reported number of TCB gaps. As can be seen from Table 3.6, this relationship is confirmed by the correlation tests and was found to be significant at the 0.05 level.

Table 3.6 Correlation between TCB system development and reported gaps

			TCB gaps	TCB system development.
Kendall's tau	TCB gaps	Correlation coefficient	1.000	0.373*
		Sig. (2-tailed)		0.0210
		N	26	26
	TCB system devpt	Correlation coefficient	0.373*	1.000
		Sig. (2-tailed)	0.0210	
		N	26	26
Spearman's rho	TCB gaps	Correlation coefficient	1.000	0.449
		Sig. (2-tailed)		0.210
		N	26	26
	TCB system devpt	Correlation coefficient	0.449*	1.000
		Sig. (2-tailed)	0.0210	
		N	26	26

Source: Interview data analyzed by author.
*Correlation is significant at the 0.05 level (2-tailed).

EFFECTIVENESS IN LEARNING IS INFLUENCED BY INDEPENDENT VARIABLES

A correlation analysis was also carried out to investigate the relationships between the level of TCB system development and certain firm-level characteristics. Tables 3.7 and 3.8 provide correlation matrices for a test of association between the number of TCB mechanisms used and a number of firm characteristics: number of years in operation; establishment size in terms of staff numbers; segment of the telecommunication services sector in which the firm operates; type of ownership; and country in which the firm operates.

Table.3.7 Correlation matrix – TCB mechanisms used, years in operation and firm size

		TCB mechanism	No yrs operational	Firm size
TCB mechanisms	Pearson correlation	1	0.547**	0.447*
	Sig. (2-tailed)		0.004	0.022
	N	26	26	26
No. years operational	Pearson correlation	0.547**	1	0.294
	Sig. (2-tailed)	0.004		0.145
	N	26	26	26
Establishment size	Pearson correlation	0.447*	0.294	1
	Sig. (2-tailed)	0.022	0.145	
	N	26	26	26

Source: Interview data analyzed by author.
*Notes: **Significant at 0.01 level (2-tailed); *significant at 0.05 level (2-tailed).*

Table 3.8 Correlation matrix – TCB mechanisms used, market segment, ownership type and country of operation

	Correlation coefficients for number of TCB mechanisms used and independent variables	Kendall's tau	Spearman's rho
TCB	1.00		
seg1	0.34	0.11	0.10**
seg2	0.40	0.05*	0.04*
seg3	-0.11	0.39	0.38
seg4	-0.24	0.27	0.26
seg5	0.17	0.31	0.29
seg6	-0.35	0.13	0.12
own1	0.40	0.10**	0.10**
own2	0.04	0.92	0.89
own3	-0.03	0.94	0.92
own4	-0.10	0.47	0.46
own5	-0.10	0.59	0.56
own6	-0.34	0.10**	0.10**
own7	-0.35	0.09**	0.08**
own8	0.25	0.15	0.14
own9	0.23	0.16	0.15
countr1	0.17	0.44	0.43
countr2	0.06	0.74	0.72
countr3	-0.51	0.01*	0.01*
countr4	0.32	0.08**	0.07**

Source: Interview data analyzed by author
*Notes: **Relationships significant at 0.1 level. *Relationships significant at 0.05 level.*

Analysis of these results confirms that firm-level factors influence the level of TCB development. Firstly, the results indicate that there is a relatively strong positive association between the level of TCB system development, the number of years of operation of the firm and the firm's size (measured in terms of staff count). The association between the firm's experience and the level of TCB development was significant at the 1 per cent level, while that for establishment size was significant at the 5 per cent level. These results are in line with expectations and provide confirmation for the conceptual framework, which considers TCB to be a learning process in which cumulative experience and critical mass in initial skills and knowledge would be expected to have a positive influence.

Secondly, a high level of TCB development was found to be positively associated with operating in multiproduct segments. This relationship was independent of the market structure in the segment, with both monopoly and competitive multiproduct segments demonstrating a positive influence on TCB system development. There was a relatively strong, positive association between the level of TCB system development and provision of multiple product services (fixed voice, data and mobile) under competitive market structure conditions. This relationship was significant at the 5 per cent level. Multiproduct firms operating in monopoly market conditions were also found to have a positive association with the level of TCB system development although this association was less strong and was significant only at the 10 per cent level. The analysis did not establish any other statistically significant relationships between other types of market segments and level of TCB system development. These results are in line with the expected positive influence that competitive market conditions and the stimulus of producing a range of services is likely to have on TCB system development.

However, as will be shown, the results of the quantitative analysis differ from the qualitative analysis insofar as the latter suggests that, even among telecommunication companies with a limited range of product offerings, for example, mobile communication and data-communication companies, it is possible to deploy TCB systems that are similar to the ideal suggested by the conceptual framework. The difference between the insights yielded by the quantitative analysis and the qualitative analysis is likely to be explained by the heterogeneity of the market segment groups. For example, among the eight firms in market segment category 3 (fully competitive national mobile communication providers), two had well-developed TCB systems, and the remaining six were evenly split between firms that had made progress in developing TCB systems and those that had no functioning TCB system.

Thirdly, only one ownership type was found to have a positive influence on the TCB system development at the 10 per cent level of significance–joint Malaysian and US shareholding. Two ownership types were found to have a negative influence on the level of TCB system development at the 10 per cent level of significance, namely firms operating as a branch of a global company and firms that were a unit of a wholly private sector, cross-border African holding company. The qualitative analysis suggests explanations for these findings. While joint Malaysian/US shareholdings benefited from systematic programmes of 'technology/knowledge transfer' from the shareholding partners, firms in the latter two categories either had no access to active technology accumulation or relied on parent firms with limited technological resources to share with the operating companies.

The results for the correlation between country of operation and the level of TCB system development are in line with initial expectations. Operating from South Africa was found to have a positive influence on the level of TCB development at the 10 per cent significance level, while operating from Tanzania was found to exert a rather strong negative influence at the 5 per cent significance level. The relationships for Uganda and Ghana were positive, but not statistically significant at the 10 per cent level. Qualitative analysis and theory suggest that the country influence on TCB system development derives from many factors, including the role of the state in provision of public knowledge goods, the influence of the size of the market and the nature of demand in stimulating learning, and the potential role of policy and regulatory bodies in facilitating TCB in firms. The results of the quantitative investigation were to some extent supportive of that analysis.

There are some surprising results among the findings. While the conceptual framework suggested that ownership by US or west European multinationals would have been strongly and positively associated with the level of TCB system development in the sample firms, since these shareholders would be expected to serve as an important source of technological capability inputs, this was not borne out by the correlation analysis. Further investigation of this result is beyond the scope of this study, but may have implications for future research.

BALANCED APPROACH TO LEARNING PROMOTES EFFECTIVENESS

The TCB system approach suggests that a balanced, systematic approach to learning and capability yields results in terms of improved effectiveness. This approach also suggests that it is possible to define an ideal system for TCB and learning. This section discusses the patterns exhibited by the sample firms and the statistical tests carried out to determine whether these patterns conformed to the hypothetical ideal.

A Wilcoxon Signed Rank Sum Test procedure, with the computations shown in Tables 3.9a and b, was applied to compare the reported patterns of usage in each of the three categories of TCB system development with the 'ideal system' suggested by the conceptual framework.

Table 3.9a Intensity scores for three categories of TCB system development and ideal

	Ideal	High	Medium	Low
I	1	0.80	0.75	0.40
II	1	1.00	0.29	0.21
III	1	0.80	0.37	0.00
IV	1	0.95	0.79	0.19
V	1	0.70	0.56	0.43
VI	1	0.70	0.67	0.05
VII	1	0.80	0.78	0.57

Table 3.9b Difference and ranks for three categories and ideal

	Ideal	High	Diff.	Rank	Med.	Diff.	Rank	Low	Diff.	Rank
I	1	0.80	0.20	*3.0*	0.75	0.25	*3*	0.40	0.60	*3*
II	1	1.00	0.00		0.29	0.71	*7*	0.21	0.79	*5*
III	1	0.80	0.20	*3.0*	0.37	0.63	*6*	0.00	1.00	*7*
IV	1	0.95	0.05	*1.0*	0.79	0.21	*1*	0.19	0.81	*4*
V	1	0.7.0	0.30	*4.5*	0.56	0.44	*5*	0.43	0.57	*2*
VI	1	0.70	0.30	*4.5*	0.67	0.33	*4*	0.05	0.95	*6*
VII	1	0.80	0.20	*3.0*	0.78	0.22	*2*	0.57	0.43	*1*

Source: Interview data analyzed by author.

This test examines the morphology of learning systems to investigate whether proportionate and balanced deployment were present. The Wilcoxon Signed Rank Sum Test is used to compare two populations when the data occur in matched pairs and do not require an assumption about the normality of the distributions. This test is used to investigate how the patterns of usage observed in the three categories varied from the theoretical ideal.

A firm with an ideal system for TCB would be expected to have a pattern of use in which the maximum intensity scores are achieved across all seven TCB groups, since this firm would be expected to balance its TCB effort across all of the key elements of the system, that is adequate and appropriate financing, facilitating management practices, supportive culture and leadership, effective management of supplier relationships and relationships within the innovation system. Interpretation of the results of the Wilcoxon Sign Test suggests that ten firms with well-developed TCB systems (firms in the high category) adopted patterns of usage that were similar to the ideal system, while 16 firms with less well-developed TCB systems did not adopt the most effective patterns of deployment of TCB mechanisms. The differences or deviations from the ideal system were found to be statistically significant at the 5 per cent level.

High vs Ideal: The rank sum for the difference between high and ideal is 17. In this case, the sample size becomes 6 because there is a difference of zero and so zero differences are excluded. The critical values for the Wilcoxon Signed Rank Sum Test for n = 6 are $T_L = 1$ and $T_U = 20$ with a rejection region: $T \le 1$ or $T \ge 20$. By comparing the test statistic with the critical values it can be concluded that at a 5 per cent significance level it is not possible to reject the null hypothesis that a high level of intensity is statistically similar to the ideal situation. This implies that the pattern of TCB system development demonstrated by firms in the high category does not deviate significantly from the hypothetical ideal.

Medium vs Ideal: The rank sum for the difference between the medium and the ideal is 28, which is T and the sample size is therefore 7. The critical values for the Wilcoxon Signed Rank Sum Test for n = 7 are $T_L = 2$ and $T_U = 26$ with a rejection region of $T \le 2$ or $T \ge 26$. By comparing the test statistic with critical values, it can be concluded that at a 5 per cent significance level, the null hypothesis of similarity is rejected. This implies that firms at the medium level of TCB systems development do have patterns of use that deviate from the ideal.

Low vs Ideal: The rank sum for the difference between the low and the ideal is 28, which is T and the sample size is therefore 7. Critical values for the Wilcoxon Signed Rank Sum Test for n = 7 are $T_L = 2$ and $T_U = 26$ with a rejection region of $T \le 2$ or $T \ge 26$. By comparing the test statistic with the critical values, it can be concluded that at a 5 per cent significance level, the null hypothesis of similarity is rejected. This implies that firms at the low level of TCB systems development exhibit patterns of use that deviate from the ideal.

These results appear to confirm that as investment in TCB increases, there is a corresponding increase in the diversity of mechanisms used and in the intensity with which different types of mechanisms are used. Firms appear to move towards the ideal system suggested by the TCB system approach, but there was variation in the level of success achieved. These are important results since they provide substantial confirmation for the argument that firms that are effective in their TCB investment employ a diverse range of mechanisms and take a balanced, systematic approach.

The results are also important since they confirm one of the main propositions of the TCB system approach, that is that there are significant morphological differences in the patterns of learning and TCB across firms. The analysis shows that there are developing country firms, such as the ten firms in this sample, that operate mature, balanced and effective approaches to TCB with equal attention given to internal and external processes. It also shows that a larger number of developing country firms, such as the 16 firms with statistically significant deviations from the hypothetical ideal, are still likely to operate unbalanced systems for TCB. As will be discussed further in the qualitative analysis, these firms with relatively underdeveloped and unbalanced TCB systems are also ineffective. The form of the TCB system used by these ineffective firms is illustrated in Figure 3.2, which varies from the proportionate and symmetrical ideal system.

Figure 3.2 An unbalanced TCB system

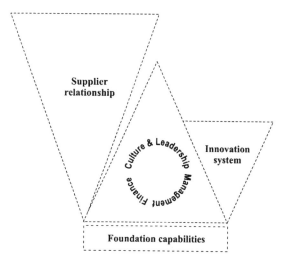

Source: Author based on analysis of empirical research.

Firms that did not conform to the ideal system lacked strategic balance in their TCB effort, their internal processes were often underdeveloped and not well integrated into a systematic approach to capability development. Their efforts were plagued by some common weaknesses:

- lack of focus on culture and leadership; absence of clear assignment of responsibility for capability development activities;
- capability development efforts were not aggregated and so, even when there were successes, these did not give rise to firm-wide benefits;
- insufficient use of integrating and coordinating mechanisms that provide systems with internal coherence;
- the TCB effort was often undertaken in crisis mode rather than as

a considered response to changes in market conditions and
technology and there were few reinforcement routines to ensure
the sustainability of learning investment;

• adoption of traditional approaches rather than support for open
learning, and investment in equipment rather than in processes
that would be likely to increase embodied capabilities.

Secondly there was an over-reliance on supplier relationships for
capability development as compared with balancing capability inputs sourced
from suppliers with other means of building capability. In addition, because
of the lack of development of internal processes, these firms did not manage
their supplier relationships well. These themes will be taken up in Chapters 4
and 5.

The firms with unbalanced systems were not able to compensate for these
weaknesses in the local innovation systems. The firms were often operating
in countries where national innovation systems were weak, relatively
undeveloped and not supportive of firm-level capability development efforts.
Under these conditions many firms relied on suppliers and other market
mediated sources of technological knowledge. Their ability to manage
relationships with the innovation system suffered and their ability to
influence or benefit from relationships with the national innovation system
also was compromised. In this study, the national institutions even in the
most-advanced country in the sample – South Africa – were considered by all
the firms in that country to be significantly less relevant and effective than
suppliers of equipment as sources of technological know-how. This suggests
that developing country firms will be encouraged to deploy more balanced
TCB systems only if there is also corresponding strengthening of national
innovation systems. This theme will be taken up in Chapter 6.

The high propensity to deploy unbalanced systems is also influenced by
the extremely challenging initial conditions under which the firms undertake
learning and capability development. Many of the ineffective firms were
starting out with such limited levels of technological knowledge and
experience in operating telecommunication networks that they were not able
to make the evolution to more effective systems.

As has been shown, the TCB system approach produces reliable indicators
and associated tests for predicting whether a firm is likely to be effective in
technological learning and capability building, where effectiveness in TCB is
defined as the ability to deploy a sustainable investment effort that is aligned
to the strategic objective of narrowing gaps in existing technological
capability and improving the ability of a firm to achieve its strategic
objectives.

The quantitative analysis in this chapter shows that there are important discernable differences in the ways in which developing country firms deploy technological learning and capability building effort and these variations influence effectiveness. In subsequent chapters the study considers the qualitative analysis of the evidence and draws out conclusions and implications.

4 Management, Culture and
Leadership for Learning

This chapter provides insights into how developing country firms establish and manage internal organizational processes for learning and TCB and explains variation in the nature and effectiveness of learning systems. This general discussion is framed within a detailed review and analysis of the experience of a sample of 26 African telecommunication firms. The qualitative assessment presented here supplements the statistical exploration in Chapter 3.

INTERNAL ELEMENTS OF LEARNING SYSTEMS

The descriptive accounts from companies confirmed that developing country firms deploy internal systems to support technological learning and capability accumulation. As shown in Table 4.1, the sample firms used 39 specific, internally orientated mechanisms for managing learning, stimulating a culture to support TCB and funding TCB investment. As can be seen from the data on the frequencies, there was considerable variation among firms in the usage of these mechanisms.

Recruitment and Retention Systems

Developing country firms actively engage in processes to identify, attract and retain personnel with technical skills, including recruiting overseas nationals and expatriates. These recruitment and retention systems were found to make a very important contribution to learning and capability accumulation. For the majority of firms in the sample, technical staffing was achieved by hiring graduates from local universities and technical colleges (M1). This most basic mechanism for getting staff with the relevant skills was the most common and traditional form of recruitment used by telecommunication companies in Africa. Many well-established firms, and particularly the publicly owned national operating companies, continued to rely on this for achievement of TCB activities. However, new entrants often brought with them other methods for attracting skilled staff. For example, in Ghana many new entrants participated in a scheme sponsored by the United Nations Development Programme (UNDP) and the Ghanaian government to attract overseas resident nationals back to Ghana (M4);[1] they also implemented a more targeted recruitment of high-level specialists (M3) and formalized the graduate recruitment programmes.

The firms in the sample provided evidence that they made investments in increasing the pool of skilled personnel by sponsoring university training for existing staff and potential recruits (M8). Nine firms from three countries used this mechanism, but they were all well-established and well-resourced firms with developed TCB systems.

Fifteen firms in the sample used recruitment of expatriates as a source of technological capability and acquired this people-based capability through short-term contracts. The expectation was that during their period of employment, expatriates would transfer skills, knowledge and information to the permanent staff. However, of the 15 firms that employed expatriates, only four had formal knowledge transfer programmes to ensure that permanent staff did acquire skills, knowledge and information from the expatriates. For the remaining firms, transfer was an unmonitored and informal process. There were other instances of considerable variation in the use made of expatriates as a source of technological skills. The majority of firms making use of expatriates were private sector companies, including those with non-African equity partners and cross-border African equity ownership. The large publicly owned firms in the sample, except for those where there was private participation through strategic investors, did not use expatriates as a source of technological skills.

The sample firms reported varying degrees of satisfaction with expatriates as a source of technological knowledge and skills. One large public network operator in a competitive market expressed concern that its firm's ability to select expatriates was compromised by the terms and conditions of technical assistance funding. In this instance, it was believed that the expatriates employed under these arrangements did not contribute to TCB, as their skills were often out-dated and their work practices did not facilitate knowledge sharing and skills transfer. However, most of the 15 firms using expatriates as a source of knowledge and capability, considered the mechanisms effective; in these cases the selection of expatriates and management of the transfer process was directed and methodical. For example, one national mobile operator that used expatriates as a core component of a network deployment team was extremely successful and it was able to build a network with national coverage on time and within budget in three months.

Table 4.1 Usage of internally orientated TCB mechanisms

Management, culture and leadership and funding TCB effort	Code/No. firms
Recruitment and retention	M1(20); M8 (9); M54 (8); M56 (8); M4 (4); M55 (4); M57 (4); M7 (4); M5 (3); M2 (1); M3 (1); M6 (1)
Training , motivation and reward systems	M9 (18); M10 (14); M19 (10); M16 (9); M12 (7); M15 (7); M17 (5); M20 (5); M18 (4); M11 (3); M14 (2); M13 (1)
Organizational design	M26 (11); M23 (9); M27 (5); M21(5); M28 (4); M29 (2);
Organizational integration	M30 (3); M31(2)
Evaluation and assessment	M33 (8)
Scan and search	M34 (7); M32(4)
Knowledge management and codification	M24 (7); M25 (4) M22 (2)
Financing TCB effort	M61(19)

Source: Compiled by author; N = 26 firms; number of TCB mechanisms = 39.

Seven firms in the sample had specific programmes designed to retain and develop staff with technical specializations (M15). The implementation of these programmes included career paths for technical specialists, remuneration systems to reward and 'incentivize' these staff and payment of 'loyalty bonuses' to retain specific individuals who were considered to be irreplaceable. One of the new entrants introduced a scheme that pegged the salaries and bonuses of technical specialists to the US dollar as an incentive. There were two firms that implemented formal career development paths for technical specialists in which promotion and career progression possibilities were designed and mapped by human resource professionals in the firm and formally communicated to staff. Firms with underdeveloped TCB systems fared less well in meeting the challenge of recruiting and retaining skilled people. These firms had not been able to diversify from their traditional sources of technical recruits and were thus likely to be affected by the sometimes lower quality and numbers of the graduates from local universities and technical colleges.

Many of the firms in the sample identified problems with recruiting information technology and computer science graduates. This appeared to be a bigger problem for well-established firms that used traditional mechanisms for recruitment of staff and had not investigated other sources of technical personnel.

Human Resource Development (HRD)

Developing country firms also use practices to train, reward and incentivize staff, to carry out performance evaluations, to implement promotion systems and to run staff development programmes, all of which increases individual motivation and performance. These human resource development systems vary in their elaborateness and effectiveness as the examples of three particular firms show. Although these firms varied considerably in size and number of years of operation, and operated in different segments of the telecommunication services sector, they had similarities in their respective approaches to HRD. Each firm had in place an extensive HRD programme designed to achieve specific objectives.

The first example is a large public network operating company, which operated several formal systems for staff development, including a leadership training programme for senior managers, a fast-track management programme for managers and staff at functional levels and a change management programme for employees at all levels. This company also had in place sophisticated reward and remuneration schemes that tied training outcomes to individual remuneration packages and, further, included training and skills development of team members as one of the evaluation criteria against which management performance was assessed. These schemes were formally managed as part of the specialist HRD function, with senior managers and executive-level employees having designated responsibility for achieving objectives.

The second example is a much smaller firm, a public network operator facing competition across all of its business lines, which had been in operation for only two years at the time that these data were collected. Because of the background and orientation of a key decision maker in the organization, start-up operations of the public network placed emphasis on organizational development activities. This individual had previously held a chair in entrepreneurship in a US business school and as the senior executive had considerable influence on the design of the corporate development systems in the company. This emphasis on organizational development and HRD is reflected in the importance given to the professional and specialized HRD function, at a relatively early stage in the life of the company, and the investment made in the implementation of remuneration systems that rewarded individual performance, denominated salaries in US dollars to hedge against foreign currency risk and implemented remuneration surveys to set reward packages for employees.

The third example is a small specialist firm providing telecommunication services to business users. This company identified its technological leadership as its competitive advantage and used organizational development methods to maintain high levels of motivation among the technical staff. In addition to the methods used by the first two example firms, this company set individually defined learning objectives and paid bonuses against achievement of these learning objectives.

These data suggest that firms with more developed TCB systems had a much more focused and individually targeted approach to HRD. Firms with less well-developed TCB systems did not employ as wide a range of human resource development mechanisms and focused on traditional approaches such as organizing classroom-based training.

Design and Implementation of Organizational Structures to Support Learning

Developing country firms often use organizational design mechanisms for learning and TCB including setting up cross-functional teams, staff rotation and specific assignment of responsibility for technological learning to line managers and special units. The last process (M27) was found in 11 firms in the sample and, particularly in small firms, was the responsibility of the chief executive of the company. Decentralization of the learning effort and assignment of responsibility for achievement of learning objectives to line mangers was found only in four companies all of which were located in South Africa. Many companies had special units responsible for TCB activities; in the larger companies these units resembled the research and development departments found in firms in industrialized countries. In smaller companies, the special TCB unit incorporated the characteristics of strategic planning, procurement and HRD. The specialized technologically advanced company, cited as an example of a firm with sound HRD programmes, also made changes to its organizational structure to bolster its TCB effort. The position of Technology Executive was created and the postholder's responsibility was to act as a bridge between the strategic concerns of the executive management and the technical specialists. The Technology Executive's job was to co-ordinate the technological scanning and search activity, to define learning objectives, to monitor their achievement, and to serve as a communication bridge between line managers and technical specialists.[2]

Efforts to Increase Organizational Integration

Firms that are seeking to stimulate learning and TCB undertake activities to increase organizational integration, including planning as an active learning mechanism, implementation of project feedback mechanisms, active environmental scanning, vision setting and future assessment. However, these approaches are often not implemented by developing country firms as illustrated by the low frequency with which these practices were used by the sample firms. Even among those firms where the TCB system was relatively well developed, the internal processes through which organizational integration of TCB effort might be achieved were often not present or not well developed. Although there was evidence of environmental scanning and assessment and design of future scenarios in the larger firms, the leadership for this activity came from the engineering side of the business and was separated from commercial and other strategic objectives. There was also evidence of disagreement as to where the focus of learning activity should be placed, with the main tension being between the engineering and purely technical aspects of capability building and the more organizational development aspects of TCB. Many firms reported lack of understanding by senior management of broadly defined learning and capability development objectives.

In the sample, there was no evidence that firms were implementing mechanisms to learn from failure and to learn how to learn. The types of practices that might assist with reflective or action learning were not in evidence either among the larger, better-established firms or among the smaller, entrepreneurial firms.

Design and Implement Technological Capability Evaluation and Assessment Systems

Evaluation and assessment systems were another area where developing country firms have not invested enough effort and resources. The large well-established public network operating companies in the sample undertook network forecasts and network planning exercizes for dimensioning their networks. These companies also often implemented formal training and skills needs assessment. However, these planning exercizes were typically carried out by engineering departments and used as inputs in developing corporate plans for the firm as whole. Although the engineering assessments of network and technology requirements were used as inputs in corporate planning, the mechanisms for arriving at a strategic assessment of technological capability requirements were very weak in the majority of the large traditional companies. Many of the senior engineers interviewed expressed the view that there was an increasing imprecision in their approach to network planning and forecasting because of the very rapid pace of technological change.

In addition, since the definitions of technological capabilities used in traditional telecommunication planning techniques are very narrow, only some of the elements of capability suggested by the TCB system approach are taken into account. In companies where HRD functions and strategic planning specialists were involved in the technological capability assessment, a fuller picture of the capability requirements of the firm was produced. Overall, there were very few examples of a more holistic approach to assessing technological capabilities and requirements.

Formal and Informal Active Technology Scan and Search Mechanisms

This is typically an area of weakness for developing country firms. One of the large public network operators maintained a well-developed search and scan facility comprising of over 400 technical professionals, who undertook technology assessment and technology review of network systems and components, carried out trials on new equipment and set performance specifications for suppliers. Many other firms carried out their search and scan activity on a project basis, triggered by the need to purchase capital equipment.

Implementation of Knowledge Management Systems

As is typical of many developing country firms, the sample firms were not very advanced in their use of formal knowledge management systems to capture, organize and disseminate technological knowledge across the firm. Systems to capture and codify technical knowledge were present only in the largest firms in the sample, and only one firm specifically identified implementation of knowledge management systems as a goal of TCB effort. Many of the firms have extensive, well developed information management systems, but few have made the transition from capturing information to explicitly capturing knowledge and documenting ways of doing things, documenting company-best practices and learning from and sharing these across the firm.

Culture and Leadership

When discussing the features of internal processes that lead to appropriate organizational culture and leadership practices, it is more difficult to isolate the effect of specific TCB mechanisms. It is the aggregate effect of several

TCB mechanisms that produces a culture and leadership that are likely to promote TCB activities. Firms in the sample reported that they were aware of the importance of making changes to the organizational culture and leadership styles and that this acted as an incentive to use certain specific TCB mechanisms. For example, when one firm introduced mechanisms to confer responsibility for TCB activities on particular functions, the respondents suggested that the rationale for this change was to give TCB efforts organizational legitimacy by making them more visible and understandable to Board members. Several firms reported seeking to encourage experimentation and learning (M26). While only four firms in the sample attempted to formally introduce development of leadership practices that could better cope with a fast-paced, commercially orientated environment (M20), several respondents identified the outmoded management style of existing leaders as a challenge. Other mechanisms, such as the monitoring of TCB expenditure and setting of targets (M29), also indirectly promote an organizational culture and values that encourage TCB activities. Some firms in the sample were supporting culture change through allocating resources for informal learning and byadopting innovative approaches to learning (M23).

While some firms in the sample had been successful in changing their culture and values using the mechanisms identified here, many of the long-established firms reported that they continued to face serious challenges in changing organizational cultures and leadership styles that were not adapted to TCB objectives. Culture and leadership are particularly important because TCB is effected by people at various levels and with many different responsibilities. In this diffuse, amorphous process it is vital that the values, norms and mental models within the firm are supportive and facilitating.

Financing TCB Effort

The data on levels of expenditure on TCB activities (see Table 4.2) often did not disaggregate the spend on embodied TCs (people related) or disembodied TCs (hardware and materials). Most companies were reluctant to disclose such information on the grounds of confidentiality and, in the vast majority of cases, the management and financial accounting systems of the sample firms did not capture information at a sufficiently disaggregated level. Estimates of spend on network equipment ranged from US$20 million to US$25 million per annum to billions of dollars and these estimates were used as a rough proxy for investment in disembodied TCs. Expenditure levels on training and staff development activities, which ranged from as low as several thousand dollars per year to millions of dollars, are used as a proxy for expenditure on embodied capabilities.

Table 4.2 Data on expenditure on TCB activities by sample firms

Code	Expenditure on TCB activities
s1	1–2% total capital equipment budget on technology assessment systems, test sets and training. Companywide in-house training providing facilities for technological training. Multibillion rand (equivalent to multimillion dollar) investment in training.
s4	US$166m. spent on SDH network funded with internal resources. US$830k technological leadership programme. US$8.3m.–USD$25m. training budget.
s5	5% total operating expenditure on training and capability development. 2% of capital expenditure for large projects on equipment supplier provided training .
s6	US$6,600 per employee per annum on training.
s7	5% total op. expend on training and capability development. Plan to increase to 7%.
t1	US$250m. over 5 years in network modernization and expansion, financed by World Bank, East African Development Bank and grants from CIDA and SIDA. This sum allocated to network equipment, technical services, technical assistance and training. Estimated that 15–20% spent on training and technical assistance. Additional expenditure from bilateral grants $110k. Internal resources 2.5% total operating expenses budget on training (TSh500m., equivalent to US$750k) and TSh1b. (equivalent to US$1.5m.) annual budget for company training school.
t2	Capital expenditure budget estimates: Base stations between US$9-12m.; Mobile switching centre US$4m.; Billing system US$3m.; Voice mail and value added service software system US$600k.
t3	Training budget set at US$100k per annum; being reduced (1% of network equipment investment). Capital investment in network equipment US$40m. over 4 years. Capital equipment to accommodate change in spectrum allocation USD$6m.
t4	Training expenditure budgeted at US$80k for 1999: spent on technical consultants, upgrading satellite communications, IT/IS skills and router configuration techniques.
t5	Very little spend on TCB activities, not able to afford. Estimates that needed overseas courses would cost company US$1,000 per person per week.
t6	Spend in start-up year US$17,000, expected to increase to US$52k in 2000. Plans to increase spend on technical information (journals, books, trade magazines) from current level of US$2,000.
t7	Joint venture partners expect to fund majority of US$90m. for national mobile network coverage.
t8	First 5 years of operation training spend estimated at US$100k p.a., now reduced to US$60-70k p.a. Spend on trade fairs, exhibitions, overseas visits est. US$40–50k p.a.
u1	Upgrading of training institute funded by institutional strengthening grant aid US$3–4m. Annual expenditure on TCB distributed in the following proportions: 70% equipment vendor supplied training; 25% overseas seminars and conferences; 5% consultancy and training by overseas experts done locally.
g1	Annual operating budget of training school 1.385b. cedis, equivalent to $US600k.
g4	Capital investment 1993-1998 totalled US$25m.; of which, 80% on non-embodied capability (equipment, software systems etc.) and 20% on embodied capability e.g. training, staff development. Expenditure on capital equipment includes US$500k. on customer care and billing system.
g5	Capital investment has been phased. Phase 1–3 US$20m.; Phase 4 US$40m. and estimates that US$100m. required for national coverage (mobile network).
g6	Estimates that 15–20% total operating expenses on TCB activities (embodied capabilities). Maintains high capital investment budget including satellite transmission equipment, and Internetworking system components.

Source: Compiled by author based on company data and interview accounts.

EFFECTIVENESS OF TECHNOLOGICAL LEARNING

The quantitative exploration in Chapter 3 confirmed that the firms in the sample varied considerably in terms of the intensity with which they used specific types of TCB mechanisms and this was found to be related to the extent to which the firm had established a balanced and systematic approach to technological learning and capability building.

From the detailed statistical exploration, the sample of 26 firms was found to consist of ten firms with well-developed TCB systems, seven firms that had made very little progress in establishing functioning TCB systems and nine firms that had made some progress in establishing TCB systems. The detailed qualitative analysis presented in this chapter sheds light on why firms with more developed TCB systems were able to increase the effectiveness of technological capability inputs and how they managed to diversify from traditional approaches to capability development. To explore the implications of these results more generally, this chapter describes the most commonly observed patterns or the prevailing systems in use[3] in the sample and then provides an analysis of the firms that performed better or worse.

Prevailing Systems in Use for Developing Country Firms

The prevailing system in the majority of developing country firms, particularly in Africa, is one that involves firms expending a great deal of effort on increasing the stock of appropriate inputs, particularly the supply of people. Firms also need to keep abreast of technological trends and ensure that their technical staff is kept up to date with knowledge and skills. In fast moving industries, such as telecommunications, this represents a major challenge because the labour market and other supply conditions are not responsive. The burden of skills development falls disproportionately on private companies and, as a result of being preoccupied with continuously ensuring that skills match the requirements for effective operation and change in technological systems, they neglect other internal processes that are required to ensure that technical personnel are used effectively.

For African telecommunication companies, the prevailing systems in use for managing technological learning and capability building had the following characteristics:

Management practices
- There was a great deal of reliance on recruitment of graduates from domestic technical colleges and universities as the main source of people-embodied technological capability. Public sector companies in

the sample often organized this recruitment effort quite rigidly and required new recruits to undertake formal induction programmes in which they were introduced to different technical disciplines through a process of rotation. These programmes in some instances lasted as long as three years.

- Formal in-house classroom based training programmes were the main method for continuous updating of skills, information and knowledge acquisition. The large firms in the sample, both public and private, conducted this in-house training through specialized departments or training colleges that were attached to the operating company. The older, more established companies often administered training programmes without reference to knowledge production institutions in the country and thus were more likely to complain that the curricula of their internal training programmes were out of date.

- Experiential training was recognized and appreciated as an important component of training, skills development and knowledge acquisition. The smaller firms in the sample were better at organizing and rewarding experiential training opportunities.

- The approach to managing the people-centred capability development process was to assign responsibility for training and knowledge development to a single specialist department in the organization, generally the HRD. The interaction between HRD and the technical specialist departments, such as network planning and information technology, was relatively irregular and there was little joint ownership of objectives for organizational learning across disciplines.

- Performance-related pay and benefits systems were used extensively to encourage and motivate capability development in individuals. Promotion of individual capability development appeared to be more effective than aggregation of this effort with teams or the organization as a whole.

- There was extensive use of expatriate employees and consultants to expand the skills base of the firm beyond the boundaries of the domestic economy. The effectiveness of internal processes to ensure genuine knowledge transfer from expatriates, even when these were the employees of shareholder companies, varied considerably across the firms in the sample. In general, African firms were relatively weak at managing the process of the flow of tacit information from expatriate staff and consultants to local employees.

- Use of open learning facilities, including resource centres, on-line training facilities and provision of internet-based resources and tools was not very widely practised by firms in the sample. Although there was widespread recognition that these facilities could provide extensive benefits, in practice African firms had not progressed beyond that recognition.

Culture and leadership

- There were diffused and amorphous approaches to managing capability development as opposed to systematic and strategic approaches. A wide range of activities was aimed at increasing capabilities available to the firm.
- There was a good understanding of the importance of capability development for meeting both competitive and defensive objectives.
- The most commonly observed patterns among these firms were those of novice rather than of experienced and sophisticated developers of capabilities. However, there was an acute awareness of the importance of technological knowledge and expertise in the ability to produce telecommunication services cost efficiently.
- There was an awareness of the imperative to develop more open learning styles and shift away from more traditional approaches to developing capability. In the publicly-owned firms, there was a sense of crisis; the impetus for this change was not experienced as being under the control of existing management. Rather it was perceived as an involuntary process associated with privatization and imminent change of ownership. Even in the privately owned companies, the most common experience was of the operating companies struggling to cope with the pace of technological change.

Allocation of financial resources

- There was much more emphasis on budgeting for the hardware and tangible inputs into the technological capability process than for the human-related needs. Telecommunication operating companies, including those in this sample, have well-established network-planning routines that allow the firms to plan and allocate resources to network expansion and maintenance. These routines were typically engineering led, and often took place in isolation from the rest of the organization. In addition to expenditure on the hard elements of technological capabilities, the operating companies also established routines for allocating resources to training and human resource development. Budgets for hardware, equipment and human resource development were often separately managed, and a common problem identified was the lack of integration between training and the technological requirements.

These prevailing systems in use were observed in 16 of the 26 firms in the sample: the remaining ten firms performed better. The factors that contributed to this better performance are discussed in the section below.

Out-Performers and Critical Success Factors

As discussed above, there were African firms that displayed best practice and compared favourably with the ideal system for TCB. These companies demonstrated breadth of routines, selectivity and integration of routines across functional disciplines and had made attempts to establish the cultural and leadership setting within which organizational learning could take place. These firms outperformed the prevailing systems in use and had very effective technological capability building efforts. The five general critical success factors and several specific characteristics that contributed to the better performance of these firms and contributed to the effectiveness of their technological learning and capability building are discussed below.

Critical Success Factors for Learning

The first critical success factor (CSF) that can be identified for out-performers is that they exhibited awareness of the importance of technological capability for the firm's survival and competitiveness. This ability was observable in the specific internal processes associated with evaluation and assessment, and the routines that aimed to direct the TCB effort in the firm. This is an important finding since it may indicate that success in TCB effort requires the following kinds of effort, noticeably absent in firms with less well-developed TCB systems.

1 Sensing of TC gaps and selecting appropriate responses
2 Implementing responses
3 Refining responses and making continuous change within TCB effort.

The second CSF is the ability to continuously address and manage change by deploying appropriate organizational culture and leadership practices. The most effective firms were those that had the ability to refine and adapt their TCB effort in response to change. This ability was not limited to large firms since, as noted, traditional public telecommunication operators (PTOs), although they had well-developed TCB systems, seemed often to be stuck with the old ways of mobilizing TCB effort and, therefore, were not able to select appropriate responses or to change over time.

Out-performing firms in the sample displayed a third key strength in terms of their willingness to experiment with organizational design and to introduce mechanisms for facilitating more openness in learning. Eleven out of the 26 firms reported providing environments conducive to organizational learning, involving, for example, making changes to organizational design. These firms provided open learning facilities such as resource centres, internet facilities, on-line tutorials and libraries. This high propensity to support open learning exceeds the forecasts of previous studies of capability development efforts by African firms. It suggests that the telecommunication sector is likely to be an outlier in terms of organizational learning and capability development in Africa.

The fourth CSF exhibited by firms in the sample with well-developed TCB system, was the existence of a high absorptive capacity for bringing knowledge and expertise from external sources into the firm and making effective use of those inputs. The firms with a well-developed TCB system appeared to be particularly good at managing the flows of tacit knowledge across organizational boundaries. The capabilities and factors that assisted with this boundary-spanning activity included management practices, such as evaluation and monitoring of expatriate contracts as well as attitudes. Firms with a well-developed TCB system reported that they cultivated a climate of willingness to learn, were not closed or suspicious, and appeared more confident in their approaches to TCB management than firms with poorly developed systems. The combination of appropriate culture and leadership, good management practices, ample financial resources and interaction with the innovation system and suppliers – the defining elements of the TCB system – appeared to have reinforcing effects that were expressed in the values and attitudes of the firms' employees. These values and attitudes were not acquired instantaneously or through a single TCB effort, but rather through a process which took place over an extended period of time and required failures and mistakes to be dealt with and the processes refined.

The fifth and final key distinction between firms with effective TCB and those without is the central importance of disciplinary-based technological knowledge. In every instance of firms that were successful in building a culture of openness and strong absorptive capacity, there was evidence that the internal capabilities of the firm were strong and resilient. The firms that had a strong foundation of in-depth technological knowledge[4] were much more confident in their boundary-spanning activities than the weaker firms and were less likely to complain of dependence on external actors. The representatives of these firms believed that their firm could respond to external changes in technology or commercial conditions. This finding has implications for how developing country firms can build technological capabilities, and lends support to the wealth of empirical evidence that suggests that indigenous capability is an absolutely essential requirement for capability development.

Specific Competencies for Effectiveness in Learning

In addition to these general features, there are some specific characteristics of the TCB effort within the firm that contributes to its relative success. These are the ability to blend traditional and non-traditional approaches, the necessity for active and purposive engagement and routines for rewarding and developing skills.

Blending of traditional and non-traditional approaches
Successful TCB firms appear to have combined traditional PTO style approaches to developing capability with specific and tailored approaches. This was particularly evident in the recruitment and retention routines of the firms in the sample. In particular, successful TCB firms recognized the weaknesses of the local labour market and education systems. They reported that they proactively engaged with the education system to try to improve the quality of staff they might employ. This is confirmed by the reported attention of firms with well-developed TCB systems to interaction with the local and global innovation systems. An example of this is a medium-sized Ghanaian firm that developed very specific routines for filling the gap in network management expertise by requiring local staff to follow an international best-practice industry-defined training programme over three years. In contrast, a large Tanzanian network operator had failed to increase its recruitment and training efforts and was reportedly experiencing the negative effects of outdated skills.

Active and purposive engagement
Successful firms with well-developed TCB systems did not leave matters to chance but reported that they managed and monitored individual TCB mechanisms and the TCB system as a whole. For example, while many firms in the sample used expatriates as a source of capabilities, few firms had management mechanisms that would increase the probability of these mechanisms being effective. In firms where there was active engagement, expatriate programmes were managed at every step from the selection of individual experts, coordination of skills transfer programmes, design of accountability measures and succession planning. The expatriate programmes where there was active and purposive engagement generally demonstrated the following attributes:

- shared responsibility between local staff and expatriates;
- mutual trust and respect;
- joint staffing of project teams;
- shared ownership of goals and objectives;

- shared accountability for outcomes;
- common vocabulary for defining project objectives and outcomes;
- similar depth of knowledge between local and foreign counterparts.

This finding is illustrated by a close examination of the medium-sized mobile network operators in the sample. For all of these firms, there was very high reliance on expatriate individuals as a source of technological capability, but there were major distinctions in their approaches to the management of this TCB mechanism. Those firms that demonstrated the characteristics of active and purposive engagement also reported greater satisfaction with expatriates as a source of capability, while for other firms of similar size, there was the same level of reliance on expatriates but less satisfaction with the performance of this mechanism. These findings are in line with the experience of firms in other contexts (see Brewster, 1991).

Developing and rewarding learning skills
The evidence appears to confirm that, of the firms in the sample, those that were able to develop the boundary-spanning skills required to bridge disciplinary and organizational boundaries were more successful in their TCB efforts. This sample of telecommunication operating firms, therefore, provides support for a well-established theoretical proposition that firms must build boundary-spanning skills or T skills.[5] The specific routines that the sample firms used to develop the T skills required for boundary spanning include tailored recruitment programmes, continuous training of technical specialists, special incentive programmes to retain specialist skills, mentoring programmes, assignment of responsibility for motivating technical specialists and team development.

The more sophisticated companies in the sample had specific routines designed to achieve better integration between budgeting for non-embodied technological capabilities and person-embodied capabilities and paid attention to gaining value from that expenditure.

Pervasive Weaknesses and Enduring Challenges

The study also identified and to analyzed persistent weaknesses and enduring challenges for technological learning and capability development in African firms. These weaknesses include: inadequate organizational integration of learning efforts, weak evaluation and assessment capabilities; limited range and inadequate stock capability inputs, imbalances among different sources of capabilities and weaknesses in sustaining cultural and leadership support for TCB. These challenges are discussed in turn.

Inadequate organizational integration and limited innovation in organizational design

The ability to ensure that there was effective organizational integration of TCB effort was found to be generally weak among the firms in the sample, even for those with a well-developed TCB system. The TCB system approach suggests that a successful TCB effort requires assignment of responsibility for learning (vision-setting and strategy development) and implementation of learning, on the basis of accountability and with appropriate evaluation systems that allow refinement of learning effort, which takes account of past failures and changing external circumstances. Figure 4.1 illustrates the relationships between these factors, with the thickness of the lines for each box indicating the relative strength across the sample firms. In the ideal system there would be symmetry across these types of effort.

Figure 4.1 Key processes in learning systems

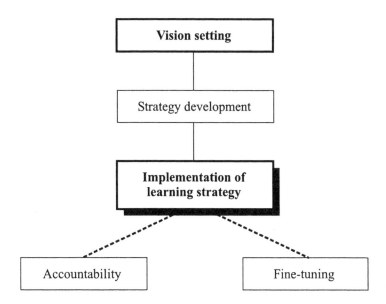

Source: Author.

The TCB system approach suggests that the vision setting aspect of organizational integration is most effective when it is undertaken at the highest level of management. The evidence from the sample firms indicates that this was reasonably effective. In many of these firms, either the chief executive, members of the Board of Directors or senior management personnel championed the learning and TCB effort. However, despite the relative strong performance on vision setting, strategy development effort among the sample firms was a major weakness. There were few examples of well-designed strategies that translated high-level visions and aspirations into consistent strategies applied at levels throughout the firm. As a result, although there was active implementation of TCB effort, it was often uncoordinated and undirected. Systems to ensure accountability and fine-tuning of TCB effort were also weak and underdeveloped. Although TCB activities took place at the line management level, there was insufficient decentralization of responsibility to enable quick recovery from mistakes.

Weak evaluation and assessment capability
The sample firms demonstrated significant expertise in their approaches to evaluating their needs and requirements for non-embodied technological capabilities, drawing upon their substantial internal engineering competencies. However, these assessments were isolated from any broader technological evaluation and did not emphasize the embodied and tacit elements of technological capabilities. This seems to have led to a mismatch in the approaches to filling the gaps in technological capabilities identified in the assessment exercizes. The qualitative and quantitative accounts suggest that there were significant gaps in both codified and tacit knowledge and in material and non-material technological capability inputs. This evidence suggests that evaluation exercizes should be balanced and well-integrated so that the TCB system can be applied to tackle problems associated with missing pieces of all the combinations of embodied and non-embodied technological capabilities and tacit and codified knowledge. Evaluation and assessment capability were elements of the learning strategy development process discussed under the theme of organizational design and organizational integration, which were discussed above.

Scarcity of different types of capabilities
As noted in the sub-section on blending traditional and non-traditional approaches, telecommunication operators have tried and tested mechanisms for attracting people into their organizations. The sample of firms reported that they used these mechanisms to overcome shortages of embodied technological inputs. However, because these firms operate in a fast moving technology space, these mechanisms were failing to provide the necessary levels of codified knowledge, for example development of wireless access technologies. Put simply, firms were bringing in people who were not familiar with new technologies. The more successful firms reported that they complemented these tried and tested methods with other mechanisms designed to increase their codified knowledge, most frequently in the form of

equipment suppliers who could provide additional knowledge inputs. Other mechanisms used were helping to improve the performance of local knowledge-producing institutions so that the people they trained acquired more up-to-date skills. Tacit knowledge was acquired through the hiring of expatriates and well-managed relationships with suppliers.

For the firms in the sample, a major weakness was the development of internal reservoirs of codified knowledge. This applied even to those firms with a well-developed TCB system. There were very few instances of firms that had successfully captured and encoded learning events and formal knowledge, and were thus able to make this available for wider dissemination across the firm. Even in the firms that reported that they had designed open learning systems, the learning materials were developed externally and so did not encompass the firm's own experiences of technological capability building. There were some repositories of formal codified knowledge in the courseware of formal in-house training programmes delivered by suppliers or internal experts.

Weakness in diversifying sources of capabilities
For developing country firms, including those in this sample, suppliers of equipment and services are the main external source of technological capability. However, the TCB system approach also suggests that managing relationships with external suppliers should be balanced with managing relationships with other external sources of technological capability inputs. The empirical evidence suggests that firms with well-developed TCB systems were better able to accumulate technological capabilities from various sources because of their ability to interact with sources other than suppliers of equipment and services, such as shareholders, other operators, regional and international organizations, industry associations and the innovation system. These firms used all of these relationships to complement knowledge they acquired from suppliers. However, the heavy reliance on commercial suppliers of equipment and services remained a persistent weakness in the majority of firms in the sample and suggests that cultivating these wider relationships is not easy for them.

Organizational culture for learning is not sustained
There is a theoretical argument that developing an organizational culture that facilitates learning requires activities, which, over time, affect the attitudes and values of individuals in the firm, making them more disposed to learning as well as increasing the number and type of learning opportunities available. In the TCB system approach this proposition is taken to mean that, while the presence of specific individual TCB mechanisms is important for an organizational culture to take root, these mechanisms must be present in

appropriate combinations so that there is continual reinforcement. Building a facilitating organizational culture involves being sensitive to the cumulative effect of many different TCB mechanisms rather than to the existence of these mechanisms in isolation.

To analyze this aspect of the TCB effort, the extent to which the sample firms demonstrated the ability to use internal TCB mechanisms in reinforcing combinations is examined using the three groups of TCB shown below.

Group 1
M23: open learning facilities
M26: organizational culture redesign aimed at supporting experimentation and learning

Group 2
M19: performance related pay
M27: assigning line responsibility for TCB
M29: TCB expenditure targets

Group 3
M20: leadership development
M21: formal change management programmes
M31: integration of TCB objectives into strategic planning.

The conceptual framework suggests that for TCB to be effective firms should deploy these mechanisms in combination. The evidence from the sample firms indicates that only five firms implemented the pair of mechanisms associated with developing open learning systems and undertaking actions to redesign culture to support experimentation and learning (Group 1). It is also worth noting that three publicly owned firms with well-developed TCB systems did not deploy this pair of mechanisms. This finding provides further support for the proposition that the publicly owned firms in the sample had not undergone the cultural change that is necessary to support effective TCB effort.

The TCB system approach suggests that the occurrence of the second group of internal processes is likely to improve a firm's ability to influence the extent to which individuals and the entire group assume accountability for TCB objectives. Only two firms in the sample had all three mechanisms in place, while four firms had two out of the three (M19 and M27, not M31). Only South African firms made an effort to improve accountability for their TCB efforts. Finally, there was only one firm in the sample that had simultaneously implemented leadership development, change management programmes and integrated TCB into strategic planning (Group 3). There were four other firms that were using two out of the three mechanisms. This is indicative of the extent to which firms formalized their TCB development effort and integrated it with planning and suggests that, among the sample firms, there was limited development of the sustainability of culture change and TCB effort. Firms had not been able to formalize their TCB efforts and closely align these with business goals and objectives. While there were informal programmes in place these often lacked legitimacy and were not able to attract resources in sufficient volume, and these factors negatively affected their effectiveness. This evidence confirms that a few firms were taking action to move beyond having strategic visions and top-level support for TCB to implementable management practice that would be expected to have an impact over time.

The study provides evidence that firms with weak TCB systems, while they may be aware of the importance of specific internal processes for supporting technological learning and capability building and often experiment with interventions, they were typically not able to deploy TCB effort in a systematic manner. For example, a small Tanzanian firm had implemented leadership development programmes and introduced facilities for informal learning, but the overall impact of these activities was not sustainable. In many of the smaller firms, TCB was managed and led by an individual champion for learning. There were five firms in the sample of 26 that demonstrated a charismatic approach to developing a learning culture. In these firms, the learning culture was associated and identified with the technical competence and knowledge of an individual or group of individuals in the firm who were frequently the founder(s) of the organization. For this sub-set of firms, the culture was dependent on the communication skills of these individuals and their ability to inspire and motivate others.

In summary, the TCB system approach suggests that the ability to effectively implement learning at company level involves transcending individual effort through processes that support and develop changed ways of 'being' and 'doing'. In this perspective, processes to aggregate the effects of learning and ways of thinking are as important as the individual learning events themselves. The evidence from this sample supports this proposition in so far as the firms that were effective in TCB and undertook learning that responded to their business objectives also reported that they introduced processes to integrate isolated learning events and developed a reinforcing culture change. In the firms that were less effective in TCB and those that were unable to align TCB with business objectives, learning experiments were in place, but the activities were not resulting in benefits.

The presence of reinforcing internal processes is considered to improve the probability of changing culture over time and producing a sustainable facilitation of learning. Together with organizational integration these features exert very important influences on the effectiveness of TCB. Operational experience and firm size were found to be positively associated with the development of effective TCB systems. The evidence illustrates that only firms that had achieved a threshold level of development of their TCB system attempted to tackle the cultural change aspects required to achieve substantial support for learning and capability development. Even for the firms that had made the most progress in the sample, there were gaps in the effort to develop facilitating cultures for capability development. A vital missing ingredient was the development of approaches that are more likely to be sustainable, because they incorporate the reinforcement features of culture development. These styles were not as widely used as the 'charismatic' approach, which was highly dependent on a single individual. Another shortcoming among the sample firms was their limited success in making learning widely accessible across the firm.

INSIGHTS FROM THE TCB SYSTEM APPROACH

This analysis has highlighted the importance of sustainable cultural change to support capability development efforts and processes to ensure that there is organizational integration of TCB effort, both of which have received rather scant attention in investigations of capability development in developing countries. By focusing on internal processes of technological learning the TCB system approach has identified factors that have the potential to explain variation in the effectiveness of TCB efforts.

The analysis of the evidence confirmed that firms with well-developed, effective TCB systems deployed internal processes in their capability building efforts and managed these processes to improve firm-wide learning. The factors that appeared to facilitate effectiveness in capability building among the sample firms included: providing leadership for learning; creating conditions that were supportive of firm-wide learning and raised awareness of the importance of technological capability for firm survival and competitiveness; introduction of open learning facilities; implementing specific management routines, such as rewarding development of boundary-spanning skills, and managing the transfer of knowledge from expatriates; implementing evaluation and monitoring systems; and proactively engaging with the local labour market and education system to provide people with the requisite education and skills, particularly disciplinary backgrounds in telecommunication engineering and information technology. The major weakness among the sample of firms was that none of the firms had made substantial progress in the organizational integration of TCB and few deployed efforts to sustain the implementation of a supportive cultural environment for learning. As a result their efforts did not achieve consistency, cohesiveness or consonance.

These results are important because, firstly, they demonstrate the fruitfulness of integrating organizational development and strategic management insights into analysis of capability accumulation by developing country firms. For example, they highlight the significance of having diverse routines for learning, co-ordinating mechanisms and supporting culture and leadership, which have not received much attention in the development studies tradition.

Secondly, the TCB system approach yields new knowledge by identifying specific internal processes (for example, introduction of open learning systems and proactive support for public education and training institutions to enable them to produce more highly trained and skilled people), which were found to be important for the sample firms and which may be important for other developing country firms operating in similar contexts of rapid technological change.

Finally, the analysis provides support for the view that it is necessary to have an appropriate balance between internal accumulation of capabilities and acquisition of capabilities from external sources. The TCB system approach operationalizes the concept of balance between external and internal accumulation by developing a measurable indicator of TCB system development, which captures both types of effort, and by using qualitative and quantitative analysis to explore why firms with a balanced approach to technological learning are more effective.

NOTES

1   For example, the government of Ghana has set up a Non-Resident Ghanaian Secretariat and actively seeks to attract investment from the Diaspora.
2   This finding confirms Watkins and Marsick's (1993) observation about the changing skill and capability mix found in 'learning organizations'.
3   The term 'systems in use' (Senge 1992) is a useful concept for describing the most commonly observed patterns that appeared to be typical of the firms in the sample. It also appears to be more meaningful to describe a prevailing kind of organizational practice than to introduce terms such as average, which tend to suggest statistical representativeness. The characteristics of the sample firms described here as being illustrative of the systems in use was drawn from a qualitative assessment of the evidence and are not based on the results of a statistical calculation.
4   In small firms in the sample, this was often a single individual – the founder.
5   See Leonard-Barton's definition of 'T skills'.

5 Managing Supplier Relationships for TCB

This chapter analyzes the part played by management of supplier relationships in facilitating developing country firms' technological learning and capability accumulation. The TCB system approach suggests that the ability to effectively manage supplier relationships is an important factor that influences whether developing country firms are able to benefit from boundary relationships and to use these relationships to advance their technological capability development objectives. There are a number of aspects that appear to account for developing country firms exercising constrained agency in their management of these relationships. These include endogenous variables, such as the level of development of their TCB system, and, in particular, the extent to which firms have acquired the specific and complementary boundary relationship management competences of technological evaluation, search, acquisition and integration. Exogenous factors, such as technological change, increasing specialization, concentration of innovation and the nature of competition, also appear to influence the contribution of supplier relationships to TCB objectives. This chapter presents empirical evidence from the sample of African telecommunications firms and interviews with four African-based supplier firms and one representative of an international firm based in Europe. These four suppliers – Lucent (South Africa), Siemens (South Africa), Altech Telecoms (joint venture with Alcatel and a South African conglomerate), and Ericsson (South Africa) are either divisions of larger international concerns or joint ventures between African private sector companies and multinational firms. The chapter analyzes the evidence in the light of the TCB system approach.

HOW DO FIRMS MANAGE SUPPLIER RELATIONSHIPS?

This section includes the selection of suppliers and specific mechanisms for acquiring technological inputs from partners, and it discusses four case studies of experiences of supplier management.

Supplier Selection

The empirical evidence confirms that only those firms with well-developed
TCB systems had well-defined criteria and systems for supplier selection and
supplier selection systems, Seven operating companies provided detailed
responses about the selection criteria they applied when choosing suppliers of
equipment and services, which are summarized in Table 5.1. Respondents
from the operating companies were asked to score the importance of each
criterion on a scale of 1 for unimportant criteria to 5 for very important
criteria. The sum of the ratings was computed for all companies and the
criteria ranked on the basis of the overall numerical score.

Table 5.1 Selection criteria ranked in order of importance

	Selection criteria	Overall ranking
1	Attractive price/cost effectiveness	*20*
2	Functionality	*18*
3	Depth of technological knowledge	*11*
4	Technical support	*11*
5	Track record in similar markets	*10*
6	Speed of delivery	*10*
7	Presence of local agent	*5*
8	Provision of training	*5*
9	Ability to finance equipment, e.g. through vendor financing arrangements	*5*
10	Reliability and performance of equipment in standardized tests	*5*
11	Preferential access to upgrades and know-how	*5*
12	Local content and local manufacturing	*5*
13	Black empowerment criteria	*5*
14	Technical novelty	*1*

*Source: Compiled by author based on primary data; N = 7 operating companies
providing responses.*

Analysis of the data in this table shows that operating companies in the
sample considered cost effectiveness, product functionality, depth of
technological knowledge, technical support, track record in similar markets
and speed of delivery to be the most important criteria. Analysis of empirical
results confirms that operating firms did not consider ability to generate
products with a high degree of technological novelty to be important and
placed more emphasis on the commercial and system execution abilities of
their suppliers. The operating companies did apply technical criteria and

these related to the functionality of the equipment. This appears to confirm that the trend toward embeddedness of knowledge and information in equipment influences telecommunication operating companies' selection of suppliers.

South African operating companies included some criteria in their selection processes that were not used by firms in other countries. For example, one data-communication company in South Africa considered preferential access to technological upgrades to be important. Speed of delivery, provision of training and ability to finance equipment were also identified by South African companies as important criteria for selecting suppliers. Operating companies in South Africa selected suppliers that conformed to black empowerment and local content rules, and considered this to be a very important variable in their selection processes, while companies in the other countries did not. This finding on the impact of policy guidelines in shaping the perception of suppliers and operators about appropriate behaviour in selecting suppliers is an important one. However, as we will see in Chapter 6, the effect derives from general industrial policy rather than sector-specific policy and regulatory requirements.

Sixteen companies identified the specific suppliers from which they acquired technological inputs (see Table 5.2). This list includes market leaders in the telecommunication industry as well as niche market suppliers in the satellite communication segment, such as Scientific Atlanta. Companies such as Tadiran, which have developed specific competencies in wireless in the local loop access technologies, were also among the list of suppliers of African telecommunication operating companies.

Table 5.2 Suppliers of equipment and services

Company name	No of operating companies
Ecrisson	4
Alcatel, Cisco, Lucent, NEC, Scientific Atlanta	2
Advent, Airspan UK Ltd (formerly DSC), AT&T, BBC, BT, Digital Equipment Corporation, Divicom, ITELCO, MAS, MCL, Mitsubishi, MSI, NDS, Nortel, NTL, Plessey, Siemens, Tadiran, Varian, Fujitsu, Hughes Network Systems, Iredeto, Irridium	1

Source: Compiled by author based on primary data; N = 16 operating companies.

A comparison of the ratings between operating companies, and suppliers' perceptions of those ratings, shows that suppliers had an accurate view of the importance of four criteria – functionality, technical support, track record in similar markets and speed of delivery – but, from their responses, they appear not to have appreciated the importance of cost effectiveness and depth of technological knowledge. While operating firms ranked depth of technological knowledge high, suppliers did not consider this to be important. Suppliers considered technical novelty to be moderately important, while for operating companies, this was of little importance. This mismatch in the importance ascribed applied to local content rules and local manufacturing, and customization of products, both ranked high by suppliers but not identified by operating companies as important for their decision making. The relatively greater importance attached to local content rules by suppliers can likely be explained by the fact these firms were based in South Africa and were subject to policy guidelines that emphasized increasing local content in manufacturing output.

In summary there appears to be a reasonably good fit in how operating companies ranked criteria for supplier selection and how suppliers thought that they would be ranked. This evidence suggests that developing country firms are not passive and do express agency in their choice of suppliers and whenever possible attempt to align their selection of suppliers with their technological needs and requirements. Further details on the main suppliers of equipment and services from whom primary data were obtained can be found in the appendix to Chapter 5.

Specific Mechanisms for Acquiring Technology from Suppliers

Eleven out of the 26 firms provided data on the specific mechanisms they used to acquire information, know-how and skills from their suppliers of equipment and services (see Table 5.3).

Analysis of these data suggests that formation of joint network design teams with suppliers, and tendering and bid evaluation processes were the most frequently used technology acquisition mechanisms. Exclusive product demonstrations, long-term attachments at the suppliers' site and interaction through social networks were among the other mechanisms that firms identified. The evidence also showed that large firms with well-developed TCB systems were more experimental in their approach to technology acquisition from suppliers, for example placing emphasis on field trials and sophisticated procurement procedures, rather than via provision of regular training programmes.

Table 5.3 Routines used for acquisition of technology capability from suppliers

	Technology acquisition mechanism	No. firms using
1	Formation of joint project teams for network planning	4
2	Tendering and bid evaluation processes including development of technical specifications	4
3	Intensive use of supplier technical support hotline	3
4	Regular communication at functional middle management level with international and local divisions of supplier firms	3
5	Short-term contracts for expatriate engineers from supplier companies during testing and commissioning on site in African country	2
6	Training on specific equipment provided at supplier premises in South Africa (regional centre)	2
7	Training on specific equipment provided at supplier premises in Sweden	2
8	Technical support services provided by supplier staff on operating company site	2
9	General technological training courses organized by suppliers and delivered overseas	2
10	Know-how transfer projects managed as part of procurement and equipment trial processes	2
11	Designation of executive with specific responsibility for managing supplier relationships	2
12	Long-term attachments with supplier companies at their premises	1
13	Shared social networks	1
14	Exclusive product demonstrations	1

Source: Compiled by author based on primary data; N = 11 operating companies.

Interviews with the five supplier firms, including the transnational company based in Europe, produced the following general features of technological knowledge acquisition.

- Technology transfer efforts were managed through indirect partnerships between international headquarters and local manufacturing or services companies. This was advantageous to the operating companies because local companies had a better understanding of local market needs and could build good relationships with the companies at no significant extra cost. The headquarters divisions maintained responsibility for high value-added services and focused on building political relationships that facilitated market entry and market development.

- Organizing formal classroom-based training programmes covering operations, installation, maintenance and network management and including overseas 'experts' in the training courses organized in developing countries.
- Working with local and expatriate staff of operating companies in joint project teams and working groups to meet project execution and implementation targets.
- Documenting project execution tasks and making work-flow improvements.
- Managing relationships with small, medium and micro enterprises (SMMEs) and providing training for the contractors and SMMEs. Introducing organizational improvements via umbrella organizations for direct liaison with SMMEs.
- Managing the division of responsibility between installation of advanced technologies, such as DECT[1] equipment, and other customer premises equipment and providing training on installation to the field SMMEs.
- Providing overseas training for customers at European headquarters.
- Implementing skills development programmes during network rollout and during the testing, commissioning and installation of equipment.
- Facilitating open sharing of non-proprietary information.
- Providing computerized technical support, including use of simulation techniques for trouble shooting and fault diagnosis.
- Providing technology forecasting and advisory services to operating companies to enable them to understand technological trends.
- Constituting a joint team for management of all aspects of post-commissioning work and to manage the transition into operation of equipment.
- Offering repeat and refresher training programmes for customers.
- Creating an organizational climate for 'technology transfer' by involving customers in the curriculum design for training courses and in network planning and delivery.
- Improving management of subcontractors and becoming involved in direct training and certification of subcontractors. Establishing minimum performance standards to improve quality of service provided by subcontractors. This approach is an innovation that the supplier is using in its worldwide operations.
- Employing expatriate 'specialists' on long-term contracts and making them responsible for skills transfer and assigning direct operational responsibility within a team that included local staff. Expatriate specialists were selected only after completing certified courses in network dimensioning and radio engineering at the company

headquarters; they were also required to have considerable practical experience.

- Making key account managers responsible for their customers' business success and encouraging them to actively support the business goals of these customers.
- Developing seminars, scenario planning exercises, product demonstrations in conjunction with their customers.
- Assigning joint responsibility for identifying learning requirements and organizing joint network planning teams.
- Running trial networks and providing rapid deployment teams for new operators during early network launch phase.
- Facilitating regular information exchange with customers.
- Providing remote diagnostics and trouble-shooting advice on a 24 hour basis.
- Undertaking and ensuring active skills development for their own staff; one supplier estimated that 3% of annual revenue was spent on internal training and at least 30% of staff time was spent on training customers.

The next section describes the methods used for technology acquisition by a number of firms in the sample.

Case Studies of Supplier Management

Four case studies are presented, the first of which is representative of companies that have built up stocks of technological capability and have a well-developed TCB system. The second case study illustrates the challenges facing companies that attempt to use supplier relationships as a means of technology acquisition, but have a less successful track record in establishing effective TCB system. The third illustrates how companies in the sample used supplier relationships to move into more traditional, better-defined innovation activities, and, finally, the fourth case is an example of firms with very close supplier–user relationships in the definition and implementation of TCB activities. These cases include examples of exceptional and of limited effectiveness in managing supplier relationships as a means of TCB. The first two case study firms are national fixed line telecommunication operating companies, operating in markets with little competition. The third case study company is a provider of private network services and does not operate in a competitive market and the fourth case is based on a mobile network operating company.

Case study one is the account of the technology transfer processes used by a large national operator during field trials for wireless in the local loop

(WLL) systems. The field trials were used to select two suppliers of WLL equipment. Two competing suppliers were selected to build a WLL network to provide 420,000 lines for rural, urban and peri-urban customers. This is the largest WLL project in Africa. The total investment for the project was R2b., equivalent to US$333m. The capital investment was shared between two suppliers in the following proportions: Altech Telecommunication 65 per cent and Lucent South Africa 35 per cent. The companies selected had to satisfy the following conditions: technical capability including provision of ISDN and caller-line identification capability on the WLL platform.[2] local manufacturing content, inclusion of black ownership and procurement to black SMMEs and a proven financial track record.

The project was organized such that the equipment suppliers provided the equipment and components, physical planning services, including site surveys and site planning, project management, all materials and installation, commissioning and testing of the network components. The operating company was responsible for overall quality control and quality assurance for the project and participated in project meetings. The staff of the operating company were not familiar with WLL as an access technology and, therefore, the project's success was dependent on their acquiring the knowledge and information necessary to make effective use of the technologies once deployed. While the network planners in this large operating company were familiar with other access technologies, prior to the field trials they had no working knowledge of WLL systems.

During the field trials, a sophisticated assessment system, using computerized tools, was used to compare the performance of each of the supplier's WLL offerings against the company's assessment of its network evolution requirements and customer requirements. This technology assessment system was also used to produce documentation of the procedures required to deploy and maintain the WLL once implemented. The technology assessment effort was managed within the specialist team of engineering professionals. This in-house team was responsible for design of technical specifications and for trouble shooting and problem resolution during the field trials. The team, known as the laboratory group, consisted of 200–250 professional engineers who provided the field engineers that were in direct contact with suppliers and contractors with advanced technological support on an 'as needed' basis. The laboratory group was also the first point for introduction of any new technology into the operating company's network. These equipment introductions were carried out under controlled conditions and always accompanied by training at the company's in-house training facilities, delivered by permanent staff and representatives of the supplier companies.

The operating company also invested heavily in computerized planning tools for effective implementation of the WLL systems provided by the selected suppliers. These tools included a geo-information system (GIS) – a planning system that produced a digital terrain model (DTM). This DTM allowed the operator to gather and collect data on household location and topography using GIS references (latitude and longitude references rather than street addresses). Having a dataset with the required level of accuracy meant the WLL systems could be deployed more cost effectively, since they could be matched to household location patterns. Thus, the operating company owned the GIS-based system, but provided the output data to its suppliers of WLL equipment in order that it could be used in the physical planning of the network.

The company reported the significance of the following areas in which learning had occurred from the field trials and deployment project:

- importance of building internal skills and carrying out network deployment in parallel. Need to maintain investment in training when the network deployment was in process;
- critical importance of documentation for all aspects of the project cycle, including the elements managed by the suppliers of equipment.

The most important processes included:

- securing environmental approvals for location of base stations;
- property acquisition;
- bulk purchasing of materials required for large-scale deployment;
- customer education for solar powered systems.

Case study two describes the implementation of another WLL project. This second WLL network deployment project was of much smaller size – 30,000 lines – and did not involve field trials for the selection of the supplier of equipment. The total investment budget for the project was US$30 m. The project team consisted of five to ten engineers provided by the supplier company and 15 engineers provided by the African telecom operating company. Training on the WLL equipment was provided in Japan as part of a factory inspection process, and allowed five local engineers to receive three weeks of training. A further 20 people received two weeks training on site at the operating company. Three Norwegian expatriates provided project management services for the project. The World Bank funded their involvement and, as a result, the operating company had no involvement in the selection of the project management consultants. The operating company believed that these arrangements and the terms of reference for engagement of the project managers severely reduced the possibility for transfer of project management and technology know-how. The expatriate consultants had been resident in the African country for several years and as a result did not have up-to-date knowledge. It was claimed that they were so out of touch with their home company that they were not useful as a source of information on state-of-the-art tools and techniques.

The African operating company was not involved in site planning, network planning or project management; the equipment suppliers and the team of expatriate project managers performed these functions. However, the local staff team was actively engaged in the field engineering and in installation. Technology transfer during the process of network deployment took place by direct involvement in joint teams for installation and testing and through observation of the network planning function.

One strength of this project was the team leader who was well qualified, very capable and had good mix of operational experience and academic training, having completed a Masters degree in telecommunication engineering. This operational project team also had the support of a new, very small business team within the operating company that had access to high-level engineering expertise.

The local team, despite the lack of formal arrangements for their participation in network planning, were able to assist with trouble shooting and problem solving, often suggested ways of integrating WLL with other access technologies and made modifications to the network deployment plans produced by the suppliers.

The WLL project was implemented on time and within budget and, in the view of the team leader of the project, was a successful example of know-how acquisition since, at the end of the project, she was confident that the African operating company would have the requisite knowledge to plan and deploy WLL networks. However, the team leader also stated that there was a need for improvement in the following aspects of the project:

- more emphasis placed on introduction of new technologies, such as WLL, as a means to motivate and catalyze TCB activity and accelerate learning on advanced technologies. Improvement was needed in the selection process for the project team: there should not be restrictions on membership – the team leader must be allowed to select the best candidates who should be relieved of other duties;
- increased spend on the number of local engineers trained on WLL technology;
- training – complement factory-based training should be integrated with classroom-based training and the scope of training widened to include principles of access network technologies and integration of WLL with other access technology solutions, network planning, large

project management disciplines and maintenance routines and procedures for the specific WLL equipment used;

• the level of technical support provided by local agents of suppliers needs to be improved, or suppliers selected that can provide better local technical support.

Case study three involved negotiation of a technology transfer agreement between an African private network operator and a UK-based supplier of radio communication equipment. Having been dissatisfied with information disclosure and know-how transfer in previous contracts, the private network operator negotiated a specific technology transfer (TT) agreement, which was costed separately from the contract for equipment.

The TT agreement was signed in 1994 and led to the development of a close relationship between the international supplier and the African private network provider. The private network operator also acted as the sales agent for radio communication equipment and its business on this front had made a positive contribution to its cash flow and profits. The 1994 TT agreement included terms for reducing declining royalty payments, for progressive disclosure of basic design information and for information exchange to transfer a fundamental understanding of the functioning, specifications and capability of the radio communication device. The management of the private network operator recognized that the signing of the TT agreement imposed an up-front financial risk and restricted the company from activity as sales agent for other radio communications equipment. However, internal evaluation of the agreement confirmed that on financial and strategic grounds it had been a success. One disappointing feature of this company's experience was that the lessons from this project had not been documented or even informally communicated across the company. As a result of poor communication and lack of visibility, the success of the project had little if any influence on organizational structure and culture. This company was not managing its TCB activities as a strategic effort and was not co-ordinating procurement and/or technology transfer efforts.

Case study four describes the implementation of a long-term supply relationship between an equipment provider and a mobile operating company operating in competitive markets. The data presented were supplied by the operating company and corroborated by primary data obtained from the supplier firm and secondary material, which analyzed the supplier relationships of this firm in different geographic regions. The mobile operator bid for and won a licence that allowed for provision of mobile, fixed and data services on a national scale in a medium-sized African country. The winning bid was supported by technical services obtained from the supplier, on the basis of a long-term supply contract between the supplier and the parent company of the mobile operator. This long-term supply contract between the two parties was considered to be mutually beneficial. The operator believed that as a result of this long-term relationship, although the absolute volumes purchased were small compared with European orders, the level of service provided by the supplier was comparable, if not superior, to that obtained in other regions. One executive of the operating company reported that 'the relationship improves access to resources and additional support needed to succeed in the difficult African market'. The supplier firm has a presence in 13 African markets and the market information and relevant know-how that was provided to the operating company in its licence bids was considered to be invaluable.

The joint approach to developing business opportunities began with the licence bid stage and continued through the network rollout and business development stages. During network rollout, which was considered to be the most intense of all the stages of the business process, the operator relied heavily on the technical skills of the supplier. The national network was installed, commissioned and launched six months after the licence was awarded, which required the close co-operation of the customer and supplier firms. A joint project team was responsible for network rollout and this team consisted of expatriates hired from among the shareholders[3] and specialist consultants who provided equipment selection and procurement services. The supplier firm was given responsibility for delivering a fully functional, integrated network so that the operating company could concentrate its managerial effort on implementing customer service systems that were superior to those of their competitors.

In the business development stage, the supplier was the main source of technical training for local staff who were hired to replace the expatriate personnel, and an on-going source of network management support and diagnostics. Key managers in the case-study company recognized the need to develop self-supporting technological capability within the country, and relied on skills transfer and training from the supplier firm and from the individual expatriates to achieve this.

The technical support provided also extended to the commercial aspects of the business. In the market where the mobile operator delivers service, prepaid rather than value added services are the core product, accounting for 97 per cent of mobile subscribers. As a result of this composition of subscribers, the business processes of the mobile operator have been redesigned and demands have been made of the equipment and software solutions providers to make product improvements. For example, the network operator has been requesting software modifications so that the prepaid offering allows audit tracking and analysis of spend on the vouchers. These types of modification would make the product more attractive to the

African customer base. In addition, since the country in which this mobile operator is located does not have credit card facilities or credit reference agencies, the information and transaction processing capability of the prepaid network offers a platform for e-commerce services, payment transaction services and validation services. The development of these information services is considered to be a possible joint venture project for the mobile operator in partnership with the equipment and service supply firm. Secondary materials obtained from the supplier represent this partnership as a 'two-way learning curve' in which the operator provides access to customer needs and the associated product development requirements in a market with characteristics unlike many others in its global network.

The success of the operating company is indicated by its performance against regulatory requirements. When the company was licensed in 1998, it was set a target of 89,000 subscribers in five years – which was achieved in 18 months. The company has also been successful in introducing aggressive tariff plans, offering mobile international calls at $1.00 per minute. By 2000, that is, in approximately two years, the case study firm was accounting for two-thirds of combined mobile and fixed line customers and had achieved national coverage of its mobile network. The range of services was expanding to include fixed line and data services in addition to the core mobile offering. The case study firm's success is attributed to its ability to adapt its product offering to local conditions, and superior customer service. The level of support from its technical partner appears to have allowed management to concentrate on the commercial aspects of the business during the crucial first two years.

WHAT CAN FIRMS DO TO INCREASE EFFECTIVENESS?

These case studies and accounts provided by other firms permit an analysis of the common features of technology acquisition efforts and identify the strengths and weaknesses of those approaches. In making this assessment the data from operating companies and the corroborating data from supplier firms and external commentators are considered.

Weaknesses and Challenges

The companies with underdeveloped TCB systems reported a number of common weaknesses in their relationships with suppliers, including poor vendor management, weak negotiation and commercial management skills; inability to integrate technology acquisition from suppliers with other TCB mechanisms; and lack of control over supplier selection processes.

In terms of the latter, companies claimed that when equipment purchases were funded through bilateral aid programmes or by loans from multilateral development agencies they were denied the ability to manage the process and to select suppliers. Publicly owned operating companies in Uganda and Tanzania, which relied on development assistance for network expansion programmes, reported the least satisfaction with the quality of the interface with suppliers. These firms identified specific problems arising from this lack of control:

- inability to specify selection criteria;
- increase in number of suppliers often resulting in poor long-term relationships, lack of integration and interoperability among equipment and network components;
- lack of co-ordination of vendor management.

The involuntary lack of control over choice of suppliers on the part of the operating company had the same effect as weak scan and search capabilities in artificially restricting suppliers. The three firms that relied on bilaterally funded or multilateral funded technical assistance programmes gave scathing accounts of the quality (or lack thereof) of the trainers provided on these programmes. They believed that funding agencies did not pay sufficient attention to quality control and screening of individuals assigned to carry out technical assistance, training and project management in developing countries. They reported that often the expatriate engineers assigned to their projects did not have up-to-date knowledge, were often close to retirement age and had not maintained adequate contact with headquarters to renew and maintain their knowledge sets and had poor communication skills.

Where search and scan abilities were weak, developing country firms make poor choices about suppliers and often select international firms that are not skilled in the design of technology dissemination projects. This flaw limits the effectiveness of codified and more particularly tacit information flows.

Firms with weak TCB systems also reported that in many instances technology acquisition processes were compressed into the commissioning and installation phase of projects rather than being staggered over a longer period of time. Independent experts corroborated the view that this approach to technology acquisition was problematic and stated that:

> Training provided by manufacturers during the commissioning process, which is a highly pressured period, is usually inadequate and ineffective. The investment in training required for effective use of new equipment, is usually underestimated, especially when the training budgets is included in total costs of purchasing new equipment. (Interview, Sept. 1999)

Firms with underdeveloped TCB systems were passive in their search and scan activities and only dedicated limited time and effort to this function. They often faced problems in negotiating attractive terms for access to upgrades of technology and new generations of technology. These companies reported that their suppliers often invoiced separately for training and technical support services and this made their investments in learning prohibitively expensive. The weaker firms reported frustrations with the poor levels of technical support provided by international suppliers. They cited examples of reports of equipment breakdowns that were not responded to for 72 hours, poor documentation and inadequate certification and maintenance of equipment. Smaller firms in the sample reported that there were inadequate numbers of qualified and experienced personnel and this hampered their ability to select appropriate staff for technology acquisition project teams.

The suppliers provided details on their assessments of the ability of an operating company to install, commission, test, operate, maintain and manage a network based on cellular switching and radio transmission or WLL access technologies as a profitable venture.

The five supplier companies identified the following areas of knowledge and capabilities as important requirements:

- project management skills and disciplines needed for large-scale network deployment, including management of installation processes;
- end-user customer education;
- radio planning;
- market analysis and market assessment;
- logistical planning, physical site planning;
- management of contractors;
- operational and maintenance documentation and routines;
- organizational stability and a commitment to a high spend on and well organized delivery of training;
- basic technological knowledge including equipment testing, first line maintenance and understanding of equipment functionalities.

As shown in Table 5.4 the majority of suppliers were of the view that the operating companies often lacked critical components of knowledge and technological capabilities, and in particular were deficient in planning and management.

Table 5.4 Suppliers assessment of operating company capability

	Su2	Su3	Su4	Su5
Operational				
Less than adequate			✓	
Adequate	✓	✓		
Superior to needs				✓
Planning and management				
Less than adequate	✓		✓	
Adequate				✓
Superior to needs				

Source: Author based on primary data; N = 4.

All the suppliers were of the opinion that the level of capability varied considerably across operators.

> some operators have superior technological knowledge, while others are more reliant ... we work within the limits of their capabilities and fill in the gaps. ... there is a formal process for assessing gaps and designing skills and knowledge transfer. (interview)

In a company periodical, the position was represented as follows:

> We build long-term relationships with the operators we support, to share technology and to increase sophistication among users ... Invariably new operators do not have practical experience, and this is remedied by establishing a very close relationship, by means of the necessary skills and knowledge being transferred to such operators. They, in turn, educate their staff according to [...] standards. This is truly a win-win situation – our African clients and their staff receive the latest in terms of network know-how and as a result we are able to provide the very best in terms of support. (*Imagine*, Aug./Sept. 2000: 20)

The views of the suppliers appear to be consistent with the organization of cellular network and WLL projects in South Africa and other African countries, where the suppliers of equipment took on responsibility for many of the higher-level planning and organizational tasks involved in the project and were not limited only to provision of equipment and training on the use of the equipment. Since supplier involvement in the introduction of advanced technologies is an important aspect, the arrangements for transferring know-how and technical information in the course of these projects would be an important TCB activity for operating firms to master.

The suppliers seemed to be prepared to respond to these challenges by organizing their WLL projects as jointly run projects in which the supplier and the operating companies shared responsibility for successful implementation. One international supplier believed that its expatriate consultants were familiar with working in developing country markets and did not believe that affordability of services and rural market conditions would impose additional pressures. However, this supplier did admit that the expatriate consultants were familiar with more formal business practices and arms-length relationships and did not trust the close relationships demanded by their African operating company clients.

Strengths and Critical Success Factors

Large firms with well-developed TCB systems were able to use their buying power and strong negotiating position to design well-managed technology acquisition programmes, often in collaboration with suppliers. Even the smaller firms with strong TCB system were able to negotiate preferential arrangements with leading international suppliers for acquisition of know-how. For example, one data communication firm exploited the good social relationships between members of the Board of the Data-communication Company and decision-makers in the international supplier to negotiate preferential access to technology in return for an arrangement to sell that company's products and services. As a distribution partner the developing country firm received preferential access to technical information and know-how, including information on product upgrades, product demonstrations, disclosure of technical specifications and information on functionality and performance of equipment. As part of this preferential agreement, the firm was also able to build relationships with personnel in the headquarters of the US supplier.

One national mobile communication network operator in Ghana cited its active participation in jointly managed network-planning projects with its strategic technology partner and equipment supplier as the key to its success. The Ghanaian company used a single supplier to equip its entire network: this supplier was also its most important source of technical information, technical support and training. However, to minimize risk the operating company jointly with its supplier created a tailor-made curriculum to build up the capabilities of those members of its staff that were selected to become technical specialists. The training was carried out over a period of years in Ghana, Sweden and South Africa and provided the successful candidates with certification, professional recognition and enhanced job prospects.

One of the South African national mobile operators identified its ability to maintain a regular information flow with its leading supplier of equipment as a key strength. The arrangements for technical information flow were maintained at the functional levels of the company and involved regular exchanges between the specialists in both companies. Many of the reporting companies emphasized the need to maintain direct relationships with international supply companies, even when there were local divisions, branches and joint venture partners in their country of operation. For example, a success factor for technology acquisition was identified as the ability to use local divisions and joint venture partners as a means of identifying sources of particular expertise in the larger international firms.

Firms with well-developed TCB systems used innovative mechanisms such as long-term attachments, where staff visited the premises of suppliers, as an effective mechanism for acquiring specialist know-how required for the deployment of a sophisticated satellite transmission system. These companies also organized specialist in-house training courses and engaged overseas experts from supplier firms to deliver these courses as a means of acquiring know-how. Companies that were effective in supplier management emphasized the need to make use of overseas training courses and seminars and to combine these with very rigorous processes for producing tender documents and evaluating tender offers.

Key and Complementary Competencies for Managing Supplier Relationships

What this evidence confirms is that firms are not born with the ability to manage supplier relationships. It has also shown that firms are able to be effective when they develop key and complementary boundary management competencies, which requires active investment. The following key competencies that are required for developing country firms to be effective in supplier management include:

- managing tacit knowledge flow;
- evaluation and assessment capabilities to analyze requirements;
- scan, search and selection capabilities.

Managing flows of tacit knowledge
Suppliers are used as a source of technological inputs; in particular, these contractual relationships are used for acquisition of equipment, software and codified knowledge and information in the form of equipment handbooks, training course materials, maintenance procedures and protocols. Although the equipment component typically accounts for a large percentage of the reported financial cost, contracts usually also include acquisition of tacit knowledge and embodied capabilities. Developing country firms typically use traditional delivery mechanisms for accessing codified knowledge and information, although a few firms, such as those identified in this research, augment these with information technology tools, such as hotlines, and web-based technology support. Through a combination of traditional and computer assisted mechanisms, developing country firms gain access to

factual information on equipment functionality and specifications, maintenance routines and equipment and software upgrades. Firms, including those in this study, use a variety of mechanisms for the acquisition of tacit knowledge and embodied capabilities ranging from formal, classroom-based instruction at the operating company site to long-term attachments of operating companies' staff at suppliers' sites. Embodied capabilities are also acquired in the person-to-person contacts that occur when suppliers provide technical support and services. Other mechanisms for acquisition of embodied capability from suppliers included site visits to supplier premises and reference sites, establishing joint project teams for network development and use of consultants and specialists from suppliers for short-term technical assistance assignments.

The most significant characteristic of these mechanisms for acquiring embodied capabilities is that they involve flows and exchange of tacit knowledge and information between supplier and operating companies. Tacit knowledge and information exchanges take place at both the formal and informal levels and the flow requires trust between parties, acknowledgement of the contextual characteristic of knowledge and information and construction of shared meanings. As a result, the design of the exchange mechanisms requires considerable skill on the part of both the operating companies and the supplier firms, and effectiveness is highly dependent on design and implementation.

The features of supplier management that appeared to improve effectiveness, particularly for transfer of tacit knowledge components, included mechanisms for:

- selecting training instructors and 'experts' with up-to-date knowledge sets, sound fundamental technological training, good communication skills and experience in similar operating contexts;
- ensuring that there is regularity of contact over all phases of network development and operation and not limiting the tacit knowledge and information exchanges to commissioning and testing phases;
- negotiating joint ownership of the technology acquisition objectives expressed in the design and staffing of project teams and the breadth of the activities that are assigned to buyers of technological inputs.

Other characteristics of supplier relationship management, which reportedly contributed to the effectiveness of managing tacit knowledge flows, included:

- ability of personnel in the telecommunication operating companies to maintain strong social networks with the staff of supplier firms;
- maintaining regular contact between the staff of operating companies and the supplier firms at all hierarchical levels, from global executives to local managers;
- implementation of mechanisms that focused on joint learning, for example, equipment trials, where suppliers and operating companies were actively involved in understanding technology requirements, and specifications prior to full commercial deployment;
- implementation of tendering processes that resulted in maximum disclosure of codified information and provided opportunities for intensive communication between suppliers and users.

Evaluation, scan, search and selection
The firms with well-developed TCB systems had formal evaluation, scan, search and selection systems and used these to improve effectiveness of supplier management. South African operating companies were the most intensive users of formal technology search and evaluation techniques with five of the firms operating in South Africa reporting the use of these mechanisms. The relatively large size of the South African companies may be an explanatory factor here, since scan and search activities require a critical mass of highly skilled technical personnel. The other distinctive feature of the large South African operating companies is that their network development was funded independent of bilateral or multilateral development assistance. In Uganda and Tanzania, the large public network operators did not operate independent search and scan mechanisms. It may be that, as reported by the interviewees, these firms were not able to exercize choice in the selection of suppliers, but were obliged to use the suppliers named by the financiers. This also applied to the Ghanaian public operator prior to privatization.

In addition to the South African companies, there were two other companies in the sample that reported using formal search and evaluation techniques. These two firms were outliers in their active approach to capability development. A Ugandan company that used formal search and evaluation routines had a technology and operational strategy that was closely influenced and directed by its major shareholder – a large South African company with operations in other parts of the continent. In the case of the other outlier, a small Tanzanian data-communication company, the implementation of formal search and evaluation was linked directly to the corporate culture of the firm. This company was part of group of companies, founded by a group of young Africans, including engineering graduates from the Massachusetts Institute of Technology. The background of the founders, their interest in technological sophistication, vision in promoting innovation and their direct involvement in influencing technological strategy had enabled this small company to extend its boundaries beyond the limits normally imposed by its small size and the deficiencies of the local innovation system.

If informal scan and search routines, such as attending trade fairs and exhibitions and participation in different communities of interest (professional bodies, trade associations, working parties of regional and international organizations), are included, the number of firms using them increases to 18. The pattern for use of informal mechanisms differed from that for formal mechanisms in so far as there was wider representation from Ugandan, Ghanaian and Tanzanian firms. For example, a small Tanzanian private network operating company reported that its owner saw trade fairs and exhibitions as a cost-effective mechanism for acquiring technological information. The owner of the firm reported that he took direct and personal responsibility for this activity drawing on his technological background. This individual was a technological pioneer in Tanzania and had a background in aviation and aeronautical engineering and he used this foundation to expand into telecommunications. Another example comes from a small Ghanaian data communication company, whose spokesperson reported an exceptionally high usage of these informal mechanisms. This firm was an active participant in technological development at the regional and international levels. The background of the founder of this business was engineering, more than 20 years private sector overseas experience in the United States and active involvement with United Nations development agencies as a technical assistance provider. This may account for the permeability of this firm's organizational boundaries and its high propensity to be actively engaged in technology scanning and search activities. The other intensive users of these informal mechanisms were large public network national operators in Uganda and Tanzania and the national mobile operators in South Africa. However, the explanations for the observed patterns differ for these two groups. For the former two, active participation in industry associations and in the working parties of the African Telecommunication Union, Commonwealth Telecommunication Organization and the International Telecommunication Union were reported to be important means for independent assessment of technological trends and evaluation of suppliers. These regional and multilateral bodies were considered by interviewees to be 'honest brokers' since they did not fund network development, but instead were mandated to share information about appropriate technological choice and to provide information on equipment standardization. Conversely, for the two national mobile operators in South Africa, participation in industry associations was said to be focused on groupings such as the GSM Association, where employees engaged in the development of standards for particular technologies on an equal footing with the other participants. The relatively strong standing of the South African participants is demonstrated by the fact that employees of one of the operators had held international office in the GSM Association at the time the data were collected.

Another community that appears to have been an important source of external inputs is the strategic investors and shareholders in the operating companies. Even companies with only moderately developed TCB systems or no discernible TCB systems at all reported that they maintained regular communication with regional headquarters, sister companies and shareholders as a means of gaining external technological input. There were some large companies, particularly in Ghana, that used formal mechanisms for acquiring technological inputs and expertise from shareholders and strategic investors, including long-term attachments for local staff at the site of the investors and formal training courses organized by the investor companies. For all the firms in the sample, supplier firms that paid close attention to the selection of trainers and technical assistant personnel and had processes for maintaining and renewing their skills, were considered to be more effective than those that failed to undertake these investments.

In summary, the evidence shows that developing country firms can develop key competencies for supplier management, and when they do they reap benefits. The foregoing analysis suggests that specific competencies such as management of tacit knowledge flows, evaluation, scan, search and selection abilities are key competencies for effective supplier management. The analysis also suggests that variation in the development of these competencies is related to features such as size, organizational culture and leadership. The next section discusses the features that are necessary to build these key competencies.

Integrating supplier inputs with other TCB effort
Effective firms are able to integrate the technological inputs provided by suppliers with their internally generated inputs. The complementary[4] competencies that are required to integrate the technological inputs acquired from external sources with the overall TCB strategy are the competencies that are required to manage the internal processes of technological learning and capability accumulation discussed in the last chapter. The empirical evidence strongly supports the view that firms that had established strong and effective management systems, particularly for organizational development, and where there was a supportive culture and engaged leadership, were also more likely to be effective at developing the key competencies required for supplier management and integrating all aspects of the TCB effort.

In particular, firms that created conditions for experimentation, reinforcement of knowledge and promotion of higher-order learning were better able to integrate external inputs. Firms with explicit technology strategies and those firms that focused their competitive strategies on developing the technological competences of their personnel were also able to demonstrate a high level of ability in integrating external inputs. Advanced capability in management development practices, such as clear definition and assignment of responsibilities, was also found to be complementary to effective supplier management.

FACTORS OUTSIDE THE CONTROL OF FIRMS

The above section discussed the factors internal to firms that influence their ability to manage supplier relationships. This evidence confirms that supplier relationships were an important source of technological capabilities and that the effectiveness of supplier management is influenced by factors that are under the control of the firms. However, as will be shown, there are also a number of exogenous factors that influence the strengths and limitations of suppliers as a source of technological inputs for developing country firms.

Limits on Suppliers as Source of Technological Inputs

Although equipment and service suppliers are a significant source of technological inputs for developing country firms, as illustrated by the evidence drawn from African telecommunication firms, there are also indications that private sector companies are less useful as sources of some types of knowledge inputs. Private sector equipment and service companies provide non-embodied and embodied technological inputs, but are not the primary source of knowledge inputs about fundamental scientific principles or the nature and direction of technological trends, and also do not provide basic technological training and literacy. Developing country firms require this type of knowledge and information, a need that cannot be satisfied through their relationships with suppliers.

Knowledge and information about fundamental scientific principles and trends ('know-why') can more effectively be sourced from innovation system institutions such as universities, training colleges and research laboratories, and from policy and regulatory bodies. The empirical evidence generated in this study also suggests that international and regional bodies might play a useful role in providing this information and knowledge. Other communities of interest and practice, such as professional and industry associations, can also make a contribution to supplying this 'know-why'.

Private sector suppliers are not particularly effective at providing access to knowledge and information about the best sources of the codified and tacit knowledge needed by operating companies, also referred to as 'know-who', because they lack objectivity and are unlikely to provide accurate and comprehensive assessments of the range of sources available. The communities of interest and practice referred to earlier have the potential to be much better placed to provide independent assessments of competing sources of technological inputs. Specialist information providers and organizers of trade fairs and exhibitions also supply 'know-who'. However, to make the best possible use of these sources of 'know-who', operating companies need to have routines for evaluation, search and scan. When operating companies used additional sources of external capability inputs, they were able to manage suppliers more effectively. Equipment suppliers became partners in technological choice, rather than taking direct ownership of this critical function.

Impact of Technological Change

The following features of technological change in the telecommunication industry also influenced the ability of developing country firms to be effective in supplier management and, in particular, determined the reliance on global market leaders as important sources of external technological inputs. As more knowledge and information are encoded or embedded in equipment and software control algorithms, suppliers have been forced to become more expert in helping their customers to understand and use this sophisticated equipment. While this characteristic of embeddedness has the effect of making knowledge required for network management increasingly product (equipment/application) specific, it also increases the possibility for fine-tuning network performance characteristics through software changes. This increasing embeddedness of knowledge in equipment has meant that the supply of embodied and non-embodied elements of technological capabilities in the telecommunication industry has become increasingly coupled. This trend has had the effect of reducing the importance of intermediaries and information brokers as sources of external technological inputs.

Telecommunication operating companies expect their suppliers to design equipment with appropriate functionalities and to provide support that demonstrates their understanding of the operational context in which that equipment will be used. There has also been a rapid and accelerating pace of technological change in telecommunication systems, subsystems and subcomponents, which has led to the need for regular, continuous interface between suppliers and operating companies. The pace of change has also had some negative consequences in that it has created unnecessary crises spurring operating companies into continuous rounds of technological upgrading.

Finally, as a result of the high levels of software controls used in switching and access networks and the huge information and knowledge content coded into equipment (devices and components), IT and project management have become core competences for telecommunication network operating companies. All professional technical employees, and particularly those in specific functions such as network management and optimization, are required to have high levels of IT literacy and skills.

In summary, the effect of technological change in the telecommunication industry has led developing country firms, such as those in this study, to be more likely to use a single supplier firm as a source of external technological inputs. The single source of supply is likely to allow operating companies to take advantage of the dual effects of access to non-embodied capabilities and embodied capabilities. These long-term, one-stop supplier relationships were common among the sample firms, but did not necessarily have the deleterious effect on access to technological capabilities implied by conventional studies on technology transfer. There appeared to be potential shortcomings in the single-supplier mode, especially for firms without technological evaluation capabilities, insofar as the operating companies could be persuaded to make regular upgrades in technological inputs at a pace determined by their supplier, rather than at a more measured pace in line with their capacity to direct and absorb the integration of these inputs. Technological change also led to the emergence of at least two areas of core competence – IT and project management.

Impact of Specialization and Concentration of Innovative Activity

Developing country firms in the telecommunication industry, including the sample firms, typically rely very much on market leaders and second-tier equipment suppliers. Even those firms with extensive search routines made most frequent use of global market leaders as their suppliers (these firms were those that had led the trend to concentrate innovative activity as measured by R&D, patents, etc.) in the equipment industry. In the telecommunication industry developing country firms have not been active in diversifying their suppliers away from market leaders and there does not appear to be a trend in favour of seeking out smaller or alternative sources of supply.[5] This pattern is consistent with the nature of competition in the telecommunication equipment supply industry. Simply put, the global market leaders were willing and able to provide the operating companies with access to up-to-date equipment and the technical services required to efficiently develop, deploy and maintain networks based on that equipment. Therefore, these market leaders were the operating companies' suppliers of choice.

While the operating companies appear not to have been interested per se in the innovative performance of the supplier companies, their keen interest in functionality and standardization of equipment led to a de facto limit on the range of supplier sources. This outcome would have been the same if they had been explicitly interested in choosing only those companies with relatively strong innovation performance. Ironically, among this sample of firms, the occurrence of multiple sources of technological inputs was more often than not involuntary and was imposed by multilateral funding agencies and heavily criticized by the purchasers.

It is important to note that the limited range of suppliers does not appear to have affected the ability of these developing country firms to exercize 'constrained agency' in acquiring technological inputs from these firms because the global market leaders in the telecommunication sector have increased their effectiveness as suppliers of non-embodied and embodied capabilities. The suppliers increasingly perceive that their success in winning business from the telecommunication operating companies in Africa and other developing countries is dependent on their responsiveness to the business needs of these companies. There was evidence from international suppliers that they recognized the importance of having joint ownership of technological development objectives with their clients. This was demonstrated by the inclusion of such features as the ability to jointly plan and manage network deployment and operation in the list of critical success factors reported by suppliers.

What is perhaps is even more interesting is the evidence that the supplier firms were themselves investing in organizational systems that aimed to improve their ability to be responsive to the technological development objectives of their developing country customers. For example, one of the supplier firms provided evidence that it had developed specialized career paths for technical assistance experts who were used to assist customers with network deployment and management. This company had also developed mechanisms whereby the employees of their customers could undertake formal certified training courses to achieve comparable levels of skill and expertise as the career network specialists in the supplier firm. There is also evidence corroborating the suggestion that this company considered its ability to design these technology dissemination mechanisms as a source of core competence in all market segments and had applied these business processes in developed markets (McKelvey et al. 1998). The evidence from this research confirms that this company was extending implementation of these business processes to its developing country markets. The organizational innovations that were perceived by supplier firms in the sample to be most effective include:

- undertaking investments in their internal technological learning and facilitation of knowledge dissemination;
- adaptation of business processes to increase knowledge and information flows between suppliers and users;
- regular and continuous interaction with customers through a variety of formal and informal interfaces;
- documentation of best practice mechanisms for knowledge dissemination;
- improved account management;
- use of computer assisted tools for dissemination of information.

In summary, the technological features of telecommunication products have influenced the changing nature of competition in the equipment supply industry. Competitive success is now considered to be increasingly dependent on the ability to assist customers in achieving their objectives and international suppliers to pursue organizational innovation to maintain and to improve their levels of responsiveness. On the evidence, it would appear that the global market leaders were satisfying their developing country customers and facilitating technological learning and capability accumulation.

CONCLUDING REMARKS

The foregoing analysis indicates that the management of supplier relationships was an important factor in determining whether developing country firms were able to benefit from boundary relationships and use these relationships to advance their technological capability development objectives. There were a number of factors that appear to account for developing country firms exercizing constrained agency in their management of these relationships. These included endogenous and exogenous variables. Among the factors that were under the control of the firm are the extent to which firms had acquired the specific and complementary boundary relationship management competences and had developed a balanced and systematic approach to TCB. Factors such as technological change, increasing specialization, concentration of innovation and the nature of competition that are outside the control of the firm also appear to influence the contribution of supplier relationships to TCB objectives. On balance, the evidence suggests that there can be an optimistic interpretation of the effects of these exogenous factors and shows how large and small firms in developing countries can interact with global market leaders to further their technological objectives. A significant factor in this interpretation is that the confluence of technological and market dynamics has led to customers and suppliers becoming more keenly interested in the exchange of tacit knowledge and information and this appears to have led to more open dissemination and greater disclosure.

NOTES

1   DECT – Digital European Cordless Telecommunication, a standard introduced by the European Telecommunication Standards Institute (ETSI), operating at 1800 MHz.
2   ISDN (Integrated Service Digital Network) is a functionality that allows different types of data to be transmitted on a single line, significantly adding to the access network's capacity. CLI (caller line identification) is a value added service feature which allows the dialled party to identify the originator of the calling party.
3   It is worth noting that the expatriates in the team were drawn from other African mobile operating companies.
4   The term 'complementary capabilities' is used in the sense that Pettigrew and Whipp (1991) use it in reference to the notion of the reinforcing effect of primary and secondary conditioning features of capabilities.
5   Tadiran, the Israeli based company, may be an exception to this general pattern, but this company was a niche market leader in wireless in the local loop access network components and systems.

6 Role of the Innovation System

This chapter discusses the importance of managing interactions with the innovation systems for facilitating learning and TCB. The analysis draws on a review of evidence from the sample firms on how they managed boundary relationships with regulatory and policy bodies as an illustration of relationships between firms and institutions in the innovation system. Details are provided of firms' varying levels of TCB system development, which gives the opportunity to contrast the performance of firms that were effective in implementing TCB effort with that of firms whose learning and TCB system required improvement.

DO DEVELOPING COUNTRY FIRMS INTERACT WITH THE INNOVATION SYSTEM?

The empirical study confirms that firms at different levels of TCB system development varied in terms of their intensity of usage of mechanisms involving interaction with the innovation system. Specifically, as can be seen from Table 3.2 in Chapter 3, by looking at the intensity of usage for Group VI (innovation system interaction), firms in the sample with the most developed TCB systems were three times more likely to interact with innovation systems than firms with fairly well-developed TCB systems, and firms with no functioning TCB system did not interact with the innovation system at all. As discussed earlier, statistical techniques confirmed that this variation across different levels of TCB system development was significant. It is also worth noting that the score for Group VI for all firms across all levels of TCB system development, was lower than for any other group of TCB mechanisms.

ARE INNOVATION SYSTEMS A SOURCE OF TCB INPUT?

This study included an empirical exploration of the actual role played by the innovation system in facilitating learning and TCB in firms, as well as an analysis of how that reality compared with the ideal and recommended role suggested by academic and policy writing on the subject. Data were collected on the roles that operating companies would like to see public sector organizations undertake in support of their TCB efforts, and on the types of interactions that were occurring between firms and public sector institutions. These data permit a useful comparison of the ideal versus the reality.

Representatives of African telecommunication operating companies were asked whether they were in favour of public sector bodies undertaking any of the following roles in support of their TCB activities.

1 **Providing subsidies** – Subsidizing operating firms in order to incentivize their TCB efforts, that is partial funding of TCB investment through indirect mechanisms whereby firms could apply for state sponsored write-offs for TCB activities

2 **Direct expenditure** – Allocating budgets to support TCB efforts in firms within line ministries and regulatory bodies. One example was of regulatory bodies organizing training for cross-industry groups on appropriate technological areas.

3 **Direct funding** – Providing the finance for public research institutions or other knowledge creating and disseminating institutions to carry out TCB activities that would benefit operating companies.

4 **Support activities** – Organizing support services and providing them to operating companies at a cost. Examples included public bodies providing technical resource information centres, supplier evaluation services and technology assessment services. A wide range of public bodies could be involved, since these services could be provided by standards bodies or national research institutions as well as by policy and regulatory agencies.

5 **Building in performance requirements** – For TCB activities in the licences of operating companies and in their contracts with suppliers.

6 **Specific measures** – other than the five categories above.

The views of operators, public sector officials and expert commentators were sought on this topic. The responses of all groups across the four countries are summarized in Table 6.1 The response rate to this question was much higher for South African and Tanzanian firms than for Ghana and Uganda.

Analysis of these summary data suggests that there was considerable variation in the perceptions of the ideal role of public sector organizations in supporting TCB activities in firms across the countries in the sample. Also, there was a high degree of variation between the operators and regulatory and public policy bodies in each of the four countries. Of the two countries with the highest responding firms, Tanzanian operating companies were much more positively in favour of a proactive role for public sector bodies, with a high proportion of the respondents favouring broad involvement in all activities designed to support TCB in firms. Responses from the South African operators were a much more qualified endorsement for public sector involvement.

Table 6.1 Desired public sector support for TCB in firm

	% operators in favour	% public officials in favour	% respondents in favour
Direct expenditure	92	100	94
Support activities	92	67	87
Direct funding of innovation institutions	75	80	76
Operator performance requirements	67	83	72
Supplier performance requirements	50	83	63
Public sector subsidies for TCB effort in firms	42	20	35

Source: Complied by author based on analysis of primary empirical data.

Analysis of these summary data suggests that there was considerable variation in the perceptions of the ideal role of public sector organizations in supporting TCB activities in firms across the countries in the sample. Also, there was a high degree of variation between the operators and regulatory and public policy bodies in each of the four countries. Of the two countries with the highest responding firms, Tanzanian operating companies were much more positively in favour of a proactive role for public sector bodies, with a high proportion of the respondents favouring broad involvement in all activities designed to support TCB in firms. Responses from the South African operators were a much more qualified endorsement for public sector involvement.

The responses of the telecommunications operating companies appear to indicate that these companies welcome active support from policy and regulatory bodies for their TCB activities, in terms of:

• organization of formal and informal training opportunities that would be available to all operators (12 out of 13 operators and five out of five public officials);
• gaining access to codified information and knowledge from technical resource centres and information services (11 out of 12 operating companies and two out of three public officials);

- improving the ability of other institutions such as universities, training centres and research centres to provide information and knowledge inputs (nine out of 12 operating companies and four out of five public officials);
- clear guidelines and standards for TCB activities being imposed through licence requirements or special purpose rules. (eight out of 12 operating companies and five out of six public officials).

The operating companies were much less in favour of policy and regulatory bodies subsidizing TCB activities in firms (five out of 12 operating companies and one out of five public officials) and were similarly lukewarm towards the proposition that public bodies should be involved in monitoring and supervizing technological sourcing contracts between themselves and their suppliers.(five out of ten operating companies).

South African and Ghanaian companies made two additional specific proposals for public sector bodies to stimulate TCB activities: (1) removing ad valorem taxes and introducing customs duty exemptions on telecommunication equipment; (2) involvement of private sector companies in public–private partnerships for large-scale networking projects.

The patterns of responses obtained from operating companies and public sector officials in any single country were broadly similar. For example, neither operators nor public officials in South Africa favoured the use of subsidies, but reportedly were in favour of setting TCB performance requirements for operators. However, while the operating companies in South Africa were strongly opposed to performance requirements on equipment supply contracts, this proposal received a qualified endorsement from South African public sector officials. For the other country with a good response rate, Tanzania, there were few clear-cut differences between the views of operating companies and public sector bodies, since the views of operating companies were not very uniform. For example, while the two public officials responded with positive support for performance requirements applying to operators, there were four operators in favour of this and two opposed to this means of facilitating TCB in firms. The empirical evidence confirms that regulatory and policy bodies are considered by telecommunications operating companies to have the potential to play a positive role in supporting their TCB activities. However, as will be discussed, the empirical research also shows that both at the time of the research and currently the relationships between public sector bodies and telecommunication operating companies do not work to optimize technological learning in these firms (see Table 6.2).

Table 6.2 Interaction between sample firms and national public policy and regulatory bodies

Means of interaction	Uganda	Ghana	Tanz	SA
Regular monthly/quarterly status reports to regulator on operations/performance; access to Board minutes and annual financial accounts and operational audits	Yes	Yes	Yes	Yes
Submission of regulatory accounts				Yes
Communicating via govt appointees to Board of Directors of large regulated companies	Yes			
Regular communication with pubic bodies via Chair, Board of Directors of large regulated companies.	Yes			
Communicating via the Chair (appointed by Head of State) of the Board of large regulated companies		Yes		Yes
Intense scrutiny during pre-qualification and bidding for issue of new licences	Yes	Yes		Yes
Intense scrutiny during licensing and agreeing licence terms			Yes	Yes
Providing information for monitoring performance against specific clauses in licences and shareholders' agreements, etc.	Yes	Yes		Yes
Participating in regular consultations with private sector, organized as industry fora convened by public sector bodies		Yes		Yes
Participating in meetings arranged by public bodies for discussion of specific technical regulatory issues, e.g. interconnection, rate filings			Yes	Yes
Getting information on/access to subsidized international training opportunities/fellowships	Yes			
Regular communication via a specific functional team in large operating company			Yes	Yes
Lobbying			Yes	Yes
Joint participation in international meetings, e.g. ITU study groups, standards setting organizations				Yes
Regular participation in fora organized outside the sector by key public sector decision makers e.g. Dept of Labour, Office of the Status of Women				Yes
Active participation in development of national testing and certification standards				Yes
Active participation in public/private funded education/training initiatives. Joint design of curriculum for education and training				Yes
Developing policy guidelines, e.g. GMPCS				Yes
Making financial contributions to HRD Fund managed by public sector body				Yes
Private sector operating companies providing technical advice to public sector bodies				Yes

Source: Compiled by author based on analysis of primary empirical data.

Table 6.2 summarizes the mechanisms that are reportedly being used by policy and regulatory bodies to interact with telecommunications operating companies in their jurisdictions, the interactions at the time of research did not conform to this ideal. This evidence suggests that public bodies can be a source of TCB input and that firms would welcome the innovation system playing a role along the lines discussed.

Operators gave detailed accounts of what they thought of the regulatory and policy making capabilities of public sector organizations that could facilitate their TCB effort. These data were used to gain a more complete understanding of firms' perceptions of the policy and regulatory environment in which they implement TCB strategies. Analysis of their responses shows that the interactions between operating companies and policy and regulatory bodies vary in intensity across the lifecycle of telecommunications projects. During the bidding, licence evaluation and licensing stages, there is intensive interaction between operating companies and policy and regulatory bodies. In addition to this phase being the most intensive in terms of frequency of contact, it often coincides with highest levels of exchange of information and is usually associated with greatest leverage for the public sector bodies. After licensing, the intensity of interaction falls off considerably, giving way to more formal, procedural interactions associated with monitoring of licence conditions. When policy and regulatory rules are being reviewed/revised, there again tends to be intense lobbying by firms, but this is infrequent.

The objectives of interactions between operating firms and policy and regulatory bodies are also context specific. Given the low levels of penetration of telecommunication services in Africa, policy and regulatory objectives in this region have tended to focus on setting explicit criteria for network rollout and have assumed that if operators were successful in meeting rollout targets they would automatically acquire capabilities. The result of this is that during the licence bidding stage and the negotiation of licence conditions, when intensity of interaction and leverage of the state is highest, the focus has not been on the technological capability of operating companies. The failure to take account of technological capability as an objective itself also means that during regular and routine interactions between public sector bodies and operating companies there is very little opportunity to influence or facilitate TCB, either at the level of a formal legal mandate or on the basis of informal best practice standard setting.

Analysis of this evidence shows that interactions between tele-communication operating companies and policy and regulatory bodies are infrequent and aimed at facilitating routine and procedural objectives rather than co-operation on strategic issues such as learning and TCB. For example, while the operating companies in all four countries were required to provide regular reports on operational and financial performance, only Uganda and

South Africa had to conform to guidelines on TCB effort in firms. None of the other three ideal roles for policy and regulatory bodies suggested by operating companies was current practice. The specific roles suggested for removing import duties on telecommunications equipment and sponsoring large projects on public–private partnership basis were also not implemented.

This evidence shows that at present the relationships between public sector bodies and telecommunication operating companies do not work to optimize technological learning in these firms. The next section identifies features that explain why the innovation system may not be performing optimally from the perspective of the operating companies and public officials.

WHY DO INNOVATION SYSTEMS UNDER-PERFORM?

This section offers an explanation of why the innovation system was not functioning as an effective source of technological capability inputs. The role of policy and regulatory bodies is taken as being illustrative of the role of the innovation system. In the telecommunication industry, which is highly regulated, these are the public sector bodies with which operating companies interact most frequently. The accounts from operating companies, public officials and external commentators are all used in this analysis. More details on the factual description of legal and policy arrangements for facilitating TCB can be found in the appendix to Chapter 6.

Uganda

The Ugandan operating companies regarded the policy and regulatory framework as broadly favouring TCB, but as being untested. Representatives of the firms were encouraged by the inclusion of detailed provisions for technology transfer in the second national operator (SNO) licence and in the policy framework for the telecommunication sector, but had reservations about the ability of the Uganda Communications Commission (UCC) and other bodies to deliver, since these institutions had only recently been established. There were also concerns as to whether or not the UCC would be able to cope with the pace of change and be able to resolve competing priorities.

Respondents from public sector bodies believed that the task of Ugandan government in balancing multiple objectives, such as increasing revenue, stimulating economic activity and creating jobs, with its desire to promote training and skills development, was difficult. It was reported that these difficulties were further compounded by the fact that Uganda was making an economic recovery after many years of turmoil and more recently of rehabilitation of economic structures. There were differences among the opinions of respondents as to the ranking of TCB within the objectives of the Ugandan national telecommunication policy. A representative of the regulatory body expressed the view that the existing regulatory framework did not prioritize TCB activities in firms because this would detract from effort to attract foreign investment. However, another respondent pointed to the weighting in the bid evaluation process for privatization of Uganda Telecommunication Ltd (UTL) whereby mechanisms to improve quality of service were more highly ranked than the financial returns, as evidence that policy makers saw TCB issues as being more important. One senior decision maker believed that the task of promoting TCB activities in telecommunication firms should be shared among several line ministries including the Ministry of Education. Public sector officials believed that the Ugandan government was willing to support TCB activities by strengthening the environmental context in which operating firms made decisions about TCB. The explicit inclusion of TCB concerns in the bidding process for the second fixed line operator licence and in the shareholders agreement with the strategic investor for UTL were considered to be favourable features of the Ugandan policy and regulatory system.

There was broad agreement among public officials and external commentators that the Ugandan institutional environment faced the following challenges and constraints:

- scarcity of available skilled, qualified people;
- limited ability of UCC to manage and maintain fair competition;
- weaknesses in local knowledge creation institutions, including lack of up-to-date knowledge and information and a specific telecommunication curriculum;
- efforts to improve penetration rates take precedence over all other policy objectives including TCB;
- shortage of funds and low levels of investment being constraints to TCB expenditures by firms;
- lack of focus on training in telecommunication fields in publicly funded scholarship programmes;
- need to improve technology transfer terms in bilateral aid projects, and technical co-operation management in these funding programmes;
- need to encourage companies to pay more attention to staff retention, staff motivation, organizational stability and creation of organizational and individual learning climate;
- lack of attention to TCB activities and customer service orientation;
- absence (or weaknesses) of specific capabilities in firms and regulatory bodies, for example familiarity with spectrum management.

Ghana

In Ghana, the operating companies' representatives expressed dissatisfaction with the institutional capacity of the regulatory body, the National Communications Authority (NCA), and believed that it was inadequately resourced to be able to facilitate TCB in firms. The overall assessment of interviewees from the Ghanaian operating companies was that, since the completion of privatization in 1996, the policy and regulatory framework had been plagued by transition problems and was characterized by 'regulatory fatigue' and inertia. The state was criticized for not providing adequate funding to knowledge creating institutions, such as universities.

Public policy bodies reported that that the objective to encourage TCB in their client firms was implicit: TCB was not set down as an explicit objective in any of the official laws or policy documents. There was general agreement among the public sector respondents that increasing private sector participation as a means of accelerating development and expansion of the telecommunication network was the overarching objective of Ghanaian telecommunication policy. These respondents also reported that the financial return from the sale of the 30 per cent stake in Ghana Telecom was also a highly weighted criterion. The government also reportedly had an objective to reduce reliance on turn-key projects. An expert commentator offered the view that the telecommunication policy was formulated on the assumption that skills would grow automatically as the industry developed, and the focus on the human resources management side was to forestall massive job losses.

This 'hands-off' approach is reflected in deliberate decisions to leave human resource development in commercial hands. For example, the Ghana Telecom Training School was not taken over by a public sector body, but was left in the hands of a privatized company. There was dissatisfaction with this arrangement. One public sector official believed that there was need for a special purpose technological training institute, that provided a wide range of training opportunities at basic and advanced levels, and whose curriculum included commercial and management training in addition to the engineering and information technology disciplines.

Public sector bodies and commentators reported that the (NCA) was plagued with difficulties in recruiting staff. It was reported that the NCA had had too much reliance on overseas consultants in the development of the regulatory framework. It was felt that these problems originated in the appointment of a team of senior members of the former monopoly telecom operator and the disbanding of the sector reform team, before establishing any continuity and learning processes. Respondents believed that the government's decision not to include specific performance requirements in terms of human resource development was understandable in the light of their concerns about political fallout if there was massive retrenchment. There was a trade-off between requirements for human resource development and investors in Ghana Telecom undertaking not to drastically reduce staff numbers. This was a very sensitive issue, made more so by a 'manpower' assessment report produced by external consultants with recommended massive layoffs. This recommendation was not implemented because of the political implications of doing so. A senior public official reported that investors had been identifying skills shortages as a bottleneck and this had raised the priority of human resource development issues. This official also reported that the Ministry of Communications was implementing steps to improve its technical capability through establishment of a specialist technical department, to allow it to be able to make more informed policy decisions on internet telephony, datacommunication services, GMPCS and other service development trends.

Public officials believed that Ghanaian companies under-invested in training and skills development. One representative of a public sector organization believed that firms spent 80 per cent of TCB budgets overseas and the remaining 20 per cent on TCB activities delivered by local suppliers. These respondents also suggested that there was need for more stability in the operating companies. Particularly among companies with public ownership, there was high turnover at senior levels of management, particularly among the political appointees, which retarded implementation of strategic focus and change management. The operating companies needed to attract managers with experience of competitive environments to complement the existing skills set and to improve their inadequate fund management and financial management systems as well as to improve poor operational routines and productivity systems. Public sector officials believed that the operating companies did not have appropriate systems for network equipment selection and technology search and evaluation. These failures were attributed to past over-reliance on turn-key projects and were thought to have increased unit cost of investment and network expansion.

The privatization programme was regarded as having put too much strain on the institutional fabric of the public sector bodies. All respondents believed that there was inadequate separation between the powers of the central government and the regulator, which was considered problematic since it was perceived as allowing political interference in decision making. One of the advantages of the regulatory system identified by these respondents was that the measurable performance targets introduced for network modernization were ambitious.

The major challenges and constraints for public sector bodies in Ghana were as follows:

- difficulties in public sector bodies providing motivation for and influencing change in firms with expatriate management teams, given their lack of cross-culture management skills and experience;
- attitudes of workers not conducive to implementation of rapid change and TCB activities;
- vested interests in the sector blocked changes, including action to promote TCB activities in firms;
- limited policy analysis capability in the Ministry of Communications;
- severe budget limitations in the Ministry and independent regulator;
- sequencing problems, insofar as the regulatory framework had not been put in place prior to the licensing of operators;
- difficulty in recruiting competent people to Ghanaian public sector bodies because of the unattractive remuneration packages;
- limited regulatory capability resulting in failure to enforce information disclosure powers and poor standards of inspection and verification;
- local universities and polytechnics unable to provide up-to-date training and skills development and needed to be upgraded and streamlined;
- lack of coordination of knowledge creation efforts in the sector;
- need for a refocused national strategy on capability development, since this has not been the focus of telecoms policy;
- indigenous capital markets tight and illiquid – not able to fund large projects;
- Board of the NCA not finalized and operational resulting in slow decision making;
- lack of clarity in the division of responsibility between Ministry of Communications and the NCA weakens credibility of the NCA;
- focus in policy making on privatization of Ghana Telecom, other objectives received little attention;
- improvements to policy development and planning capabilities needed;
- national telecommunication policy failed to identify human resource development as a priority;
- Information and communications sector not given sufficiently high visibility in national planning and development efforts.
- too much political interference in management of the operating companies.

Tanzania

Tanzanian operating company interviewees gave a broadly negative assessment of the Tanzanian Communications Commission (TCC) and rated its performance and level of capability as poor. It is worth noting that, while in Uganda and Ghana the assessments of public officials and commentators and respondents from operating companies were fairly similar, there were significant differences in the opinions of these two groups in Tanzania. The public officials in Tanzania considered that the regulatory body was adequately resourced and was capable, while the operating companies' view of its capability and performance was negative. Operating company interviewees and external commentators in Tanzania criticized the policy and regulatory institutions for their arbitrariness in decision making and lack of transparency, for allowing central government interference in licensing decisions, and they also considered the TCC to be severely lacking in technical capabilities.

The TCC was seen as being bureaucratic and inefficient. Interaction between the employees of the operating companies and the policy and regulatory bodies had no basis of mutual respect or trust. Rather than being regarded as a source of technological know-how, the regulatory bodies were considered to be a "policing" nuisance, not up to performing their core tasks. This perception was pervasive for interviewees from firms operating in the competitive market segments, but was not shared by those from the large state owned public network operator.

With respect to basic and specific provisions, public officials in Tanzania were of the view that, while there was a political commitment to these goals, there were also significant difficulties in implementing this mandate. The national objectives in the telecommunication sector were to expand the communications infrastructure and use this as a lever for social, economic and political change; to diversify away from donor-funded infrastructure development, through attracting high-quality private investors to competitive segments of the market; and, finally, to improve the commercial and financial performance of the publicly owned operating company.

The public officials assessing regulatory and policy capabilities reported that the TCC had undertaken a formal training needs assessment and had identified the requirements for extensive regulatory and policy training. The staff of the TCC had received training from bilateral and international organizations including the United States Telecommunication Training Institute (USTTI), University of Michigan, PARUC, Omnitel, Finnish Telecoms, Cable and Wireless, the Adam Smith Institute, The UK Department of Trade and Industry, Oftel, the Radio Communications Agency and AFRALTI. Staff members had also benefited from exchanges with the US Federal Communications Commission (FCC), and the state Public Utility Commissions of Vermont and California and from the regulatory bodies in India, Singapore and Malaysia. US dollar annual expenditure on training in the regulatory body was reported to be: 1995–96 $150k; 1996–97 $300k;

1997–98 $98k. The result of this training was believed by the staff of the TCC to have improved their capabilities, enabling them to intervene more effectively in the market place.

Despite the perceptions of the staff of the regulatory body, external commentators characterized the TCC as weak, timid, as having poor governance and management systems and as being not sufficiently independent of central government. External commentators welcomed proposals to implement a cross-regulatory model of regulation, in which a cross-sectoral regulatory body would fall under the oversight of a parliamentary committee, claiming that the proposed changes in the definition of regulatory responsibilities, process of appointments and renewal of Commissioners would reduce direct interference from line Ministries and improve accountability and effectiveness.

In addition to these general comments, one respondent gave a very detailed assessment of the problems and failings of the regulatory system in Tanzania, including the following problems:

- limited adherence to the rule of law, which introduces arbitrariness in the institutions and allows for personality centred decision making;
- lack of thorough scrutiny of potential investors and absence of transparency in systems for selecting and evaluating prospective investors. This respondent believed that the failure of the regulatory body to provide clear prequalification guidelines prevented it from screening unsuitable investors;
- central government interference in the details of regulatory decision making, in contravention of publicly stated rules and licensing guidelines, has weakened the system. For example, the rules specifying that there was to be a minimum 35 per cent local shareholding in mobile cellular operating companies and that there were to be set guidelines for migration of analogue systems to digital systems were changed to accommodate potential entrants and existing operators of analogue networks. The government also acted to summarily dismiss Commissioners of the TCC after they made licensing decisions that were out of favour.

The following challenges and constraints were identified for Tanzania:

- staff shortages in the TCC;
- lack of financial resources in public sector bodies;
- relatively small size of the economy and the sector, which stifles TCB investment;
- independent regulator circumscribed by the executive branch of

government, including by the legislative provision for ministerial veto of TCC decisions;

- absence of legally binding guidelines for TCB makes it difficult for public bodies to facilitate TCB
- monitoring TCB activities in firms would impose an impossible burden on TCC unless its resources were increased;
- taxation systems do not provide any incentive to reinvest earnings in TCB activities: there are no rewards or incentives for undertaking human resource development and technological capability building – specifically targeted incentives needed;
- training at tertiary level in local institutions still inadequate and expensive and there is little involvement between university and operating companies, except for TTCL where professors sit on its Board of Directors;
- operating companies have not invested in succession planning or skills transfer mechanisms, resulting in badly managed technical assistance programmes and poor results from transfer of technology programmes;
- financial constraints at the University of Dar es Salaam restrict the supply of qualified graduates and this provides a bottleneck to TCB activities. Despite shortages in supply, there has also been inadequate absorption of graduates;
- user community in Tanzania is not very sophisticated in their requirements and this reduces the incentive for TCB activities. The exceptions to this are the banking and tourism sectors and within the telecoms sector itself.

In addition public officials and commentators believed that operating companies in Tanzania were too preoccupied with short-term commercial pressures and not focused on long-term strategic actions such as TCB. As a result, TCB activities are under funded in the parastatals and in private sector companies. The operating firms also lack experience of operating in competitive markets and lack change management systems and capabilities. Between 1993 and 1999 there has been considerable capital investment in the broadcasting and telecommunication sectors, but the spend on human resource development has not kept pace. There has also been little institutionalization of human resource development issues. Within operating companies, expenditure on training is still treated as recurrent expenditure rather than as an investment in intellectual capital. Training budgets are too small, especially in large capital-intensive projects and there is an over reliance on factory training during commissioning and testing of equipment as a means of TCB. When not complemented by technology search and evaluation, this can result in poor choice and selection decisions and little technology transfer. An example is provided from purchase of a switching system from a Japanese company, where the functionality for CCITT-7[1] features was suppressed on the equipment and delivered without that feature and with no training. The companies often lack customer orientation and commercial skills and this poses many problems and results in low productivity levels and poor quality of service levels, even when capital infrastructure has been improved.

South Africa

South African operating companies regarded the policy and regulatory framework for TCB as fair and fundamentally sound. The major achievements at the sectoral level were considered to have been accomplished by the inclusion in operating company licences and shareholder agreements of specific terms and conditions to encourage capability development. However, the operating companies volunteered the view that well-enforced general legislation and policy, such as the Skills Act and the Employment Equity Act, had greater influence on their investment spend on capability development than sector specific proposals, because the telecommunication industry arrangements and provisions were not monitored or enforced.

However, opinion differed among officials of the South African Telecommunication Regulatory Authority (SATRA) as to whether or not there was a legal mandate to influence TCB activities in firms. Those officials who felt that influencing TCB activities was outside the scope of the regulator adopted a literal interpretation of the provisions of this section, while their counterparts believed that the provisions in the section supported actions by the regulator and public policy bodies. In particular, the sections on encouraging participation by people from 'historically disadvantaged communities', and the clauses to set up a Human Resource Development fund and to encourage training and skill development were cited. One SATRA official believed that the regulator had a firm mandate to facilitate TCB and used it in the licensing of new entrants by paying particular attention to skills development. This respondent also claimed that the authority uses its licensing powers to set out performance targets for technology transfer and skills transfer. This view was similar to that of a senior public policy official who believed that since the policy environment in South Africa was adaptable and responsive to change, even if there were no explicit requirements for TCB because these could not have been anticipated, the objectives could be accommodated by current practices within the sector.

It was only operating companies in South Africa that identified some strengths in the policy and regulatory institutional framework. These included the specific legal mandate for TCB, which was enshrined in primary legislation and supporting legal documents, and the high priority afforded to this issue as reflected in the active involvement of key public bodies. In South Africa skills development provisions were one of the conditions of partial privatization of a state-owned company and were used to remedy discriminatory access to skills training during apartheid. After 1994, the democratic government introduced explicit provision for funding of skills development through its HRD fund and established specialist skill development and training agencies on a sectoral basis. The ministry responsible for telecommunication in South Africa also had a proactive approach to implementing training programmes with firms.

A senior policy-making official reported that TCB was among the top priorities of the national telecommunication policy. In his view, the evidence for this high ranking is reflected in the budget for direct expenditure on TCB activities of R3–4 million or US$500k. The optimism about the perceived importance of TCB was not reflected in the views of the regulatory officials, one of whom stated that, 'TCB activities fall near the bottom of the list of priorities, but perhaps SATRA should be more proactive'. The same regulatory official went on to state that the South African Telecommunications Regulatory Agency (SATRA) could take leadership in facilitating co-operation between tertiary education institutions and operating companies and ensuring that there was alignment between curriculum development initiatives and the needs of industry. This role was believed to be an important adjunct to the proposed active involvement in setting standards for training qualifications and certification in the industry.

Officials from South African public sector bodies assessed the performance of the independent regulator as fair, given the budget constraints under which it operates. The regulatory body was considered to have had success in encouraging service quality improvement and in stimulating innovation. Among the improvements made in the system was the introduction of regulatory accounts that provided an incentive for firms to improve their cost allocation systems and improve quality of management information. Some of the problems that these commentators identified included SATRA's inability to compete effectively for talented staff and to invest in staff development. As a result of staff shortages and high rates of attrition, the regulator has not been able to carry out its core functions, such as frequency monitoring at the level required by industry players. This has resulted in reluctance of licensees to pay fees and has increased the sensitivity of operators to any signs of SATRA extending its mandate beyond core regulatory functions. The sector-specific regulator was considered to have shown very weak performance in policing, monitoring and enforcing licence conditions. The internal assessment of respondents within the regulatory body was that the activities of the authority were being compromised by funding arrangements and they were in favour of making changes to SATRA's funding base.

There were conflicting opinions among the public sector officials as to the effectiveness of capacity development activity within the regulatory body. At least one respondent reported that the mechanisms used for building capabilities, including skills transfer from consultants, internships, study tours, training programmes, conferences and seminars, had been successful. In his view, while these mechanisms had made improvements, there were still gaps in legal and economic analysis, interconnection and tariffing, engineering and technological assessment and in the organizational efficiency of the regulatory authority. It was reported that the authority was attempting to speed up its internal skills development programmes and, in particular, trying to develop the skills of black staff to counteract the loss of skilled white staff members to industry.

South African operating companies also identified specific weaknesses in the regulatory environment including:

- The need to increase funding and strengthen the human resource capabilities of the sector-specific regulator and improve its ability to attract and retain high calibre staff.
- Lack of clarity around the shared roles and responsibilities of the Department of Communications and the sector-specific regulator, SATRA.
- The need to review regulation to make it compatible with a multi-operator environment.
- All respondents identified a number of general constraints and challenges.
- Daunting pace of technological change imposes a high performance standard for regulators and policy makers and requires that the intention of regulatory intervention changes to enabling rather than directing behaviour of operating companies.
- Need to accelerate the in-house capability for technology and applications development.
- TCB was not a core regulatory function, and its promotion would not be given priority over those legally defined functions. Training and empowerment were subordinate functions of the regulatory body and so received less attention than frequency allocation, tariff setting, licensing, setting quality of service targets and making choices of service range.

- Companies did not welcome interference from public bodies and take a legalistic definition and interpretation of SATRA's jurisdiction to ensure that it did not exceed its legal mandate.
- Regulatory body faces serious financial constraints. SATRA staff are overburdened by existing functions and would not be physically able to extend into other areas, within present resource limits. To worsen the situation, SATRA has lost a number of key senior staff to industry and this has severely weakened its technical capacity.
- Regulatory body would have to devote more dedicated staff resources to TCB-related activities and this has not been a stated intention, despite the understanding of the issues at Council level.
- Lack of clarity in division of responsibilities between Department of Communications and SATRA and perceived competition for leadership on issues of human resource development and crowding out of the independent regulator. The regulator's role and credibility are compromised by present financing arrangements and these also weaken its accountability, and its independence and strength in the market.
- SATRA unable to perform its core functions to the desired standard, and can be characterized as a 'toothless bulldog'. Government ownership of one of the largest licensees also compromises SATRA's regulatory responsibilities, since conflicts of interest arise between these multiple public sector roles. The regulator also does not have sufficient influence over the legislative process, for example bills for number portability and roaming were rejected by Parliament and the regulator was not consulted on the reasons for this rejection of its proposals.
- Perception of 'regulatory capture' by TELKOM, the national fixed line operating company, weakens SATRA's standing with other operating companies and reduces its ability to influence TCB activities.
- The growing trend for litigation in the sector, diverts attention and resources away from TCB activities.
- TCB activities are not accorded high enough priority among competing policy objectives; it is regarded as 'nice to have but not terribly important', while it should be regarded as a key requirement.
- Developing common approaches to TCB promotion in the rest of Africa will take considerable time.
- SATRA will need to remain involved in the development of sector qualification and certification standards, and in the operations of the Sector Education and Training Authority (SETA), despite its budgetary and staffing constraints.

- Scarcity of skilled labour and the solutions to this problem lie outside the control of players within the telecoms sector. SATRA can play a role through ensuring that the HRD Fund is used in accordance with the stipulations of the Telecoms Act Section 80/3. These provisions are a vital tool for ensuring that the majority black population enjoys fair access to training and skills development opportunities.
- Small companies lack the financial base to undertake TCB activities and can be supported through affirmative action in procurement policies of large operating companies. Therefore TCB can be promoted directly as well as indirectly, but this requires creative thinking in the design of instruments to encourage skills development and transfer of technology to SMMEs during the procurement cycle.

The foregoing evidence shows that in developing countries the legal mandate for public policy support for TCB in firms is often non-existent and when present is weak and unclear. In South Africa TCB was included under the rubric of skills development and in Uganda it came within technology transfer. Unlike the requirements for network rollout, these targets for skill development and technology transfer were not well defined and often did not include measurable targets, indicators or mechanisms for enforcement or monitoring.

The shortcomings of the policy and regulatory environment are illustrated by the responses from the telecommunication operating companies with Malaysian investment partners that operated in Ghana, Tanzania and South Africa. These companies expected African governments to pursue long-term objectives, such as the promotion of TCB, through implementing specific guidelines for public–private partnerships. Their expectations, however, were not being met and, ironically, the absence of attention to detail in public policy, rather than promoting inward investment flows, lessened the confidence of the Malaysian investors.

In summary, this evidence shows that overall weaknesses in the policy and regulatory framework rather than in specific measures to facilitate TCB, limit effectiveness. There was significant agreement across all countries and all types of firms that the failure of public efforts to facilitate TCB activities in firms stemmed from the inability of public institutions to implement policy objectives and co-ordinate responsibilities across different arms of government. The limitations to TCB facilitation were perceived to be generally low levels of competence and execution capability, which did not come near to matching the specific requirements of this functional area. A general problem reported by all companies was the inability of policy and regulatory bodies to monitor and enforce regulation. In each of the four countries, private sector firms rated the capabilities of the regulatory and public sector firms much lower than did publicly owned firms and public sector officials and commentators.

The views solicited from public officials and expert commentators in South Africa were similar to those of the operating companies in South Africa. In Ghana, Uganda and Tanzania, however, both these groups dwelt on skills shortages, weakness of local knowledge creation institutions and unwillingness of the operating companies to become involved in TCB. Public officials in these three countries saw prioritizing TCB, given other competing objectives, as a significant challenge, and maintained that the role of foreign advisors undermined the possibility of including long-term objectives that might conflict with maximization of financial profit.

In addition to the efficacy of specific institutions in the innovation system structural features contribute to underperformance. In all four countries, promotion of TCB was considered to be an indirect, but automatic, benefit of network expansion that would accrue from growth and expansion of the network. Policy makers in the countries under investigation were not able to justify placing any special emphasis on TCB promotion since other policy objectives, such as network expansion, were seen as priorities.

There was a commonly held perception that inclusion of specific requirements for TCB might reduce the chances of attracting private external capital and, in a region that was constrained by debt burdens and capital scarcity, this effectively would reduce freedom for action for policy makers. While policy makers seemed to understand that the licensing of new operators gave the state the opportunity to impose requirements for TCB, this was often not followed up because the licensing negotiation involved difficult and politically sensitive decisions about the restructuring of state-owned companies, which were overstaffed. Policy makers, therefore, frequently claimed that they made a trade-off between not highlighting TCB and reducing the levels of job losses that accompanied privatization and corporatization. The financial objectives of privatization and the state requirement to maximize proceeds often took precedence over such long-term objectives as facilitating TCB efforts.

HOW CAN FIRMS BE EFFECTIVE IN INTERACTIONS WITH THE INNOVATION SYSTEM?

Compared with the other three African countries in the sample, South African firms seemed to have made more progress in managing boundary relationships with the innovation system to facilitate TCB. The interaction between South African operating companies and the policy and regulatory bodies extended beyond the procedural level and worked in such a manner as to provide tangible technological inputs for the TCB efforts of firms. It is worth noting that the most proactive institution in the South African innovation system was a ministry, which had extended its mandate of policy setting beyond the traditional interpretation and had established skills training programmes in partnership with firms.

There were many specific examples of South African firms implementing TCB activities in collaboration with public sector institutions or under the influence of institutional rules. These included:

- a large public network operator that was an active participant in a three-way learning experiment, which arose out of a public sector requirement to trial telecommunication technologies prior to implementation. The trials involved the operating company, suppliers and the state and resulted in the public network firm improving its understanding of wireless access technologies;
- a former incumbent public network operator that undertook a significant skills development programme, mandated by the terms and conditions in the shareholder agreement, which underpinned the sale of 30 per cent of its equity to an international strategic investor;
- all South African operating companies, which are bound by the conditions for skills development and human resource development set out in primary legislation for the sector and in general legislation as an attempt to redress the skills imbalances of the apartheid era;
- operating companies, which were required to contribute to a HRD Fund that partially financed the skills development programme championed and organized by the responsible ministry.

South African firms welcomed state involvement in the provision of 'public goods' such as standardized training, technological literacy and certification of training programmes, but were resistant to state direction or intervention in the management of their TCB effort. While operating companies in South Africa supported public sector involvement in TCB on the basis on technological neutrality, they did not relish the state becoming active in specifying technological choice, generally because firms did not regard public sector institutions as being abreast with the changes in technologies. However, there were sharp differences between firms operating in competitive segments of South African telecommunications and those in monopolistic or duopolistic segments. The latter were more pragmatic and accepting of public policy involvement, while the former were resistant to any public sector role, and identified government's restrictive interpretation of the 1996 Telecommunications Act as a critical barrier to TCB efforts.

Although South African firms appear to have made the most progress, there are examples of successful management of boundary relationships with regulatory and policy bodies in all four countries. In Tanzania, there was evidence that the public network operating company managed boundary relationships with public bodies through its board of directors rather than through its relationship with policy and regulatory bodies. The Tanzanian public network company used appointments to the board of directors as a mechanism for accessing technical skills and knowledge and, by this means, secured the services of prominent and well-respected professors from the local university. The state was then able to exercize influence over TCB activities through the board of directors more effectively than through its policy making or regulatory role. In Ghana, operating companies found informal consultation and regular communication with the policy and regulatory bodies valuable in soliciting information and know-how. The importance of utilizing shared social networks and of increasing trust between public officials and operating company decision makers stood out as a feature of the TCB system of Ghanaian companies.[2] In Ghana, the state undertook the role of providing training that was accessible to all firms by mandating the majority-owned public network operator to open access to its training college facilities. In the three smaller African countries, the scarcity of training resources and skilled personnel in knowledge centres, meant that the resources of individual firms was greatly superior and opening access to the knowledge resources of the operating firms was therefore an important effort. In Uganda, the large state-owned company achieved success in acquiring technological inputs from the global innovation system by having a knowledgeable senior executive take responsibility for interaction with international sources of technical information, such as international organizations and standards-making bodies as a representative of the Ugandan state. Representation of the country at the highest levels by an executive of the operating company was unusual, but accelerated technological capability development in the firm. These examples also illustrate another feature of TCB effort in African firms. In all four countries in the sample, companies with some state ownership had more interaction with policy and regulatory bodies than companies that were 100 per cent privately owned.

Across the four countries there was a high level of correlation between size of the company and the reported level of interaction with the regulatory and policy bodies. Analysis of the responses to open-ended questions on recommendations for facilitating TCB effort in firms indicates that smaller firms, 100 per cent privately owned firms and firms operating in competitive segments were less satisfied with the efforts of the policy and regulatory bodies than larger firms and those firms that had some degree of state ownership and/or monopoly control. Small firms in the smaller countries with the least developed institutional systems, reported the highest levels of distrust and disaffection with the innovation system and displayed the least ability to compensate for the institutional failings of the national innovation system. We believe that this finding is consistent with the argument of the TCB system approach, which suggests that firms with clearly designated, professional responsibility for managing the interface with public and regulatory bodies would be better able to benefit from these interactions and to compensate for institutional failures. It is also consistent with the findings and analyzes, which were discussed in Chapter 3, indicating that the level of development of TCB systems is highly correlated with firm size. The relative high level of disaffection on the part of small firms might also be explained by the tendency for policy and regulatory bodies to be genuinely more solicitous of large firms that have greater economic impact and wield more political influence. The evidence has confirmed that some firms are able to benefit from boundary relationships with the innovation system, even when public sector institutions provide support that is far removed from what is desired by firms.

CONCLUSION

For developing country firms and their national innovation systems, the importance of promoting interaction and exchange of knowledge and information across organizational boundaries in order to encourage learning and capability building appears to have been understood and accepted at the rhetorical level, but has made only limited progress at the implementation level. This underperformance can be explained by structural barriers, strategic limitations within firms and the ineffectiveness of innovation system institutions.

NOTES

1   CCITT-7 is an international standard for switching systems in telecommunication networks.
2   This feature of Ghanaian telecommunication companies appears consistent with business practices in other sectors. See Kuada (1994).

7 Strategic Balance

The technology capability building (TCB) system approach provides a conceptual framework for understanding processes of learning and capability development in firms that do not produce equipment or technologies and operate in local innovation systems far removed from the technological frontier. The approach is consistent with evolutionary theories of the process of innovation, but amplifies these theories by considering and examining the innovation processes within firms operating outside the frontiers of knowledge. This chapter presents the main empirical insights that emerged from the study. It also discusses the theoretical implications and policy relevance of these findings and identifies avenues for further research.

HOW DO FIRMS IN DEVELOPING COUNTRIES BUILD TECHNOLOGICAL CAPABILITIES?

The research described in this book sheds considerable light on patterns of technological learning in developing countries. The analysis suggests ways in which developing country firms can improve their effectiveness.

Balance Increases Effectiveness in Learning

The research findings provide substantial confirmation that developing country firms accumulate technological capabilities through a systematic investment process involving learning, uncertainty, trial and error, multiple motivations and diverse practices. The analysis shows that developing country firms have many motivations to undertake TCB and their technological strategies are dissimilar from those of firms at the technological frontier. The 26 firms studied undertook TCB to monitor technological trends, to maintain pace with technical change and to improve their understanding and use of technological knowledge. It was not evident that any of the firms had undertaken TCB in order to generate new knowledge in the form of products or processes. All of the firms in the sample appeared to recognize that, although they had little or no direct control over technological change, it was imperative that they should invest in technological capability development. Even those firms that had made little progress in establishing TCB systems acknowledged the importance of capability development. This suggests that since developing country firms do not build capabilities for the sole purpose of improving their competitive position in the marketplace, a conceptual framework that allows for multiple objectives for TCB is needed if we are to understand how and why such processes take place.

A suitable framework requires that TCB be defined more broadly to encompass much more than research and development (R&D). This characterization of technological capability accumulation as a non-R&D centred process makes the TCB system approach presented in this book relevant to developing country firms in a number of industries, where production of knowledge at the frontier is not the main goal. Such industries would include other technologically intensive service sectors, such as banking and information technology, as well as manufacturers producing for domestic or niche export markets.

The research described in this book also explains how developing countries can improve the effectiveness of their technological learning and capability building. It offers strong support for the claim that it is the extent to which the capability process is organized in a coherent and balanced system that influences its effectiveness. There is evidence that ten of the 26 firms in the sample had made good progress in establishing effective learning processes for TCB; the remaining 16 had 'unbalanced' TCB systems, which departed from the proposed 'ideal'. Quantitative analysis confirmed that firm-level and country-level factors influenced the level of TCB system development. A number of independent variables, such as operating experience, size, range of service offerings and ownership profile, were found to have positively influenced technological capability accumulation. Operating in a supportive national innovation system also contributed to the effectiveness of technological learning in the firms examined.

This study was successful in explaining the variation in the effectiveness of technological learning in developing country firms and, therefore, adds to the knowledge on capability accumulation processes. It shows that there is a structural requirement for improving effectiveness in TCB by identifying a number of differences between out-performers and underachievers in terms of technological learning. The out-performers proportionately, simultaneously and systematically directed their efforts towards five key elements of technological learning, that is financing, management and co-ordination, culture and leadership and managing relationships with suppliers and with the innovation system. This conclusion is applicable to other industry settings.

The TCB system approach developed TCB system indicators to measure variance between a firm's 'systems in use' and the hypothetical 'ideal' systems for learning. The TCB system indicators also have predictive value and were used to identify whether a firm was likely to have a 'balanced' and effective system for learning or an 'unbalanced' and ineffective one.

Management, Co-ordination, Culture and Leadership are Crucial

Analysis of the evidence confirmed that firms with effective TCB systems deployed internal processes in their capability building efforts and managed these processes to improve firm-wide learning. The factors that facilitate effectiveness in capability building included:

* providing leadership for learning;
* creating conditions that supported firm-wide learning and raised awareness of the importance of technological capability for firm survival and competitiveness;
* providing of open learning facilities;
* implementing specific management routines including remuneration and reward systems that encourage development of boundary-spanning skills and manage the knowledge flows from expatriates;
* implementing evaluation and monitoring systems; and
* proactively engaging with the local labour market and education system to increase the number of people with requisite education and skills, particularly those with disciplinary backgrounds in telecommunication engineering and information technology.

A major weakness of the firms studied was that none had made much progress in the organizational integration of TCB and, as a result, could not achieve consistency, cohesiveness or consonance. These results are important because they demonstrate the fruitfulness of integrating organizational development and strategic management insights into the analysis of capability accumulation by developing country firms. Without the insights from these academic traditions, analyzing the differences between firms with an ideal system for TCB and others whose attempts were less effective in accumulating capabilities would not have identified many of the intra-firm contributing factors. For example, the importance of having diverse routines for learning, co-ordinating mechanisms and supportive culture and leadership has received little attention in the development studies tradition. Also, the TCB system approach yields new knowledge by identifying specific internal processes (for example, the introduction of open learning systems and proactive support of public education and training institutions to provide access to skilled people) that were found to be important to the firms studied and which may be important for other developing country firms operating in similar contexts of rapid technological change.

Supply Conditions Change but Supplier Management Remains Critical

Managing relationships with international suppliers of equipment and services was found to be a critical component in the TCB systems in developing country firms. While this finding is in line with the conventional understanding of the role of external capabilities in capability development, the TCB system approach produces a more nuanced view.

Firstly, the TCB system approach suggests that technology-specific and industry-specific characteristics significantly influence the commercial relationship between developing country firms and their suppliers. As has been shown (see Chapter 1) market structure and technology developments in the telecommunication industry have fundamentally altered the nature of the production process in the telecommunication services sector and the commercial relationships between equipment suppliers and operating companies. Telecommunication operating companies, including those in developing countries, source their technological inputs, that is the components required to construct, operate and maintain telecommunication networks, from external suppliers operating in the international market. These inputs typically take the form of physical plant and equipment, software and professional services and are widely available in the international marketplace. Since the early 1980s the market for these components has become increasingly concentrated in terms of the number of firms offering these inputs and there has also been an increasing trend toward the adoption of global standards in technology. Operating companies generally source technology from a limited range of suppliers and there is intense competition among the few market leaders for access to markets. In this context, the development of long-term relationships between suppliers and operating companies has become a central feature of competition dynamics in that it is the ability to manage and secure mutual benefit from large projects of long duration that gives suppliers of telecommunication equipment an edge. Given the importance of the components provided by a relatively small number of suppliers, firms' management of these supplier relationships becomes a core competence, without which the maximum technological capability benefits from the relationship cannot be achieved.

The evidence in this study suggests that these shifts in technological trends and competitive forces have positively influenced the ability of developing country firms to exercize constrained agency in their relationships with international firms. There is evidence of developing country firms that were able to effectively source technological inputs with the assistance of global market leaders that were actively investing in organizational innovation, which improved their ability to transfer knowledge to developing country customers. These findings suggest that in designing policy interventions to support trade in information and knowledge, emphasis should be placed on industry features, competitive dynamics and technological trends.

Secondly, the approach suggests that improving knowledge management and tacit knowledge flows is a critical element of supplier management. The application of the TCB system approach to the investigation of supplier relationships yields new knowledge by identifying specific management routines that developing country firms can use to improve knowledge management and tacit knowledge flows in technological intensive environments. The study shows that the employees of supplier firms are the main conduits of externally sourced technological capability. The highly valued specialized engineering and information technology knowledge and the skills to apply this knowledge in network implementation and operation reside in people. Developing country firms, therefore, need to improve their abilities to manage interactions with the persons embodying these critical components of technological knowledge and skills. To achieve this firms must screen and select among expatriate staff and consultants and actively engage in designing the programmes through which these individuals are expected and required to share knowledge. It has been shown, however, that the ability of developing country firms to incorporate these elements into their TCB systems is not entirely under their control. Examination of the telecommunication industries in Uganda, Ghana and Tanzania provided examples of conditions attached to intergovernmental loans and grants that acted as barriers to recipient firms playing an active role in the selection of expatriate persons providing technological knowledge services. This finding that external constraints may influence a developing country firm's ability to undertake effective supplier management is important and has policy relevance.

Thirdly, the TCB system approach suggests that a more disaggregated notion of 'absorptive capacity' of recipient firms is needed to explain effectiveness in supplier management. In line with organizational development research, the absorptive capacity of a firm is considered at a detailed level in terms of the skills, attitudes and abilities of the individuals managing and participating in capability development. It has been shown that developing country firms can increase absorptive capacity by investment in individuals and by taking steps to increase their level of motivation and confidence. In the sample firms it was the young, highly educated African staff members that were able, because of their comparable social capital and social networks, to interact with expatriate staff and gain access to their technological knowledge. When these local technical professionals were, motivated by being given authority and a pro-learning cultural environment, they facilitated the flow of technological knowledge. Under such conditions local staff were able to be effective and successful conduits and transformers of knowledge. This individual aspect of absorptive capacity is emphasized in the TCB system approach and has policy implications.

The research identified the importance of the role of returning nationals and national technological champions in increasing the absorptive capacity of developing country firms. Although the mobility of highly skilled nationals has received attention in analyzes of Asian capability development efforts, this has not been closely examined in the African context. The empirical evidence from the study described in this book confirms that members of the African Diaspora often returned home as technological champions and played vital roles in energizing the capability development efforts in firms. For the private sector firms in this research, returning nationals who had acquired skills, knowledge and experience from working with international equipment suppliers in developed markets were an important source of external knowledge and were effective intermediaries in relationships with suppliers. Of the four countries in the study, Ghana stands out as an example of a country with a formal government policy to increase the benefits that can be realized from recruitment of returning nationals. The skill and technological knowledge of these individuals was very much in evidence in the Ghanaian firms in the study.

Organizational development theorists stress the importance of the availability of 'boundary spanning' skills for capability accumulation. This research confirms that developing countries can and should accumulate these specialist skills. The TCB system approach yields new knowledge by identifying boundary-spanning aptitudes that are required for supplier relationships to be effectively managed. These include confidence, assertiveness, problem-solving ability, intellectual curiosity, interest in experimentation and willingness to take risks. Given the cultural and political distance between participants in information exchange between external suppliers and developing country firms, these 'soft' factors appear to be critical. The research findings confirm that in firms where some staff had these characteristics, the likelihood of establishing technology and knowledge flows was greater. Representatives of technology suppliers also reported that lack of these aptitudes and characteristics was a barrier to capability development.

In the next section, the implications for public policy of these features of supplier relationships are discussed. These findings are in line with organizational development theorists' conceptualization of capability accumulation in the context of firms at the technology frontier. The contribution that the TCB system approach makes is to confirm that soft factors associated with technological confidence are important user capabilities for developing country firms operating in industries facing rapid technological change.

Fourthly, in addition to having the appropriate human factors to capture and share tacit knowledge from external sources, effective management of supplier relationships required firms to have access to a number of complementary competencies. Applying the TCB system approach identified mechanisms that facilitated the development of those complementary competencies. The research findings from this study confirm that developing country firms require technology search and scan mechanisms, systems for technological evaluation and routines to integrate inputs sourced from suppliers with other technological knowledge. These integration and co-ordination routines are also the methods used to facilitate higher-order learning, to encourage experimentation and to ensure coherence of internal capability building and appear to reinforce the aptitudes and absorptive capacity of those individuals involved in supplier management. Management practices such as equipment trials, joint projects with equipment suppliers and policies and practices to ensure that operating company staff are involved in all aspects of network projects from planning to implementation, were among the most important supplier management techniques. Firms that reported satisfactory supplier relationships also had mechanisms for feedback and evaluation of interaction with suppliers. There appears to be a relationship between the size of the initial stock of technological capability and the reported success in managing supplier relationships.

Finally, the TCB system approach suggests that there are limitations to the contribution that management of supplier relationships can make to overall capability development effort. The ideal system for capability development is a finely tuned integrated system in which the central elements' internal processes, supplier relationships and interaction with the innovation system are in balance, that is they receive proportionate attention and financial investment and are implemented with reference to the specific initial conditions that obtain within the firm and the strategic objectives of the firm. Sixteen firms in this sample of telecommunication operating companies did not conform to this ideal. In the 'unbalanced' TCB system that was characteristic of those firms, greater attention was given to supplier relationships and the financial commitment made to this element was disproportionate to the other elements of the TCB system. In particular, supplier relationships received much more attention and investment than relationships with national innovation system institutions. This pattern is likely to be similar in other industries in developing countries, particularly those involving rapid changing technology. This pattern of over-emphasis and over-reliance on the supplier relationships, although it can be explained in part by the unavailability of alternative sources of technological inputs, has negative consequences for overall capability effort. As noted in the analysis in Chapter 5, suppliers of equipment are unlikely to provide access to several important types of knowledge, namely general technological principles and understanding of trends ('know-why') and knowledge related to sources of technological input ('know-who'). Therefore, the relative lack of effort in developing relationships with national innovation system institutions can be said to hamper the effectiveness of the capability development investment.

Innovation Systems are not Automatically Relevant

The analysis presented in this book suggests that managing relationships with institutions within the national innovation system has not been an important source of technological capabilities for telecommunication operating companies in developing countries in Africa. The national innovation systems in Uganda, Ghana and Tanzania did not appear to be conducive to the TCB efforts of their telecommunication operating firms. In these three countries, firms that were able to develop effective TCB systems undertook many activities that can be characterized as 'compensating mechanisms' to overcome the failings of the national innovation system, and there were very few examples of a positive influence of the local innovation system on firm-level TCB efforts. The respondents from the operating companies inUganda, Ghana and Tanzania did not perceive their TCB effort to be a response to signals or inducements from the local innovation system. Although the South African firms operated in a more favourable environment, the representatives of these firms also did not regard local public sector institutions, such as regulatory authorities and policy-making bodies, as sources of technological inputs. This result requires further exploration, since it appears to be at odds with the existing literature on capability development.

Firstly, it appears that public sector bodies have not been able to keep up with the rapid pace of technical change in the telecommunication industry and, therefore, firms that are engaged in production activities do not regard them as repositories of useful knowledge. The evidence presented confirmed that the skills and knowledge base of individuals within public sector institutions often lagged behind those of staff in operating companies.

In addition to not keeping pace with technological change, in the four countries in this study, the public institutions were made more ineffectual by a weak legal mandate to support technological capability building in firms. Where there were provisions to support technological capability development in firms, these focused almost exclusively on skill development, and were administered by institutions with very weak enforcement and compliance capability. The evidence shows that facilitating TCB through general industrial development policy and regulations, such as that administered by the Department of Trade and Industry in South Africa, was more successful.

Telecommunication operating companies require specific information regarding the operating conditions and functioning of network components, which is likely to be vendor specific and proprietary. Public sector bodies, therefore, are unlikely to be sources of this type of information. This suggests that evaluation of the usefulness and importance of institutions in the national innovation system requires an assessment of the types of information and knowledge required by firms. The TCB system approach encompasses this and concludes that there are important distinctions between the type and nature of knowledge required by service organizations and that required by manufacturing firms. Previous studies of capability development in the telecommunication industry have been based on analysis of the requirements of aspiring telecommunication equipment producers, and, in such settings, the role of national research laboratories has been significant. This study does not match their conclusions; instead it suggests that public sector research centres were more dependent on telecommunication operating companies as a source of knowledge and information. This result departs from the expected relationship between innovation systems as a source of technological capability inputs and has important policy implications.

Although the evidence indicates that for telecommunication operating companies in Africa national innovation systems were not in the forefront of the TCB effort and certainly did not play the strategic role envisaged in previous studies of capability development, the firms in the sample were all in favour of public sector organizations playing a more proactive role in facilitating TCB efforts. In particular, there was support for public sector organizations becoming focused on providing independent assessments of technological trends. The evidence also suggests that developing country firms are keen for public sector organizations to provide assistance with vendor selection, technology search and scan and information and skills sharing across different firms and communities of interest.

Managers of publicly owned operating companies who were part of the same social networks as regulators and policy-making bodies used mutual trust and respect to facilitate access to knowledge even in weak national innovation systems. These individuals, therefore, were less critical of the national innovation system than their private sector counterparts.

The role of the national innovation system in influencing TCB effort at firm level is also affected by initial conditions. In the 1990s, the national university systems in Uganda, Ghana and Tanzania were plagued by underfunding and structural problems; despite efforts to achieve curriculum reform, restructuring of engineering degree programmes and attempts to work more closely with the operating companies these institutions were unable to provide the appropriate support for firms' TCB efforts. Universities and technical colleges in South Africa were relatively better funded and achieved some success in facilitating TCB in firms by improving mechanisms for joint execution of projects and, in some instances, undertaking applied research at universities within projects funded by industry. The South African case, therefore, aligns much more closely with academic writings on how national innovation systems institutions and firms can be more effectively integrated. In Uganda, Ghana and Tanzania, the relative immaturity and fragility of institutions in the national innovation system suggest that more direct approaches to supporting the TCB effort in firms are likely to be more effective in the short term. Therefore, the policy recommendations suggested here, while supportive of investment in institutional development, emphasize the need to give support to inexperienced firms through direct action.

The research findings indicate that the ability of firms to manage boundary relationships with the national innovation system varied with firm size, with larger firms reporting greater interaction with public sector bodies. Interaction between public sector bodies and telecommunication operating companies appeared to be intense during the bidding and licensing stages and tailed off after networks became operational. This pattern may have contributed to the inability of sector-specific bodies to be effectively involved in long-term strategic issues, such as technological capability development.

KEY THEORETICAL INSIGHTS AND POLICY RELEVANCE

The TCB system approach offers support for adopting a people-centred approach to understanding capability development in firms. The analysis shows that individual effort and creative leadership can substantially improve the facility of firms to develop technological capability. The analysis has shown that it is useful to see TCB as process of investment the efficacy of which depends on improving the ability of individuals to absorb technological knowledge and circulate that knowledge throughout the firm.

This empirically based analysis has confirmed that, when developing country firms organize technological learning through coherent, balanced systems, the value of these efforts improves. The systematic approach required firms to invest proportionately in internal elements of TCB, such as financing mechanisms, culture, leadership, management and co-ordination processes, as well as boundary spanning elements, such as supplier management and relationships with the innovation system.

The TCB system approach differs from other approaches to understanding capability development in firms. First, it links the insights of organizational learning, most of which have emerged from studies of firms operating at the technological frontier, to the ideas in the development studies tradition, arising from several decades of research on capability development. Second, the operationalized TCB system approach permits quantitative exploration of patterns of technological learning in developing country firms. Using statistical analysis the study confirms that internal processes and boundary relationships are equally important for effective capability development. Finally, the approach delves more deeply into the variations in capability development at firm level by examining internal processes. It concludes that underdevelopment of the strategic and systematic management of capability development is a major constraint. These distinctive features lead to the conclusion that if developing country firms are to improve their navigation of technological frontiers they must deploy a coherent, systematic approach to capability development incorporating the strategic management of change.

The approach developed in this book is applicable to both the manufacturing and service sectors and explores an under-researched area. The vast majority of the existing studies of capability development by developing country firms has examined the conditions necessary for acquiring capability building in manufacturing production technologies. The TCB system approach adds to the knowledge by producing a framework which considers the specific requirements of service sector firms. This enhancement matters. We have seen that telecommunication operating companies and manufacturing firms require different types of technological knowledge and learning systems. The study has also identified, at a considerable level of detail, the learning processes by which service sector firms acquire and build user capabilities, such as system integration and other process and change management abilities.

Applying the TCB system approach has yielded a fresh analysis of how developing countries gain access to technological inputs through commercial transactions with international suppliers and concludes that the trading environment for service sector firms has improved. There are many accounts of African telecommunication operating companies successfully acquiring capability inputs from international equipment suppliers. The combined effect of technical change and competition dynamics in the global market, which has led international equipment suppliers to develop core competencies in joint technological project management, has also helped developing country firms.

The TCB system approach examines the role of the innovation system in facilitating technological learning. It offers a provocative conclusion that the intervention of the policy making and regulatory apparatus has made little difference or, in some instances, has made things worse.

Several key implications for policy and ideas that can be implemented by developing country firms and public sector bodies in national innovation systems emerge from this research. These recommendations could contribute to the transformation of the capability development effort by making investments in learning come closer to the theoretical 'ideal' envisaged in the TCB system approach.

Firstly, firms should improve their technological capability accumulation effort by paying attention to the individual aspects of absorptive capacity. This requires developing a culture in which employees are supported and given confidence, are encouraged to acquire technological knowledge and to develop boundary-spanning skills. Features of this learning culture include leadership and involvement from senior management, clear assignment of responsibility and careful design of widely available learning programmes, which include higher-order and 'transcendent' aspects of learning. Secondly, firms must adopt a diverse range of learning mechanisms and align them such that they are coherent with business objectives and capability gaps. Investment in learning must be sustained over time. Thirdly, given the unfavourable local contexts of the majority of developing country firms, they need to be proactive in increasing the pool of technically skilled persons. This can be achieved by joint development with universities and technical colleges of technological training courses, regular industry involvement in and support for curriculum development in education and training, and implementation of formal and informal cross-industry training programmes, where costs are shared among the beneficiaries. Fourthly, firms should treat supplier management as a specific aspect of capability development. By being proactive in technological search and scan and vendor selection, developing country firms can increase the benefits derived from external sources of technology. An important aspect of supplier management involves developing country firms becoming involved in a broad range of technological functions in partnership with suppliers of equipment and services. This should lead to a cumulative improvement in technological knowledge and levels of understanding. Finally, since public sector bodies in the national innovation system can supply complementary types of knowledge, that is 'know-why' and 'know-who', firms should develop mechanisms for more effective interaction with the national system of innovation.

The research described in this book also suggests that in developing countries national systems of innovation require considerable reinforcement in terms of the range of institutions involved and the tools used to support capability development in firms. This is particularly so in the case of technology-intensive sectors, such as the telecommunication industry, in which technical change takes place rapidly. To improve effectiveness, the employees of public sector knowledge producing institutions should update their skills, and improve their level of familiarity with and understanding of technological trends. Public sector institutions, such as universities and technical colleges, must also improve their technological training curricula making them more suited to producing people with an understanding of technological trends and fundamental principles as well as applied skills and industry-specific technological knowledge. In their interactions with industry, public sector institutions should become more facilitating and supportive of technological knowledge exchange.

FOUNDATIONS FOR FUTURE RESEARCH

This research has shed new light on how developing country firms undertake learning processes that are important for fostering competitiveness, innovation and economic development. Its strengths are that the conceptual framework developed extends the development studies work on capability development by including intra-firm and endogenous factors in the analysis of capability development processes. The approach focuses on soft skills, aptitudes and analyzes TCB at the human level. The TCB system approach also integrates the notion of organizational coherence and the strategic management of change, and the transcendent aspects of learning into the analysis of capability accumulation by developing country firms. These areas of organizational development and strategic management theory have hitherto not been emphasized or examined in detail as possible explanations for success or failure in capability development. The conceptual framework builds on and extends the non-linear approach to understanding capability development by adding two boundary relationships as necessary elements of capability development. The approach developed in this study argues that effective management of firms' relationships with suppliers and with the innovation system must coexist with internal processes of capability accumulation. The TCB system approach further suggests that the management practices associated with internal processes also confer complementary competences that are needed to manage boundary processes appropriately.

The conceptual framework developed for this study was operationalized and used to develop indicators of the level of TCB system development. The process of computing these indicators identifies specific routines that firms use for developing internal processes and managing boundary relationships. This is important since it allows for quantitative exploration of how firms go about technological learning and capability building. In addition to permitting a detailed examination of the routines used in capability accumulation, the indicators developed in this study were sufficiently robust to allow them to be used in quantitative tests of patterns of capability development.

The TCB system approach is applicable to a number of industry settings, because the ideal system proposed contains generalizable features of the capability accumulation process in developing countries. To apply the approach in other contexts, the appropriate technology- and industry-specific features would have to be incorporated. The study thus provides a foundation for future research.

Although there was a focus on the individual aspects of capability development, the psychological dimensions of learning and capability development were not fully explored. Integrating insights from the discipline of psychology is likely to further understanding of the barriers to capability accumulation in developing country firms by allowing greater disaggregation and unpacking of the contribution of individuals in terms of their motivation and development of confidence in increasing the absorptive capacity of firms.

The methodology used in this research primarily involved a cross-sectional analysis of firms in one industry across four countries. As a result this study does not analyze how TCB investments yield benefits cumulatively over time. Future research could apply a time-series research design, which would enable researchers to analyze the relationships between the development of TCB systems and variables, such as profitability, revenue growth and market share over time. The TCB system indicators developed here use counts of routines and practices as the basis for assessing the level of development of a TCB system. Although this extends existing research, and the quantitative measures of capability development were robust enough to be used in statistical tests, there is still room for improvement. It may be useful to develop these indicators so that they capture more nuanced aspects of the TCB process, in particular to represent the degree of effort expended in any TCB routine rather than a simple count of the existence of a routine.

CONCLUSION

The main finding of the research was that firms that invested in developing systematic, balanced approaches to learning were effective in technological learning and capability development. The TCB system approach was able to establish this by paying attention to specific and general organizational learning routines and practices within firms as well as to exogenous factors outside the control of the firm. This approach shows that it is internal competencies, such as the ability to manage strategic change and develop coherent systems, that enable developing country firms to navigate technological frontiers, the network of global suppliers and weak national innovation systems. In particular, the ability of developing country firms to strike a strategic balance between developing a diverse range of internal learning routines and managing boundary assets over which they have only partial control, was found to be of critical importance.

The study extends existing knowledge by developing a reasonably robust diagnostic tool – the TCB system development indicator – which is used to predict whether a firm's investment in technological learning is likely to be effective. When applied to a sample of 26 firms, it was found that ten had deployed TCB systems that met the requirements of the theoretical ideal, nine firms had made moderate progress and seven firms had made little progress. The firms that were the most effective were those that had a balanced, coherent approach to capability accumulation with investment effort deployed in all of the key elements, that is the internal processes – finance, culture and leadership, and specific management practices – and management of boundary relationships with suppliers and the innovation system. In addition to producing this diagnostic tool to differentiate between novices and firms that have learned to be effective in technological learning, the study also identified specific routines that are contributed to effectiveness.

The study also showed that firms can compensate for unfavourable environments. For all firms in the sample, operating in South Africa was found to have a positive influence on the effectiveness of their TCB, while having a base in Tanzania was found to be negative. Despite the inhibiting environmental factors, there was at least one Tanzanian firm that was effective in its technological learning and TCB effort. This suggests that explanations of 'effectiveness' in capability development must consider endogenous variables as well as country-level factors. The Tanzanian firm that was effective in deploying a range of learning routines integrated these across the firm. This firm outperformed the level of technological learning that corresponded to Tanzania's weak national innovation system, small market size and unfavourable macroeconomic conditions. This firm ensured that learning and TCB have an appropriate and effective structure.

The study offers a convincing explanation of why developing country firms struggle to build technological capabilities. It demonstrates that developing country firms must learn to master many of the approaches to learning and competence development that would put them on a level with firms at the technological frontier and at the same time put in place specific mechanisms to cope with their challenging local environments. In particular, developing country firms need to build confidence, encourage experimentation, support open learning, integrate learning across firms and align this learning with their overall business strategy. They must also develop routines for sharing responsibility for joint learning and knowledge acquisition with suppliers, and manage relationships with institutions in the innovation system. It is essential that these behavioural, structural and environmental enablers coexist and are managed as a balanced, systematic, coherent and integrated effort if they are to yield maximum benefit.

Appendices

A1.1 DATES OF INTERVIEWS AND INTERVIEWEES

Uganda

June 1998
Hope Abbie Kyoya, General Manager HR, Uganda Telecommunications Ltd
Patrick Masambu, Managing Director, Uganda Telecommunications Ltd
A.M. Mubiru, Director , Nakawa Training Institute/Uganda Telecommunications Ltd
Francis Kazinduki, General Manager, Marketing, Sales and International Services, Uganda Telecommunications Ltd
Edward Ssali, General Manager Planning and Development, Uganda Telecommunications Ltd
Sam Tusabe, Operations Manager, Celtel Ltd
David Sserunjogi, Financial Controller, Celtel Ltd
Paul Meredith, Technical Director, MTN Uganda Ltd
Hon. Minister John Nasasira, Minister of Works, Housing and Communications
Robert Kibukka, Senior Official, Ministry of Works, Housing and Communications
Paul Nalikka, Co-ordinator UPTC Restructuring, Ministry of Finance, Privatisation Unit
Simon Bugaba, Senior Official, Uganda Communications Commission
David Iverson, Consultant, Booz Allen and Hamilton
Dr Z.M. Nyiira, Director, Ugandan National Council on Science and Technology
Mary Mabweijano, Senior Investment Officer, Uganda Investment Authority
Charles Musisi, Director, Uganda On-Line
Dorothy Okello, Lecturer, Makerere University, Department of Electrical Engineering

November 1999
Margaret Wanyama, Acting Director, Uganda Communications Institute

Ghana

July 1998

Lai Ki Tong, Chief Strategy Officer, Ghana Telecommunications Co. Ltd
Mr K.A.Boateng, Financial Comptroller, Ghana Telecommunications Co. Ltd
Ing. Abrefa Kodon, Director , Ghana Telecom Training School
Dr J.A.M. Cobbah, Director Corporate Development, ACG Telesystems Ghana Ltd (Westel)
Beatrice Bridget Ofei, Human Resources Manager, ACG Telesystems Ghana Ltd (Westel)
Prince Kofi Kludgeson, Chief Executive Officer, Celltel
Phil Dunglinson, Managing Director, Mobitel (Ghana) Ltd
Mustapha Houri, Technical Director and founder, ScanCom Ltd
Dr Nii Quaynor, Executive Chairman, Network Computer Systems Ltd (NCS)
Hon Cdr (Rtd.) P.M.G. Griffiths, Deputy Minister, Ministry of Communications
G.K. Adanusa, Telecommunication Advisor, Ministry of Communications
J.K. Gyimah, Acting Director General, National Communications Authority
T.A. Botchway, Telecommunication Advisor, National Communications Authority
Mavis Ampah, CEO and former co-ordinator privatization programme, Spectrum International Ltd
Mr Agganium, Director of Training, Ministry of Education
Prof. Christine Kisiedu, Information Systems, Dept of Library Studies, University of Ghana (Legon), and Chair Ghana Internet Society
Mohammed Sani Abdulai, Lecturer, Dept of Computer, Science University of Ghana (Legon)
Dr Okyere, Head of Department, Kwame Nkrumah University of Science and Technology (Kumasi)
Rev. Dr J.K. Oppong, Senior Lecturer, Kwame Nkrumah University of Science and Technology (Kumasi)
Dr Joseph Gogo, Director, Science and Technology Policy Research Institute (CSIR/STEPRI)
George Essegbey, Scientific Secretary, Science and Technology Policy Research Institute (CSIR/STEPRI)

Tanzania

July 1999

Edward Mallango, Human Resources Director, TTCL
Priscilla Chilipweli, Acting Director Network Development, TTCL
Asenath Mpatwa, Director of Privatisation, TTCL
F. Stefano, Head Regulatory Interface Unit formerly Head of Design Engineering, TTCL
Toby Jack, Acting Technical Manager, Mobitel (Tanzania) Ltd
Azlan Bin Abd. Wahab, Chief Technical Officer Network Division, TRITEL
Said S. Abdullah, Deputy General Manager, Datel Tanzania Ltd
Salum Akida, Head of Operations, Datel Tanzania Ltd
Greg Almeida, Operations Manager, East Africa, Afsat Communications Ltd
Heinrich Nothnagel, General Manager East Africa, Afsat Communications Ltd
Abdallah Mnende, General Manager, Wilken Afsat Tanzania Ltd
Charles Ogutu, General Manager, Africa On-Line (Tanzania) Ltd
R. Ng'humbi, Director and founder, Planetel Communication Ltd
Steve Mworia, Chairman and founder, Computer Corporation of Tanzania Ltd
Andrew Mpaplika, Director Telecommunications Development, TCC
Goodluck Medeye, Chief Personnel and Admin, TCC
Eng. E.N. Olekambainei, Communications and Transport Specialist, former Director General TCC, Ministry of Communications and Transport
Prof. Chambega, University of Dar es Salaam, Dept of Electrical Engineering
Prof. M. Luhanga, Vice Chancellor and Chair of Electrical Engineering, University of Dar es Salaam, member of Board TTCL, University of Dar es Salaam
Dr Titus Mteleka, Director of Science and Technology Policy, Ministry of Science and Technology
Enock Yonazi, Principal Scientific Officer, National Council on Science and Technology COSTECH
Prof. Benno Ndulu, Technical Specialist, World Bank Resident Mission
Prof. Sam Wangwe, Executive Director, Economic and Social Research Foundation (ESRF)

South Africa

Aug. 1999
Myron Keller, Executive Wireless Technology, Telkom SA Ltd
Gabrielle Celli, Executive Regulatory, Planning and Support, Telkom SA Ltd
Paula Doublin, Executive, Centre for Learning, Telkom SA Ltd
Victor Booysen, Executive Human Resources, Telkom SA Ltd
Zolisa Masiza, Legal and Regulatory Affairs, Transtel
Mlamli Booi, Company Director and networking specialist, Zakheni Communications Strategies cc. (Z-Comms)

Sept. 1999
Wanda Miles-Davis, Executive, Employment Equity and Affirmative Action Human Resources, Telkom SA Ltd
Dr Angus Hay, Divisional Manager, Technology, Transtel Mobile Communications
Alf Karrim, Managing Director, Orbicom Pty Ltd
Soraya Millen, Strategic Support Executive, Orbicom
Dr Sebiletso Matabane, Chief Executive Officer, Sentech
Deon Conradie, Manager Business Development, Sentech
Suresh Maharaj, Manager Human Resource Development, Sentech

Oct. 1999
Grant Theis, Strategy Director, UU-Net (SA) Pty Ltd
Khaya Dlukulu, General Manager Africa, ICO Global Communications
Thabo Makhake, Acting Head of Economic Planning, SATRA
Isaak Coetzee, Manager, Economics, SATRA
Eddie Funde, Deputy Chairperson, Councillor, SATRA
Siphiso Dabengwa, Managing Director , MTN SA Ltd
Adu Zeh, Group Executive Network Group, MTN South Africa
Dave Smith, Chief Engineer, Transmission , ESKOM
Ron Coney, Head Telecommunications, ESKOM Enterprises
Dr Rocky Skeef, Manager THRIP Programme, National Research Foundation

Nov 1999
Thomas Beale, Head Policy and Regulatory, Vodacom Pty Ltd South Africa
Jean-Marie Blanchard, Regional Director Middle East & Africa, Alcatel
Ian Braid, Strategic Planning, Altech Telecommunications Ltd (AAT)
Mokgubudi Masilela, Divisional Manager, Business Development, Siemens Telecommunications (PTY) Ltd
Hennie Huisman, Director, Marketing and Sales, Lucent Technologies

Sept 2000
Christer Hohenthal, Managing Director, Ericsson South Africa Ltd

Oct 2000
Barry Vlok, Head of Engineering Services, Vodacom South Africa
Lydia Schmidt, Human Resource Development Manager, Vodacom South Africa
Barry Blackburn, Sales Director, Vodacom South Africa

A1.2 INTERVIEW GUIDES

Interview Guide for Firms and Public Sector Officials

Technological capabilities are defined in this research very broadly as:

> a collection of skills, knowledge, aptitudes and attitudes which confer the ability
> to operate, to understand, to change and to create production processes.

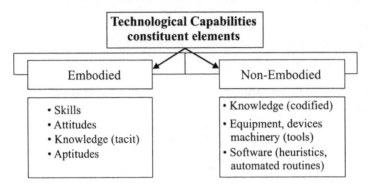

The activities that firms undertake to organize individual elements of technological capability into a systemic integrated and directed effort are included in the definition and are considered to be important. Further, this research assumes that development of organizational capability is a vital element of technological capability building since it is likely that firms that possess organizational capabilities are better able to transform elements of technological capability into meaningful and desired outcomes. Elements of organizational capability would include team effectiveness, clarity of organizational goals and purposes, effective resource allocation and implementation processes, responsiveness to external environment, etc. The definition also takes into account, that the elements of capabilities can take various forms, that is they can be codified (formalized and documented) or can be tacit (non-formal, transferred and exchanged without use of documentation). This research has two main aims:

- to improve understanding of the nature of learning and technological capability building (TCB) processes under conditions of dramatic industry restructuring and institutional development; and
- to produce research findings and recommendations that contribute to making improvements in firm-level effectiveness in TCB in the telecommunications industry, through design and implementation of regulatory and policy initiatives and firm strategies.

The research results will make a contribution to the theory and practice of operation and regulation of telecommunications companies in developing countries, where there are many challenges including the need to improve the ability to cope with and respond to rapid technological change.

> *This interview guide documents the questions asked of different types of respondents (managers in telecommunications companies, policy makers, regulators, academics and civil servants in capability development organisations). Questions are intended to cover many aspects of the core research problem and are asked to elicit responses that can be compared. The guide is used, as is common in elite interviews, to provide a frame for a conversation in which the researcher probes, asks basic questions and ensures smooth flow of information gathering. Not all questions are asked of each respondent. Question order will vary depending on the interview situation. Statements/questions that are italicized, are notes for the interviewer to follow-up when the basic question does not elicit sufficient information. The guide is in three main sections: an introductory context setting section and one for each main research question. The introductory page describing the purpose of the interview was given to all respondents, including information giving the institutional affiliation of the researcher.*

UNDERSTANDING THE PROCESS OF BUILDING TECHNOLOGICAL CAPABILITY IN PRODUCTION OF TELECOMMUNICATIONS SERVICES

1   Does the definition of technological capability (TC) provided adequately capture your understanding of the concept? Are there any other elements of TC which you view as being important? Do you have any other preliminary comments on how technological capability building works in the context of your organization, and how this should be taken account of in the definition of TC?

2   What in your view, are the most important technological capabilities required by firms operating as telecommunications service providers?
   - *Introduce specific areas such as skills of employees, access to up-to-date technical specifications.*

3   What are the main processes and/or mechanisms used for acquiring technological capabilities?
   - *Interviewer gives some of the standard and most common used types and asks whether any of these are used.*

4   If there are different processes, how are they ranked in terms of importance, frequency of use and effectiveness?

5   Do you believe that your ranking of the most important process of TCB would be shared by others (in your firm, in the government (regulator/policy bodies etc.)?

6   What are the main incentives for firms to invest in TCB? How does your

company benefit from undertaking TCB? Are there any measures used to quantify this?

7   Does your firm have a budget for TCB activities? If yes, what is the size of this budget. If no, what is your estimate of annual expenditure on activities related to TCB activities.
    • *Interviewer seeks to get detailed information (in writing) on composition of TCB budget, e.g. training budget.*

8   Do you vary the process for TCB depending on the type of capability you are trying to acquire? Are there many different types of TCB processes or a main one, e.g. training staff, using vendors of equipment?

9   Can you describe in more detail the main features of technological capability building in your organization, indicating whether strategies have shifted over time?
    • *For this question, it will be important to distinguish between perceptions of strategic behaviour held by middle and senior management staff.*

10 How are TCB activities organized in your firm? Is there centralized planning for these activities within your organization, or is decision making decentralized? Please give details of lines or responsibility and reporting, and the skills and qualifications of main decision makers responsible for TCB activities. Has this organization changed over time? Does it depend on the type of TCB activity?

11 What would you regard as being the most important gaps in technological capability in your firm?
    • *When this question is posed to regulators/policy makers the emphasis is on these public officials giving their view for the sector as a whole.*

12 What are the main challenges your organization faces in building technological capability?

13 What are some of the most important sources used for acquiring elements of technological capability, outside of your organization? How are these ranked in order of importance, effectiveness, frequency of use?

14 Is the process of TCB continuous or are there significant variations over time, in level of attention, effort and expenditure on TCB activities? If there are variations, what accounts for these variations, and what internal/external events lead to acceleration in TCB activities?

MANAGING RELATIONSHIPS WITH SUPPLIERS OF EQUIPMENT AND SERVICES

1   How much has your organization invested in WLL over the last year, and how much do you plan to invest over the next 5 years? How is that expenditure shared among the suppliers?

- *What percentage share of total capital investment/network expansion budget does this represent?*
2 How do you select WLL suppliers? What criteria are used to compare competing suppliers? Were the different criteria given weights or were they considered to be equally important?
3 Did you use a formal tender process in selecting your chosen suppliers?
4 How important was price and financing options in your selection decision?
5 Please consider these aspects of quality of supplier and rank in order of importance.
   - wide range of services/technology products offered by a single firm (scope);
   - specific functionality or technological superiority of the product/service offering;
   - demonstrated depth of technological knowledge;
   - novelty of the product/service offering;
   - track record in countries and/or companies similar to your own;
   - ability to serve small or special-purpose markets, e.g. topography requirements;
   - speed of delivering system components (performance guarantees);
   - timeliness of suppliers response to queries, requests for technical assistance;
   - local presence of representatives or branch offices.
6 Does your firm consider acquiring technological capability to be an objective of effective management of relationships with suppliers? Has your firm used supplier relationships in TCB?

This section of questions focuses on relationships with suppliers as a source of technological capability. If firms have indicated that this is NOT an important or frequently used source, the interviewer will ask questions to assess the level of experience of the respondents with this source and will elicit views on why this source proved to yield unsatisfactory results. For respondents who have experience of TCB activities through supplier management, the following questions apply.
7 Can you describe in more detail how your organization uses supplier relationships to build technological capability? Have these strategies changed over time?
8 How is the supplier management process organized in your firm? Is there centralized planning for these activities within your organization, or is decision-making decentralized? Please give details of lines or responsibility and reporting, and the skills and qualifications of main decision makers responsible for 'supplier management'.

9   What would you regard as being the most important gaps (if any) in the technological capability needed for successful implementation of WLL systems?
     • *When this question is posed to regulators/policy makers the emphasis is on these public officials giving their view for the sector as a whole.*
10   What strategies does your firm use to acquire technological capabilities through suppliers of WLL systems? What are the critical success factors in this process?
11   Would you expect 'effective supplier management' to have any impact on the following, and if so how?
     • access to technical information;
     • staff time devoted to managing relationship with suppliers;
     • staff time spent of study visits, technical training;
     • supplier provided in-house technical training, overseas technical training courses;
     • expenditure on training.
     Does your firm have any other expectations of effective supplier management?
12   Does your company have any plans for making significant changes in how it manages relationships with suppliers of WLL systems? What have been some of the significant outcomes of past changes?
13   What are the main challenges your organization faces in using supplier relationships as a means of building technological capability?
14   Where there have been problems with using supplier relationships for TCB, what in your view are the main causes of those difficulties?

MANAGING RELATIONSHIPS WITH REGULATORY BODIES AND THE TECHNOLOGICAL CAPABILITY BUILDING PROCESS

1   What is your view on whether or not regulatory bodies should be proactive in attempting to influence TCB in their client organizations?
2   If you believe that regulators and policy makers should seek to influence TCB in firms, which if any, of the following actions should they take:
     • provide subsidies to firms undertaking TCB expenditure;
     • undertake direct expenditure on TCB activity;
     • provide direct funding to organisations which build TCs such as national research labs, science and research councils etc.;
     • provide other support activities (technical information sourcing, technical assistance, funding scholarships, building training centres, disseminate policy research findings providing evidence of the benefits of TCB;

- introduce performance requirements into operator/service provider licences;
- introduce performance requirements into supplier contracts.

Are there other actions which regulators and policy makers can take to influence TCB in firms?

3 Are there any potential negative impacts of regulatory bodies taking steps to influence TCB? How should these dangers be minimized?

4 Does the legal mandate of the regulatory body in your country permit taking steps to influence technological capability building? Please give examples of how this mandate might be implemented.

5 Do the policy objectives for the telecommunications sector support technological capability building activities?

6 Where does TCB rank in order of priority for the sector regulator in your country?
   - *Is there an understanding and/or desire to include capability building among policy objectives for the telecoms sector?*

7 Are you aware of any specific clauses in legislative or policy documents that give the regulatory bodies powers to be active in promoting TCB?

8 How do policy makers and regulators currently attempt to promote TCB in the telecommunications sector? What are the expected outcomes from any of these efforts to promote TCB in client firms?

9 Which organizations are involved in these activities? How are the responsibilities divided among these various organizations?

10 There are many new entrants into the industry in your country. In your view, at what stage would actions to promote TCB be most effective: prequalification, bid evaluation, issue of licence conditions, and, finally, on-going review of licence conditions and performance evaluation. Can you comment on whether you are aware of the regulatory body in your country taking steps to influence TCB at any of these stages of the licensing process?

11 Please provide more details about how policy intervention or regulatory instruments have been used to influence TCB by firms? Please provide details of the nature of the intervention, timing, the basis of your evaluation and any other comments and documentation. Did these interventions produce the expected outcomes, and if not, why not?

12 What are the major bottlenecks faced by policy/regulatory organizations in attempting to successfully influence TCB by client firms?

13 How can the bottlenecks identified be removed?

14 Do these actions require legislative change? Organizational reform or other fundamental change?

15 What capabilities must regulatory bodies possess if they are to be effective in these interventions?

16 What, in your view, are the important elements of a relationship between policymakers/regulators and their client firms that would lead to greater TCB?

Interview Guide for Suppliers of Telecommunication Equipment and Services

Questions to corroborate information from telecommunications operators
1   Basic information (company details and market data)
    1.1   Volume of sales in Africa and as % of total
    1.2   Average size of contract in African region
    1.3   Average duration of project implementation for negotiation to deployment
2   What is the distribution of your customer base, as a percentage, across the following categories:
- Telecommunication operators (fixed line operators);
- VANS (value-added service providers, private network solutions companies, data communications companies);
- Mobile network operators;
- Other.
3   What criteria are used by your customers in the tender processes used to select suppliers?
    3.1   Are these criteria given equal weight?
4   What aspects of your service offering, do you believe to be most important in securing contracts?
    4.1   How important is pricing terms in your customers' selection processes?
    4.2   What about the ability to offer financing options for your customers?

5   What are the most important elements of quality in your service/product offering?
6   How would you rate the level of technological knowledge possessed by your customers?
- Less than adequate
- Adequate
- More than adequate
- Superior
7   What are the most important areas of knowledge, skills and other capabilities required by your customers, if they are to make effective use of your equipment and services?
8   Are there any other elements of technological capability (as defined in the introductory text), which are important for customers making effective

use of your services and equipment?

- *Interviewer reminds about categories of embodied and non-embodied capabilities, e.g. attitude, aptitude, organizational routines, specific equipment and software systems.*

9   What role does your company play, if any, in enhancing the capabilities of your customers?

9.1 How is this implemented?

9.2 What have been the successes and/or challenges of this type of interaction?

10 In your view should equipment and services suppliers to telecommunications companies be pro-active in technological capability building TCB activities for the sector as a whole? If yes, how do you play this role? Do you play this role in response to any regulatory requirements?

- *Ask about interaction and relationships with R&D centres, universities, technical training colleges.*

11 How does your company develop and build its own internal technological capabilities?

12 Has your company's strategy with respect to technology transfer to/capability development of your customers changed over time? What accounts for these changes?

13 How do your customers organize their supplier interface? Is there a single point of contact with central control or is it decentralized with multiple points of contact? From your perspective, which structure of interface is more effective, and why?

14 What are the main factors which lead to effective supplier–customer interface?

15 What are some of the main challenges you face in effectively offering products and services to African telecommunications firms?

16 Should there be regulatory rules governing your relationships with customers, which, for example, would specify and guide on technology transfer and capability development?

17   What in your view are the main advantages of WLL as an access technology for delivering rural telecommunications?

A1.3 SUMMARY PROFILES OF TELECOMMUNICATION MARKET STRUCTURE

UGANDA

Policy-making authority: Ministry of Works, Transportation and Communications
Regulator: Uganda Communications Commission
Mobile cellular operators: Celtel, MTN Uganda Consortium – second national operator
Fixed network operator: Uganda Posts and Telecommunication Corporation – state-owned national operator.

Liberalization index (1998)	
Local fixed service	Monopoly
Long distance fixed service	Monopoly
International fixed service	Monopoly
Leased lines	Competitive
Mobile cellular service	Monopoly
Data service	Competitive

Source: ITU/BDT (1998a).

Country data	1996	1997	1998	1999
Population ('000)	20,039	20,296	20,554	21,143
Key telecommunication data	1996	1997	1998	1999
Main telephone lines in operation	47,927	54,829	56,919	57,100
Main lines per 100 inhabitants	0.2	0.3	0.3	0.3
% of digital main lines	75.2	75.5	90.6	
% of main lines equip. for IDD	11	n/a	n/a	
Cellular mobile subscribers	4,000	5,000	30,000	56,400
Analog cellular subscribers	0.0	0.0	0.0	
Digital cellular subscribers	4,000	5,000	30,000	56,400
Public packet data network subscribers	1996	n/a	n/a	
Public pay phones	799	1,158	1,333	
International outgoing telephone traffic (million minutes)	5.8	6.3	6.4	
International incoming telephone traffic (million minutes)	13.7	14.4	17.9	
Estimated modems in use	n/a	n/a	n/a	
Number of internet hosts	17	30	113	
Telecom revenue (US$ million)	43. 4	34.4	32.8	

Source: ITU/BDT (2000).

GHANA

Policy-making authority: Ministry of Transport and Communications
Regulator: National Communications Authority
Mobile cellular operators: Mobitel (analogue mobile services)
Celltel (analog mobile services)
Scancom (GSM mobile services)
Fixed network operators: Ghana Telecom – partially privatized in April 1997. SNO-ACG Telesystems

Liberalization index (1998)	
Local fixed service	Competitive
Long distance fixed service	Competitive
International fixed service	Competitive
Leased lines	Competitive
Mobile cellular service	n/a
Data service	Competitive

Source: ITU/BDT (1998a).

Country data	1996	1997	1998	1999
Population ('000)	17,800	18,500	19,200	19,700
Key telecommunication data	1996	1997	1998	
Main telephone lines in operation	77,886	105,534	144,218	158,600
Main lines per 100 inhabitant	0.4	0.6	0.8	0.8
% of digital main lines	90.9	93.8	70	
% of main lines equip. for IDD	n/a	n/a	n/a	
Cellular mobile subscribers	12,766	21,866	41,800	70,000
Analog cellular subscribers	12,766	n/a	n/a	
Digital cellular subscribers	0.0	n/a	n/a	
Public packet data network subscribers	n/a	n/a	n/a	
Public pay phones	453	483	1,815	
International outgoing telephone traffic (million minutes)	20.8	21.9	n/a	
International incoming telephone traffic (million minutes)	64.0	79.2	n/a	
Estimated modems in use	n/a	n/a	n/a	
Number of internet hosts	203	252	192	
Telecom revenue (US$ million)	99.9	132.9	145.9	

Source: ITU/BDT (2000).

TANZANIA

Policy-making authority: Ministry of Communications and Transport
Regulator: Tanzania Communications Commission (TCC)
Mobile cellular operators: Zanzibar Telecom Ltd; IC Tanzania Ltd; TRI Telecommunication Tanzania Ltd
Fixed network operator: Tanzania Telecommunication Company Ltd, the corporate state-owned national operator.

Liberalization index (1998)	
Local fixed service	Partial Competition
Long distance fixed service	Partial Competition
International fixed service	Partial Competition
Leased lines	Partial Competition
Mobile cellular service	Competitive
Data service	Competitive

Source: ITU/BDT (1998a).

Country data	1996	1997	1998	1999
Population ('000)	30,799	31,506	32,102	32,792
Key telecommunication data	1996	1997	1998	
Main telephone lines in operation	92,760	105,095	121,769	149,600
Main lines per 100 inhabitant	0.3	0.3	0.4	0.5
% of digital main lines	64.7	72.5	82.3	
% of main lines equip. for IDD	n/a	n/a	n/a	
Cellular mobile subscribers	9,038	20,200	37,940	51,000
Analog cellular subscribers	6,338	14,000	25,940	
Digital cellular subscribers	2,700	6,200	12,000	
Public packet data network subscribers	n/a	n/a	n/a	
Public pay phones	579	494	706	
International outgoing telephone traffic (million minutes)	6.4	10.2	111.7	
International incoming telephone traffic (million minutes)	20.1	22.7	22.1	
Estimated modems in use	n/a	n/a	n/a	
Number of internet hosts	3	25.5	129	
Telecom revenue (US$ million)	73.1	98.7	109.9	

Source: *ITU/BDT (2000).*

SOUTH AFRICA

Policy-making authority: Ministry for Posts, Telecommunication and Broadcasting
Regulator: South African Telecommunication Regulatory Authority (SATRA)
Mobile operators: Vodacom; MTN
Fixed network operator: Telkom SA Ltd, the private national operator.

Liberalization index (1998)	
Local fixed service	Monopoly
Long distance fixed service	Monopoly
International fixed service	Monopoly
Leased lines	Competitive
Mobile cellular service	Competitive
Data service	Competitive

Source: ITU/BDT (1998a).

Country data	1996	1997	1998	1999
Population ('000)	42,390	41,543	40,713	
Key telecommunication data	1996	1997	1998	1999
Main telephone lines in operation ('000)	4,258	4,645	5,075	5,492
Main lines per 100 inhabitants	10	11.2	12.5	13.77
% of digital main lines	74	82	n/a	
% of main lines equip. for IDD	n/a	n/a	n/a	
Cellular mobile subscribers ('000)	953	1,600	2,500	5,269
Analog cellular subscribers	0.0	0.0	0.0	
Digital cellular subscribers ('000)	953	1,600	2,500	5,269
Public packet data network subscribers	21,006	n/a	n/a	
Public pay phones	94,937	127,272	153,476	
International outgoing telephone traffic (million minutes)	353	469	n/a	
International incoming telephone traffic (million minutes)	385	450	n/a	
Estimated modems in use	n/a	n/a	n/a	
Number of internet hosts	99,284	122,025	144,445	
Telecom revenue (US$ million)	3,802	4,375	5,971	

Source: ITU/BDT (2000).

APPENDIX TO CHAPTER 3

Definition of TCB mechanisms

Code	Summary description of mechanism
M1	Recruitment of university, technical-vocational school and college graduates
M2	Implement formalized graduate recruitment programmes
M3	Targeted recruitment of high-level specialists
M4	Targeted recruitment of overseas nationals
M5	Offering internships to university students
M6	Implementing long duration induction programmes (pupillages, and/or apprenticeships) for recruits into technical functions
M7	Organizing short-term induction programmes for new recruits
M8	Sponsorship of university undergrad and postgrad training through scholarships, bursaries and study loans
M9	Organizing formal in-house training (classroom-based)
M10	Providing informal on-the-job training opportunities (non-formal and experiential)
M11	Using distant learning programmes for staff training
M12	Organizing training of trainers programmes
M13	Improving supervision of technical recruits
M14	Improve administrative co-ordination of training programmes
M15	Implementing programmes to maintain and develop cadre of technological specialists
M16	Making use of mentoring programmes
M17	Implementing formal, individualized training plans/programmes
M18	Using individualized career development programmes
M19	Integrating performance-related remuneration systems linked to achievement on TCB activities
M20	Organizing leadership development programmes
M21	Organizing change management programmes
M22	Using formal knowledge management and intellectual capital management systems and programmes
M23	Creating conditions for informal learning, providing support facilities, e.g. in-house libraries, documentation centres, resource centres and access to Internet
M24	Providing access to technical journals, periodicals, handbooks
M25	Developing standard operating procedures and documentation of technical processes

Code	Summary description of mechanism
M26	Implementing cultural/organizational structure, change to support TCB, e.g. assigning TCB to function, creating specific job functions & open styles of leadership, encouraging and supporting experimentation and learning
M27	Line management responsibility for implementing TCB objectives
M28	Introducing formal QM systems, e.g. ISO-9000, ISO-1400
M29	Establishing TCB expenditure targets and processes for monitoring spend on TCB activities
M30	Running staff rotation programmes
M31	Integrating TCB objectives in strategic planning processes
M32	Maintaining active involvement with international industry associations
M33	Conducting formal technology needs, training needs, staff skills and customer technology requirements assessments
M34	Conducting formal active technology search/evaluation processes
M35	Implementing skills transfer projects during commissioning and installation of equipment
M37	Undertaking pilot projects and field trials for network equipment
M38	Participating in training courses delivered by suppliers of telecommunications equipment & services offered locally
M39	Participating in training courses delivered by suppliers of telecommunications equipment & services offered overseas
M41	Making active use of technical support hot-lines, vendor presentations and access to technology upgrades and technical information from suppliers
M42	Participation in training programmes offered by bilateral programmes USTTI, TEMIC, TELIA academy, UK Academy of Training, Cable and Wireless, BT training programmes.
M43	Participation in workshops, seminars, and conferences offered by international organizations (e.g. ITU, CTO)
M44	Participation in training courses offered by private sector training providers, e.g. Microsoft certified courses, business process reengineering courses and leadership training
M45	Participation in ITU Study Groups; technical assistance from ITU
M46	Participation in regional training programmes, e.g. AFRALTI & ATU (formerly PATU)
M47	Undertaking site visits to overseas telecom operators
M48	Attending trade-fairs and exhibitions

Code	Summary description of mechanism
M49	Undertaking short-term exchange visits to companies owned by strategic investors, joint venture partners and shareholders
M50	Undertaking long-term placement of staff with companies owned by strategic investors, joint venture partners and shareholders
M51	Participating in formal training programmes run by strategic investors, joint venture partners and shareholders overseas.
M52	Accessing technical skills from regional headquarters staff, staff of group headquarters and maintaining regular communication on technological issues across regional companies, group of companies. Contact included troubleshooting queries.
M53	Long-term placements/internships with other operators and suppliers of equipment
M54	Recruiting expatriate staff on contracts averaging 2–5 years in duration
M55	Recruiting experts on assignment 6 months to 1 year
M56	Recruiting experts on specialised short term consultancy assignments of less than 6 months in duration
M57	Formal skill transfer programmes to transfer skills from expatriate staff
M58	Carrying out TCB activities in partnership with local universities
M59	Establishing and maintaining contact with international universities (research, training and professional networking)
M60	Establishing and maintaining contact with local training institutes (technical and vocational colleges, 'Technikons')
M61	Maintaining capital investment levels for network modernization, technology upgrades, network and service range expansion.

Source: Author based on primary data.

APPENDIX TO CHAPTER 5

Key financial and operating data for African based suppliers

Variable	Altech Telecom (JV with Alcatel)	Siemens SA Ltd	Lucent SA Ltd	Ericsson SA Ltd
Employee base in telecoms	1,300	1,800	130 staff 1,500 contrac- tors	230
No engineers/technicians	480	n.a	n.a.	n.a.
Overall telecom revenues 1999	R3.0 b.	R2.9b.	n.a.	1.5b.
Revenues (WLL equip. & services) 1999	R1.2 b.	n.a.	R0.8b.	
Export sales	n.a.	5%	n.a.	20%
Av. size of WLL contract	n.a.	R50m.	10,000- 20,000 subs equiv. to US$15m.	n/a
Typical duration WLL project	2 years	6 months	3 years	n/a
Distribution of customer base %:				
Public fixed line operators	88	60	75	15
VANS operators		2		
Mobile communications providers	5	30	20	85
Other including exports and private corporate networks	7	8	5	
Manufacturing operations	Yes	Yes	No	Yes
Local R&D activity	Yes	Limited	No	Yes

Source: compiled by author based on primary and secondary data.
Notes: N = 4. n.a.= not available. n/a = not applicable.

The main lines of business for these firms are as follows:

Altech: production and sale of switching and routing products, transmission products and radio-based systems, including DECT subscriber terminals and base station container integration systems. The company also resells imported Alcatel equipment and offers technical support and repair services.

Siemens South Africa Ltd: provides network solutions for public network operators including equipment, systems infrastructure and integration services, enterprise solutions to the corporate sector, including equipment for PABXs, routers, hubs and call centre systems; technical services, including network planning, configuration, and testing, software development; and systems integration and technical support.

Lucent South Africa Ltd: presently offers wireless access technology systems including radio access and customer premises equipment, PABXs, WAN/LAN equipment and office cabling systems. Plans to expand range to include fixed line switching and transmission equipment and IT systems for telecommunication operators, including network management, billing and voice messaging systems.

Ericsson South Africa Ltd: is a provider of integrated telecommunication solutions, including transmission, GSM switching and base stations, energy systems, data-communication equipment and related professional services, including R&D, applications software, network operations services, technical training and project management. The company through its R&D and applications development centres offer design and development of intelligent networks and GSM services. The South African operating company manufactures power and microwave equipment.

APPENDIX TO CHAPTER 6

Summary of legislative and policy provisions for facilitating TCB in telecommunication firms in Uganda, Ghana, Tanzania and South Africa

Legislative & policy frame-work for public sector support of TCB in firms	Uganda	Ghana	Tanzania	South Africa
Telecom Legislation	Comms Act (1997)	Comms Act (1997)	Comms Act , TTCL Act (1993) Section 22.3	Telecom Act (1996) Section 2
Telecom policy		Nat'l Telecom Policy (1996)	Nat'l Telecom Policy (1997)	
Licence provisions in operators licences and performance agreements	*	*	*	*
General provisions in shareholders agreements	*	*		
Specific provisions in shareholder agreements	*	*		*
Clauses in overseas dev assistance & loan agreements	*	*	*	
Labour laws				Employment Equity Act (1999) & Skills Devlt. Act (1998)
Industrial development policy				Jnt Econ Devpt Agreement by Dept Trade & Industry
Immigration laws	*			

Source: compiled by author based on interviews, public domain and confidential secondary sources, including Republic of Uganda, 1997; Republic of Ghana, 1996; United Republic of Tanzania, 1993, 1997; Republic of South Africa 1996, 1997a,b, 1998, 1999; South African Regulatory Authority 1998; Telkom SA 1998, 1999; Essegebey and Atubra 1992; Frempong 1996, 1997; Kilaba 1996; Wangwe 1995b.

References

Abiodun, A.A. (1997), *Human and Institutional Capacity Building and Utilization in Science and Technology in Africa. Part One: An Appraisal of Our Performance to Date.* Abidjan, Cote D'Ivoire: United Nations Development Programme–Africa's Future.

Amsden, A. (1989), *Asia's Next Giant: South Korea and Late Industrialization*, Oxford: Oxford University Press.

Argyris, C. (1993a), *Knowledge for Action: A Guide to Overcoming Barriers to Organizational Change*, San Francisco: Jossey-Bass.

Argyris, C. (1993b), 'Seeking Truth and Actionable Knowledge: How the Scientific Method Inhibits Both', in C. Argyris (ed.), *On Organizational Learning*, Cambridge:MA: Blackwell pp. 286–94.

Argyris, C. (1993c), 'Teaching Smart People How to Learn', in R. Howard (ed.), *The Learning Imperative: Managing People for Continuous Innovation*, Boston, MA: Harvard Business School Press, pp. 177–94.

Argyris, C. (1996), 'Prologue: Towards a Comprehensive Theory of Management', in B. Moingeon and A. Edmondson (eds), *Organizational Learning and Competitive Advantage*, London: Sage, pp.1–6.

Argyris, C. and D. Schon (1978), *Organizational Learning*, Reading: MA: Addison-Wesley.

Argyris, C. and D. Schon (1996a), 'Turning the Researcher/Practitioner Relationship on Its Head', in C. Argyris and D. Schon (eds), *Organizational Learning II, Theory, Method and Practice*, Wokingham: Addison-Wesley, pp. 30–51.

Argyris, C. and D. Schon (1996b), *Organizational Learning II, Theory, Method and Practice*, Wokingham: Addison-Wesley.

Arrow, K. (1962), 'The Economic Implications of Learning by Doing', *Review of Economic Studies*, **29**(2): 155–73.

Baden-Fuller, C. and J.M. Stopford (1994), *Rejuvenating the Mature Business*, Boston, MA: Harvard Business School Press.

Barnett, W.P. and R. Burgleman (1996), 'Evolutionary Perspectives on Strategy', *Strategic Management Journal*, **17**: 5–19.

Barney, J. (1991), 'Firm Resources and Sustained Competitive Advantage', *Journal of Management*, **17**(1): 99–120.

Bell, M. (1984), '"Learning" and the Accumulation of Technological Capability', in M. Fransman and K. King (eds) *Technological Capability in the Third World*, London: Macmillan, pp. 187–209.

Bell, M. and K. Pavitt (1993), 'Accumulating Technological Capability in Developing Countries'. Paper presented at the World Bank Annual Conference on Development Economics 1992, Washington, DC.

Bell, M. and K. Pavitt (1997), 'Technological Accumulation and Industrial Growth: Contrasts between Developed and Developing Countries', in D. Archibugi and J. Michie (eds), *Technology, Globalisation and Economic Performance*, Cambridge:

Cambridge University Press, pp. 83–137.

Bhagavan, M.R. (ed.) (1997), *New Generic Technologies in Developing Countries*, London: Macmillan.

Brewster, C. (1991), *The Management of Expatriates*, London: Kogan Page (with Cranfield School of Management, Human Resource Research Centre).

Brock, G.W. (1981), *The Telecommunications Industry: The Dynamics of Market Structure*, Cambridge, MA: Harvard University Press.

Brusoni, S. and A. Prencipe (2001), 'Unpacking the Black Box of Modularity: Technologies, Products and Organizations', *Industrial and Corporate Change*, **10**(1), 179–205.

Carlsson, B. and R. Stankiewicz (1991), 'On the Nature, Function and Composition of Technological Systems', *Journal of Evolutionary Economics*, **1**: 93–118.

Chiesa, V., R. Manzini and A. Rangone (1996), 'Assessing and Monitoring Strategic Competence', in J. Butler and A. Piccaluga (eds), *Knowledge, Technology and Innovative Organisations*, Milan: Geurini E Associati, pp. 89–104.

Cohen, W., and Levinthal, D. (1989), 'Innovation and Learning:The Two Faces of R&D', *Economic Journal*, **99**, 560–96.

Cohen, W.M. and D.A. Levinthal (1990), 'Absorptive Capacity: A New Perspective on Learning and Innovation', *Administrative Science Quarterly*, **35**: 128–52.

Cooper, C. (1980), 'Policy Interventions for Technological Innovation in Developing Countries', World Bank Staff Working Paper No. 441, December, World Bank, Washington, DC.

Cooper, C. (1991), 'Are Innovation Studies on Industrialised Economies Relevant to Technology Policy in Developing Countries?', UNU/INTECH Working Paper No.3, Maastricht.

Cooper, C. (1994), 'Science and Technology in Africa under Conditions of Economic Crisis and Structural Adjustment', UNU/INTECH Working Paper No.4, Maastricht.

Crandall, R.W., and K. Flamm (eds.) (1989), *Changing the Rules: Technological Change, International Competition, and Regulation in Communications*, Washington, DC: The Brookings Institution.

Davies, A. (1996), 'Innovation in Large Technical Systems: The Case of Telecommunications', *Industrial and Corporate Change*, **5**(4): 1143–80.

Davies, A. (1997), 'The Life Cycle of a Complex Product System, *International Journal of Innovation Management*, **1**(3): 229-56.

Davies, A. and T. Brady (2000), 'Organisational Capabilities and Learning in Complex Product Systems:Towards Repeatable Solutions', Unpublished monograph, SPRU/CENTRIM, Brighton.

Dodgson, M. (1993), 'Organizational Learning: A Review of Some Literatures', *Organization Studies*, **14**(3): 375–93.

Dosi, G., C. Freeman, R.R. Nelson, G. Silverberg and L. Soete (eds) (1988), *Technical Change and Economic Theory*, London: Pinter.

Dosi, G., R.R. Nelson and S. Winter (2000a), 'Introduction: The Nature and Dynamics of Organizational Capabilities', in G. Dosi, R.R. Nelson and S. Winter (eds), *The Nature and Dynamics of Organisational Capabilities*, Oxford: Oxford University Press, pp. 1–22.

Dosi, G., R.R. Nelson and S. Winter (2000b), *The Nature and Dynamics of Organisational Capabilities*, Oxford: Oxford University Press.

Dutrenit, G. (2000), *Learning and Knowledge Management in the Firm*, Cheltenham: Edward Elgar.

Economist Intelligence Unit (1999a), 'Ghana Country Report' (Client services on-line report available at http://www.eiu.com), dated 12 July 1999, Economist Intelligence Unit, [last accessed 24/02/2000].

Economist Intelligence Unit (1999b), 'South Africa Country Report' (Client services on-line report available at http://www.eiu.com), dated 12 November 1999, Economist Intelligence Unit [last accessed 24/02/2000].

Economist Intelligence Unit (1999c), 'Tanzania Country Report' (Client services on-line report available at http://www.eiu.com), dated 12 November 1999, Economist Intelligence Unit [last accessed 24/02/2000].

Economist Intelligence Unit (1999d), 'Uganda Country Report' (Client services on-line report available at http://www.eiu.com), dated 26 November 1999, Economist Intelligence Unit [last accessed 24/02/2000].

Edmondson, A. and B. Moingeon (1996), 'When to Learn How and When to Learn Why: Appropriate Organizational Learning Processes as a Source of Competitive Advantage', in B. Moingeon and A. Edmondson (eds), *Organizational Learning and Competitive Advantage*, London: Sage, pp. 17–37.

Edquist, C. (ed.) (1997), *Systems of Innovation: Technology, Institutions and Organisation*, London: Pinter.

Enos, J. (1991), *The Creation of Technological Capability in Developing Countries*, London and New York: Pinter.

Enos, J. (1995), *In Pursuit of Science and Technology in Sub-Saharan Africa: The Impact of Structural Adjustment Programmes*, London: Routledge and UNU-Press.

Enos, J. and W.H. Park (1988), *The Adoption and Diffusion of Imported Technology – The Case of Korea*, London: Routledge.

Ernst, D. and B.-Å. Lundvall (1997), 'Information Technology in the Learning Economy - Challenges for Developing Countries', DRUID Working Paper No. 97-12, Aalborg, Denmark.

Ernst, D., L. Mytleka and T. Ganiatsos (eds) (1998), *Technological Capabilities and Export Success: Case Studies from Asia*, London: Routledge.

Essegbey, G. and W. Atubra (1996), 'The State of Ghana Telecommunications and Prospects for Private Enterprise', unpublished paper presented at seminar organized by Institute of Social Sciences, Technical University of Denmark under the Technology Assessment Project sponsored by DANIDA, Lyngby, Denmark, November.

Forje, J. (1991), 'The Three Decades of Africa's Science and Technology Policy Development', in M. Huq, P. Bhatt, C. Lewis and A. Shibli (eds), *Science, Technology and Development : North–South Co-operation*, London: Frank Cass, pp. 107–115.

Foss, N. (1999), 'Incomplete Contracts and Economic Organization: Brian Loasby and the Theory of the Firm', in S. Dow and P. Earl (eds), *Contingency,Complexity and the Theory of the Firm. Essays in Honour of Brian J. Loasby, Vol. II*, Cheltenham: Edward Elgar, pp.40–66.

Fransman, M. (2000), 'Evolution of the Telecommunications Industry into the Internet Age', Unpublished seminar manuscript, presented at University of Sussex, 24 October.

Freeman, C. (1995), 'The "National System of Innovation" in Historical Perspective', *Cambridge Journal of Economics*, **19**: 5–24.

Freeman, C. and C. Perez (1988), 'Structural Crises of Adjustment: Business Cycles and Investment Behaviour', in G. Dosi, C. Freeman, R. Nelson, G. Silverberg, and L. Soete (eds), *Technical Change and Economic Theory*, London: Pinter, pp. 38–66.

Freeman, C. and L. Soete (1997), *The Economics of Industrial Innovation* (3rd edn), London: Pinter.

Frempong, G. (1996), 'Developing Telecommunications in Ghana', *IEEE Technology and Society*, **Spring**: 23–31.

Frempong, G. (1997), 'Assessing Ghana's Telecommunication Policy', *IEEE Technology and Society*,**Winter 1997/98**: 37–45.

Garvin, D. (1993), 'Building a Learning Organization', *Harvard Business Review*, **July–August**: 79–91.

Girvan, N. and G. Marcelle (1990), 'Overcoming Technological Dependency: The Case of Electric Arc (Jamaica) Ltd, a Small Firm in a Small Developing Country', *World Development*, **18**: 91–107.

Hobday, M. (1990), *Telecommunications in Developing Countries: The Challenge from Brazil*, London and New York: Routledge.

Hobday, M. (1995), *Innovation in East Asia: The Challenge to Japan*, Camberley: Edward Elgar.

Hoffman, K. and N. Girvan (1990), *Managing International Technology Transfer: A Strategic Approach for Developing Countries*, Ottawa: IDRC.

Hughes, T.P. (1987), 'The Evolution of Large Technical Systems', in W.E. Bijker, T.P. Hughes and T.J. Pinch (eds), *The Social Construction of Technological Systems*, Cambridge, MA: MIT Press, pp. 51–82.

ITU/BDT (1996), *The Africa Green Paper Telecommunications Policies for Africa*, Geneva: International Telecommunication Union.

ITU/BDT (1998a), 'Chapter 2: Africa', in ITU/BDT (ed.), *General Trends in Telecommunications Restructuring 1998: World Volume 1*, Geneva: International Telecommunication Union.

ITU/BDT (1998b), *General Trends in Telecommunications Restructuring 1998: Africa Volume II*, Geneva: International Telecommunication Union.

ITU/BDT (1998c), *African Telecommunication Indicators*, Geneva: International Telecommunication Union.

ITU/BDT (2000), 'World Telecommunication Indicators', available at http://www.itu.int/publications/online.htm [last accessed 24/02/2000].

Johnson, B., E. Lorenz and B.-Å. Lundvall (2002), 'Why All This Fuss About Codified and Tacit Knowledge?, *Industrial and Corporate Change*, **11**(2): 245-62.

Jovanovic, B. (1995), 'Learning and Growth', NBER Working Paper Series, Working Paper 5383, NBER, Cambridge, MA.

Katz, J. (ed.) (1987), *Technology Generation in Latin American Manufacturing Industries*, London: Macmillan.

Kilaba, J. (1996) 'Telecommunication Sector Reform in Tanzania', CTI Working Paper No. 16, Centre for Tele-information, Lyngby, Denmark.

Kim, L. (1997), *From Imitation to Innovation. The Dynamics of Korea's Technological Learning*, Boston, MA: Harvard Business School Press.

Kim, L. (1999), 'Building Technological Capability for Industrialisation: Analytical Frameworks and Korea's Experience', *Industrial and Corporate Change*, **8**(1): 111–35.

Kim, L., and R.R. Nelson (eds) (2000), *Technology Learning and Innovation*, Cambridge: Cambridge University Press.

Kuada, J. (1994), *Managerial Behaviour in Ghana and Kenya - A Cultural Perspective*, Aalborg: Aalborg University Press.

Kumar, N. (1996), 'Foreign Direct Investments and Technology Transfers in Development: A Perspective on Recent Literature', UNU/INTECH Discussion Paper # 960, UNU/INTECH, Maastricht.

Lall, S. (1987), *Learning to Industrialise: The Acquisition of Technological Capability by India*, London: Macmillan.

Lall, S. (1992), 'Technological Capabilities and Industrialization', *World Development*, **20**(2): 165–86.

Lall, S. (1997), 'Policies for Industrial Competitiveness in Developing Countries: Learning from Asia', unpublished report, prepared for the Commonwealth Secretariat.

Leonard-Barton, D. (1988), 'Implementation as Mutual Adaptation of Technology and Organization', *Research Policy*, **17**: 251–67.

Leonard-Barton, D. (1992a), 'Core Capabilities and Core Rigidities', *Strategic Management Journal*, **13**: 111–25.

Leonard-Barton, D. (1992b), 'The Factory as a Learning Laboratory', *Sloan Management Review*, Fall: 23–38.

Leonard-Barton, D. (1995), *Wellsprings of Knowledge: Building and Sustaining Sources of Innovation*, Boston: MA: Harvard Business School Press.

Levinthal, D. (2000), 'Organizational Capabilities in Complex Worlds', in G. Dosi, R.R. Nelson and S. Winter (eds), *The Nature and Dynamics of Organisational Capabilities*, Oxford: Oxford University Press, pp. 363–79.

Lundvall, B.-Å. (1988), 'Innovation as an Interactive Process: From User–Producer Interaction to the National System of Innovation', in G. Dosi, C. Freeman, R.R. Nelson, G. Silverberg, and L. Soete (eds) (1988), *Technical Change and Economic Theory*, London: Pinter. pp. 349–69.

Lundvall, B.-Å. (1995), 'The Social Dimensions of the Learning Economy' Inaugural Lecture, Department of Business Studies, Aalborg University, Denmark.

Lundvall, B.-Å. (ed.) (1992), *National Systems of Innovation: Towards a Theory of Innovation and Interactive Learning*, London: Pinter.

Lundvall, B.-Å. and B. Johnson (1994), 'The Learning Economy', *Journal of Industrial Studies*, **1**(2): 23–42.

Mansell, R. (1987), *Telecommunication Network-Based Services: Policy Implications*, OECD ICCP Series Report #18, Paris: OECD.

Mansell, R. (1993), *The New Telecommunications: A Political Economy of Network Evolution*, London: Sage.

Mansell, R. (1995), 'Innovation in Telecommunication: Bridging the Supplier–User Interface', in M. Dodgson and R. Rothwell (eds), *Handbook of Industrial Innovation*, Cheltenham: Edward Elgar, pp.232–242.

Mansell, R.and U. Wehn (eds) (1998), *Knowledge Societies: Information Technology for Sustainable Development*, Oxford: Oxford University Press.

McKelvey, M., F. Texier and A. Hakan (1998), 'The Dynamics of High Tech Industry: Swedish Firms Developing Mobile Telecommunication Systems', unpublished research report prepared for Systems of Innovation Research Program (SIRP) at Linkoping University, Sweden.

McNamara, J. (1991), *The Economics of Innovation in the Telecommunications Industry*, New York: Quorum Books.

Miyazaki, K. (1995), *Building Competences in the Firm*, New York: St Martin's Press.

Moingeon, B. and A. Edmondson (eds) (1996), *Organizational Learning and Competitive Advantage*, London: Sage.

Mowery, D.C. (1994), *Science and Technology Policy in Interdepdendent Economies*, Boston: Kluwer Academic.

Mytelka, L. (ed.) (1999), *Competition, Innovation and Competitiveness in Developing Countries*, Paris: OECD Development Centre.

Nanda, A. (1996), 'Resources, Capabilities and Comptencies', in B. Moingeon and A. Edmondson (eds), *Organizational Learning and Competitive Advantage*, London: Sage, pp. 93–120.

Narduzzo, A., F. Rocco and M. Warglen (2000), 'Talking About Routines in the Field: The Emergence of Organizational Capabilities in a New Cellular Phone Network Company', in G. Dosi, R.R. Nelson and S. Winter (eds) *The Nature and Dynamics of Organisational Capabilities*, Oxford: Oxford University Press, pp. 27–50.

Nelson, R.R. (1991), 'Why Do Firms Differ, and How Does It Matter', *Strategic Management Journal*, 12: 61–74.

Nelson, R.R. (ed.) (1993), *National Innovation Systems: A Comparative Analysis*, Oxford: Oxford University Press.

Nelson, R.R. and S. Winter (1982), *An Evolutionary Theory of Economic Change*, Cambridge MA: Harvard University Press.

Nonaka, I. (1994), 'A Dynamic Theory of Organizational Knowledge Creation', *Organization Science*, 5(1): 14–37.

Nonaka, I. and Takeuchi, H. (1995), *The Knowledge Creating Company*, New York: Oxford University Press.

OECD (1992), *Information Networks and New Technologies – Opportunities and Policy Implications for the 1990s*, OECD ICCP Series, Paris: OECD.

Oppenheim, A.N. (1992), *Questionnaire Design, Interviewing and Attitude Measurement*, London: Pinter.

Patel, P. and K. Pavitt (1994), 'National Innovation Systems: Why They Are Important and How They Might Be Measured and Compared', *Economics of Innovation and New Technology*, 3: 77–95.

Pavitt, K. (2002), 'Innovating Routines in the Business Firm: What Corporate Tasks Should They Be Accomplishing?', *Industrial and Corporate Change*, 11(1): 117–33.

Perez, C. (1983), 'Structural Change and the Assimilation of New Technologies in the Economic and Social System', *Futures*, 15(5): 357–75.

Perez, C. (1985), 'Microelectronics, Long Waves and World Structural Change: New Perspectives for Developing Countries', *World Development, Special Issue on Microelectronics*, 13(3): 441–63.

Pettigrew, A. and R. Whipp (1991), *Managing Change for Competitive Success*, Oxford: Blackwell.

Pickett, J. (1991), 'Indigeneous Technological Capability in Sub-Saharan Africa', in M. Huq, P. Bhatt, C. Lewis, and A. Shibli (eds), *Science, Technology and Development: North–South Co-operation*, London: Frank Cass, pp. 31–46.

Prahalad, C. and G. Hamel (1990), 'The Core Competence of the Corporation', *Harvard Business Review*, **May–June**: 79–91.

Prahalad, C. and G. Hamel (1994), *Competing for the Future*, Boston:MA: Harvard University Press.

Prencipe, A. (2000), 'Divide and Rule: Firm Boundaries in the Aircraft Engine Industry', Unpublished DPhil thesis, SPRU, University of Sussex.

Republic of Ghana (1996), *National Communications Authority (NCA) – Act 524*, GPC/A618/300/11/96, Government Printer, Accra: Assembly Press.

Republic of South Africa (1996), 'No. 103 of 1996 Telecommunications Act', Capetown: Government Gazette.

Republic of South Africa, Department of Communications (1997), *Notice 768 of 1997 Licence Issued to Telkom SA Limited to Provide Telecommunication Services under Section 36 of Telecommunications Act (1996)*, Capetown: Government

Gazette.
Republic of South Africa, Department of Trade and Industry (1998), *Technology and Human Resources for Industry (THRIP) Strategic Plan 1997–2001*, Pretoria: DTI.
Republic of South Africa, Department of Trade and Industry (1999), *National Research Foundation Annual Report, 1998–99*, Pretoria: DTI.
Republic of South Africa, Ministry for Posts, Telecommunications and Broadcasting (1997), *Partnership for the Future*, Pretoria: Ministry for Posts, Telecommunications and Broadcasting.
Republic of Uganda (1997), *The Uganda Communications Act, 1997, Acts Supplement, 26 September 1977*, Entebbe: GPCC.
Rosenberg, N. (1982), *Inside the Black Box: Technology and Economics*, Cambridge: Cambridge University Press.
Rumelt, R.P. (1984), 'Towards a Strategic Theory of the Firm', in R.B. Lamb (ed.) Competitive Strategic Management, Englewood Cliffs, NJ: Prentice-Hall, pp. 556–70.
Salter, A. (1999), 'Faint Expectations: Science and Technology Policy in Ontario', Unpublished DPhil Thesis, SPRU, University of Sussex.
Sayer, A. (1992), *Method in Social Science* (2nd edn), London and New York: Routledge.
Schein, E. (1992), *Organizational Culture and Leadership* (2nd edn), San Francisco: Jossey-Bass.
Senge, P., C. Roberts, R. Ross, B. Smith, G. Roth and A. Kleiner (1999), *The Dance of Change: The Challenges of Sustaining Momentum in Learning Organizations*, London: Brealey.
Senge, P.M. (1992), *The Fifth Discipline: The Art and Practice of the Learning Organization*, London: Century Business.
Silverberg, G. and B. Verspagen (1994), 'Learning, Innovation and Economic Growth: A Long-Run Model of Industrial Dynamics', *Industrial and Corporate Change*, 3(1): 199–223.
Starkey, K. (1996), *How Organizations Learn*, London: International Thomson Business Press.
Stewart, F. (1984), 'Facilitating Indigenous Technical Change in Third World Countries.', in M. Fransman and K. King (eds), *Technological Capability in the Third World*, London: Macmillan, pp. 81–94.
Stewart, F. (1990), 'Technology Transfer for Development', in R. Evenson and G. Ranis (eds), *Science and Technology: Lessons for Development Policy*, Boulder, CO: Westview Press, pp. 301–24.
Stewart, F., S. Lall and S. Wangwe (eds) (1992), *Alternative Development Strategies in Sub-Saharan Africa*, London: Macmillan.
Tanzania Telecommunications Co. Ltd (1997–1999) *Connect Quarterly*, various editions.
Teece, D.J. (1987), 'Profiting from Technological Innovation: Implications for Integration, Collaboration, Licensing and Public Policy', in D.J. Teece (ed.), *The Competitive Challenge: Strategies for Industrial Innovation and Renewal*, Cambridge, MA: Ballinger, pp. 185–219.
Teece, D.J. and G.P. Pisano (1994), 'The Dyanamic Capabilities of Firms: An Introduction', *Industrial and Corporate Change*, 3: 537–56.
Teece, D.J., G.P. Pisano and A. Shuen (2000), 'Dynamic Capabilities and Strategic Management', in G. Dosi, R.R. Nelson and S. Winter (eds), *The Nature and Dynamics of Organisational Capabilities*, Oxford: Oxford University Press.
Thomson, R. (1993), 'Epilogue: Institutions, Learning and Technological Change', in

R. Thomson, (ed.), *Learning and Technological Change*, London: Macmillan, pp.,267–79.

Tidd, J., J. Bessant and K. Pavitt (1997), *Managing Innovation: Integrating Technological, Market and Organizational Change*, London: Wiley.

Tushman, M. and D. Nadler (1996), 'Organizing for Innovation', in K. Starkey (ed.), *How Organizations Learn*, London: International Thomson Business Press, pp. 135–55.

UNCTAD (1996), *New Technologies and Technological Capability Building at the Enterprise Level:* Some Policy Implications, Geneva: United Nations.

United Nations (1997), 'Report of the Working Group on Information and Communications for Development', E/CN.16/1997/4, March, United Nations ECOSOC.

United Nations (2000), 'Report of the High Level Panel on Information and Communication Technology New York' 17–20, United Nations, High-Level Panel on Information and Communication Technology.

United Republic of Tanzania (1993) 'Acts Supplement, No. 6 An Act to Amend the Public Corporation Act', promulgated 24 Dec. Arusha.

United Republic of Tanzania, Ministry of Communication and Transport (1997) *National Telecommunication Policy (1997–2020)*, dated October, Dar es Salaam.

Vaill, P. (1996), 'The Purposing of High-Performing Systems', in K. Starkey (ed.) *How Organizations Learn*, London: International Thomson Business Press, pp. 60–81.

Wangwe, S. (ed.) (1995a), *Exporting Africa – Technology, Trade and Industrialization in Sub-Saharan Africa*, London: Routledge and UNU-Press.

Wangwe, S. (1995b), 'Fostering Technological Capacity Building: The Case ofEthiopia and the United Republic of Tanzania', ESRF Discussion Paper Series No. 006, November.

Watkins, K.E. and V.J. Marsick (1993), *Sculpting the Learning Organization: Lessons in the Art and Science of Systemic Change*, San Francisco: Jossey Bass.

Weick, K.E. (1987), 'Substitutes for Strategy', in D.J. Teece (ed.), *The Competitive Challenge. Strategies for Industrial Innovation and Renewal*, Cambridge, MA: Ballinger, pp. 221–33.

Winter, S.G. (1987), 'Knowledge and Competence as Strategic Assets', in D.J. Teece (ed.), *The Competitive Challenge: Strategies for Industrial Innovation and Renewal*, Cambridge, MA: Ballinger, pp. 159–84.

World Bank (1998a), 'World Bank Annual Report 1998: Africa' (on-line edition) http://www.worldbank.org/html/extpb/annrep98/africa.htm [last accessed 28/02/2004].

World Bank (1998b), 'World Bank Brief: Sub-Saharan Africa' (on-line edition) http://www.worldbank.org/afr/regional_brief.htm [last accessed 30/09/1999].

World Bank (2000), 'Global Economic Prospects and the Developing Countries 2000, Appendix 1 Regional Economic Prospects Sub-Saharan Africa' (on-line edition) http://www.worldbank.org/prospects/gep98-99/appx1/safrica.htm [last accessed 28/02/2004].

Index

Abidoum, A.A. 5, 59
absorptive capacity 163
acquiring 42
active technology scan 89
activities, iteration of 35
adaptation 49
Africa 12, 13, 59
  innovation system 140, 152
  management, culture and leadership
    83, 92, 93–4, 96
  quantitative exploration of
    technological learning 71, 76
  strategic balance 164, 169
  supplier relationships 107, 114, 116,
    117, 118–19, 122, 129
  Telecommunication Union 127
Alcatel 107, 195
aligning 42
Altech Telecom 107, 114, 195–6
Amsden, A. 58
ANOVA 10, 68, 69
Argyris, C. 6, 31, 34
Asia 13, 58, 164
assessment 100
AT&T 38

Baden-Fuller, C. 31
Barnett, W.P. 28
Barney, J. 31, 34
Bell, M. 4, 33, 43–5, 55, 56,
  57, 58
Bhagavan, M.R. 21
boundary
  processes 55–60
  spanning skills 164
Brady, T. 18, 19
Brazil 46, 47, 50, 51
Brewster, C. 98
Brock, G.W. 17, 47
Brusoni, S. 39
Burgelman, R. 28

capability 100–101
catch-up strategies 46, 50
challenges 119–23
change management 41
Chi-Square test 69
choosing ability 42
co-ordination 161–2
Cohen, W.M. 31, 56
Commonwealth Telecommunication
  Organization 127
competencies 97–8, 124–9
complementary skill sets, tight coupling
  of 35
constrained agency 56, 132
Cooper, C. 5, 55, 59
Crandall, R.W. 17, 47
critical success factors 35, 95–6, 123–4
culture 54, 89–90, 94, 161–2

Dar es Salaam University 148
Data-communication Company, Board of
  123
Davies, A. 17, 18, 19, 20
definitions of TCB mechanisms 192–4
designing 49
developing country firms 92–5, 135
development of organization 42
digital terrain model 115
diversification 101
Dodgson, M. 31
Dosi, G. 30
Dutrenit, G. 4

East Asian crisis 13
economic structure and performance
  12–14
Edmondson, A. 34
Edquist, C. 58
effectiveness 119–29
  competencies 124–9
  improvement 33–46

strengths and critical success factors
123–4
weaknesses and challenges 119–23
electronic capital goods 48
empirical context: empirical
environment and industry specific
factors 12–20
economic structure and performance
12–14
knowledge, policy and practice,
implications for 21–2
technical change in
telecommunication industry
15–20
telecommunications policy and
regulatory environment 14–15
Employment Equity Act 149
engaged leadership 36
engagement, active and purposive 97–8
Enos, J. 5, 58, 59
equipment suppliers and services 182–4
Ericsson 107, 195–6
Ernst, D. 4, 19, 33, 55, 58, 59
Europe 9, 19, 76
supplier relationships 107, 111, 118
evaluation 100, 126–8
executing ability 42
existence indicators 28
expenditure, direct 136

finance/financial 90–91, 136
data for suppliers 195–6
mechanisms 52–3
resources, allocation of 94–5
Finland 146
firms 180–86
Flamm, K. 17, 47
Forje, J. 5, 59
Foss, N. 28
Fransman, M. 15, 17, 18, 19, 20, 47
Freeman, C. 32, 55, 58
funding *see* finance/financial

generating ability 42
geo-information system 115
get-ahead strategy 50
Ghana 2, 6, 7–8, 12, 13, 14, 59
innovation system 136, 138, 139,
143–5, 146, 153, 154, 156
interviews and interviewees 176

legislative and policy provisions 197
management, culture and leadership
83–4, 97
Ministry of Communications 144–5
National Communications Authority
143, 145
quantitative exploration of
technological learning 76
strategic balance 163, 164, 166, 167,
168
summary profile 189
supplier relationships 125, 126, 127,
128
Telecom Training School 143
Girvan, N. 4, 55, 56
gross domestic product 12, 13, 14
GSM Association 128
GTE 38

Hamel, G. 55
higher-order learning, promotion of 35–6
Highly Indebted Poor Countries Debt
Initiative 12–13
hiring 49
Hobday, M. 4, 17, 18, 20, 39, 46–50, 58
Hoffman, K. 4, 55, 56
Hughes, T.P. 21
human resource development 86–7, 93
fund 149–50, 153, 155

implementing ability 42
India 146
information
and communication technology 21
feedback systems installation 49
technology 72, 131
innovation 41, 99–100, 131–3
innovation system 58–60, 135–57, 166–8
effectiveness in interactions 154–7
Ghana 143–5
and interaction with developing
country firms 135
source of TCB input 135–41
South Africa 149–54
Tanzania 145–9
Uganda 141–2
inputs 128–9
interactions 154–7
International Telecommunications Union
12, 127

interview guides 180–88
interviews and interviewees 175–9
islands of progress 37

Japan 19, 115, 149

Katz, J. 58
keeping-up strategies 47, 50
Kim, L. 4, 33, 55, 58
know-how 58
know-who 58, 130, 166, 170
know-why 58, 129, 166, 170
knowledge 35
Kruskal–Wallis test 10, 69
Kumar, N. 55

Lall, S. 5, 56, 58
leadership 54, 89–90, 94, 161–2
learning 27–33, 41, 48–9
    ability 42
    by setting up electronic capital goods
        48
    by training and hiring 49
    cells 37
    effectiveness 159–61
    skills, developing and rewarding of 98
    see also learning systems, internal
        elements of
learning systems, internal elements of
    83–91
    active technology scan and search
        mechanisms 89
    culture and leadership 89–90
    finance 90–91
    human resource development 86–7
    organizational integration 88
    organizational structures, design
        and implementation of 87
    recruitment and retention systems
        83–6
    technological capability evaluation
        and assessment systems 88–9
Lebanon 9
legislative provisions 197
Leonard-Barton, D. 3, 4, 31, 34, 35–6,
    40, 52
Levinthal, D. 28, 31, 56
loyalty bonuses 85
Lucent 107, 114, 195–6
Lundvall, B.-Å. 19, 55, 58

McKelvey, M. 18, 132
McNamara, J. 19, 47
Malaysia 9, 75–6, 146, 153
management 161–2
management, culture and leadership for
    learning 83–105
    learning systems, internal elements
        of 83–91
    technological learning, effectiveness
        of 92–104
management practices 53, 92–4
managing supplier relationships 107–34
    case studies 113–19
    effectiveness 119–29
    mechanisms, specific for technology
        acquisition 110–13
    selection 108–10
    specialization and innovative activity
        131–3
    technological change 130–31
    technological inputs 129–30
Mansell, R. 6, 17, 18, 20, 21, 47
Marsick, V.J. 34
Massachusetts Institute of Technology
    126
measures, specific 136
mechanisms, specific for technology
    acquisition 110–13
Moingeon, B. 34
Mytelka, L. 17, 46–7, 50–51

Nadler, D. 3, 4, 38
Nanda, A. 39
Narduzzo, A. 19
national innovation system 55
Nelson, R.R. 28, 29, 31, 46, 55, 58
non-governmental organizations 7
non-traditional approach 97
Nonaka, I. 32

operating data suppliers 195–6
Oppenheim, A.N. 6
organization design 99–100
Organization for Economic Cooperation
    and Development 47
organizational
    culture 101–4
    integration 88, 99–100
    structures, design and
        implementation of 87

out-performers 95

Park, W.H. 58
Patel, P. 55, 58
Pavitt, K. 4, 33, 39, 43–5, 55, 56, 57, 58
Perez, C. 32
performance requirements 136
Pettigrew, A. 3, 4, 28, 31, 32, 34, 36–8,
    45
Pickett, J. 5, 59
Pisano, G.P. 3, 31, 34
policy
    provisions 197
    relevance 168–71
portfolio of basic abilities 42
Prahalad, C. 55
Prencipe, A. 39
product designs 49
public sector officials 180–86
public telecommunications operators 95,
    97

quantitative exploration of
    technological learning 63–81
    balanced approach and effectiveness
        76–81
    development, variation in reflected
        in system indicator 68
    independent variables 73–6
    patterns of learning variation 69–70
    routines, wide range of 63–7
    technological capability, gaps in
        70–73

recognizing ability 42
recruitment systems 83–6
regulatory bodies 184–6
research and development 19–20, 28, 35,
    43–4, 46, 57, 58, 160, 187
research strategy, method and analysis
    5–11
resources identification and allocation
    52–3
retention systems 83–6
Rumelt, R.P. 31, 34

Salter, A. 59
Sayer, A. 6
scanning 41, 126–8
Schein, E. 31, 34

Schon, D. 6, 31, 34
Schumpeter, J. 32
Scientific Atlanta 109
search/searching 48, 126–8
    mechanisms 89
second national operator 141
selection 108–10, 126–8
Senge, P.M. 31, 34
Siemens 107, 195–6
Singapore 146
Skills Act 149
small, medium and micro enterprises
    112, 114, 153
soft factors 164
South Africa 2, 6, 7–8, 12, 13, 14, 59,
    195–6
    Department of Communications 151,
        152
    Department of Trade and Industry 167
    Employment Equity Act 149
    innovation system 136, 137, 138, 139,
        141, 149–54, 155–6
    interviews and interviewees 178–9
    legislative and policy provisions 197
    management, culture and leadership
        87, 102
    quantitative exploration of
        technological learning 70, 72, 80
    Sector Education and Training
        Authority 152
    Skills Act 149
    strategic balance 166, 168, 173
    summary profile 191
    supplier relationships 107, 109, 110,
        114, 122, 125, 126, 127, 128
    Telecommunication Regulatory
        Authority 149, 150–51, 152, 153
South Korea 19, 46, 47
southeast Asia 58
specialization 131–3
specific competencies 97–8
Starkey, K. 31
Stewart, F. 5, 56, 58
Stopford, J.M. 31
strategic balance 159–74
    future research 171–2
    innovation systems 166–8
    learning, effectiveness in 159–61
    management, co-ordination, culture
        and leadership 161–2

supply conditions and supplier
management 162–6
theoretical insights and policy
relevance 168–71
strengths 123–4
Sub-Saharan Africa 12, 14
subsidies provision 136
summary profiles 188–91
supplier/suppliers
interaction 55–7
management 162–6
relationships *see* managing supplier
relationships
supply conditions 162–6
support activities 136
Sweden 125
system approach 3–5

tacit knowledge flows 124–6
Tadiran 109
Tanzania 2, 6, 7–8, 12, 13, 14, 59
Communications Commission (TCC)
145, 146, 147–8
innovation system 136, 139, 145–9,
153, 154, 156
interviews and interviewees 177
legislative and policy provisions 197
management, culture and leadership
97
quantitative exploration of
technological learning 76
strategic balance 163, 166, 167, 168,
173
summary profile 190
supplier relationships 120, 126, 127
technical change in telecommunication
industry 15–20
technological capability evaluation
and assessment systems 88–9
technological change 130–31
technological inputs 129–30
technological leap-frogging 46
technological learning, effectiveness of
92–104
critical success factors 95–6
out-performers 95
prevailing systems in use for
developing country firms 92–5
specific competencies 97–8
weaknesses and challenges 98–104

technology acquisition 110–13
technology capability building system
approach 25–61
effectiveness improvement 33–46
ideal system 51–60
as learning 27–33
and learning in telecommunication
sector 46–51
Technology Executive 87
technology transfer 41, 117
technology/knowledge transfer 76
Teece, D.J. 3, 31, 34, 55
Telebras 47
telecommunication network-based
services 6
Telecommunications Act (1996) 153,
155
telecommunications policy and
regulatory environment 14–15
theoretical insights 168–71
Thomson, R. 29
Tidd, J. 31, 40–43, 52
traditional approach 97
training 49
TTCL 148
Tushman, M. 3, 4, 38

Uganda 2, 6, 7–8, 12, 13, 14, 59
Communications Commission 141,
142
innovation system 136, 139, 140,
141–2, 146, 153, 154, 156
interviews and interviewees 175
legislative and policy provisions 197
Ministry of Education 142
quantitative exploration of
technological learning 76
strategic balance 163, 166, 167, 168
summary profile 188
supplier relationships 120, 126, 127
Telecommunications Ltd 142
United Kingdom 117, 146
United Nations 127
Development Programme 84
United States 9, 19, 75–6, 146
management, culture and leadership
86
supplier relationships 125, 127

Vaill, P. 31

Wangwe, S. 5, 59
Watkins, K.E. 34
weaknesses 119–23
Wehn, U. 21
Weick, K.E. 32
Whipp, R. 3, 4, 28, 31, 32, 34, 36–8, 45

Wilcoxon Signed Rank Sum Test 10, 76–8
Winter, S. 28, 29, 30, 31, 46
wireless in the local loop systems 113–15, 116, 117, 121–2, 182–4, 187
World Bank 12, 115